Essentials of Risk Control

Volume 2

Essentials of Risk Control

Volume 2

Edited by
George L. Head, Ph.D., CPCU, ARM, CSP, CLU
Vice President
Insurance Institute of America

Third Edition • 1995

Insurance Institute of America
720 Providence Road, Malvern, Pennsylvania 19355-0770

Contents

Chapter 8

Controlling Liability Losses

Educational Objectives

1. Define the liability peril and distinguish it from liability losses and expenditures for liability risk control.

2. Illustrate why, when, and how an organization should reduce the *frequency* of its liability losses.

3. Illustrate why, when, and how an organization should reduce the *severity* of its liability losses.

4. Describe how to select and apply appropriate strategies for managing liability claims.

5. Describe the characteristics and uses of decision trees in making choices among risk control techniques.

6. Construct and apply decision trees to given situations.

7. Define or describe each of the Key Words and Phrases shown in the course guide for this assignment.

Outline

Fundamental Concepts

Legal Liability

Legally Protected Interests of Others and Legal Wrongs

Liability Risk Control Techniques, Control Points, and Control Measures

Control of Events Creating a Liability Loss

Act or Omission Generating Legal Responsibility

Resulting Harm to Others

Form of Legal Action

Control of Events Increasing Liability Losses

Selection of Jurisdiction

Resolution of Claims

Severity of Harm

Degree of Organization's Culpability

Legal Defense

Liability Claims Management

Summary

Controlling Liability Losses

An organization's liability losses are the amounts of money it pays for legal claims brought against it. Controlling these losses is an important risk control responsibility because an organization can be legally responsible for the conduct of many people, including employees, subcontractors, other agents, and even volunteers. Adding to the complexity of the task are the many kinds of legal wrongs for which an organization can be held legally responsible (breaches of contract, crimes, and torts); the multitude of claimants to whom an organization can be legally responsible (employees, customers, neighboring property owners, members of the general public, and the state); and the almost unlimited dollar amounts for which an organization can become liable.

To reduce the frequency and severity of such losses, an organization's risk management professional must work with others to implement a systematic program for liability risk control. This chapter presents such a program.

Regardless of who commits the legal wrong, the nature of that wrong, or who is harmed as a result, only a few events or factors influence the frequency and the severity of liability losses. If the organization commits a legal wrong or if a suit is filed against the organization, the organization suffers a liability loss. Those events affect liability loss *frequency*. The extent of harm done to a claimant or the negotiating abilities of those representing the claimant and the organization determine the amounts of an organization's liability losses. Those factors affect liability loss *severity*.

The purpose of liability risk control, therefore, is to identify, analyze, and control those liability-producing and liability-increasing events, thus decreasing the number of situations that lead to liability and reducing the effects of those situations. This chapter examines liability loss events and analyzes how each can be controlled at a reasonable cost so that liability loss control costs do not become excessive.

Fundamental Concepts

To best control liability losses, risk management professionals should understand the fundamental concepts of liability. Therefore, this section describes the concepts of legal liability; the legally protected interests of others; and liability risk control techniques, control points, and control measures.

Legal Liability

Liability is an obligation imposed by law. Controlling liability losses requires some understanding of legal concepts and procedures. Particularly important are the relationships among the liability peril, a liability loss, and liability risk control.

Liability Peril

The peril that causes a liability loss is the filing of a legal claim against an organization. Filing a legal claim incurs expenses that constitute the **liability loss**. That definition of a **liability peril** implies that any legally wrongful act is not itself the liability peril. Instead, any legally wrongful act is a **liability hazard** because it increases the likelihood that the liability peril, the filing of a claim, will occur.

Even if an organization has not committed a legal wrong, it can suffer a liability loss. A claimant might, for any reason, file an unfounded claim against an organization. Filing the claim, even though the claim is completely unfounded, means a liability loss because the organization must spend money in response to the claim. Much of liability risk control focuses on preventing legal claims from being made against an organization.

> **What are liability perils, liability losses, and liability risk control?**
>
> **What are the legally protected interests of others?**
>
> **What are effective liability risk control techniques, control points, and control measures?**

Liability Loss

A liability loss is money paid to investigate or defend against a legal claim, to pay an out-of-court settlement or satisfy a court verdict, or to comply with an injunction or other court order from such a claim. The definition implies that an organization (or any other entity) that is sued need not lose the suit, or even agree to a negotiated settlement, to have a liability loss. As soon as an organization spends money in response to a particular legal claim, it has suffered a liability loss. Even a relatively modest amount spent to determine that the claim is totally unfounded is still a liability loss.

The expenditures incurred after a legal claim has been filed can be categorized as (1) legal expenses, (2) the cost of complying with injunctions and court orders for specific performance, and (3) money for settlements, verdicts, or fines. Loss of the organization's reputation and/or market share is another important financial consequence of legal liability. That financial consequence is treated as a net income loss, which, along with appropriate control measures, will be described in Chapter 10.

Legal Expenses

When an organization faces a civil suit or a criminal charge, the organization must investigate the circumstances and prepare a legal defense. Investigation and defense costs are perhaps the most easily overlooked liability exposures of organizations. Because of the complexities of modern society, cases often require many hours of investigation and legal work to avoid, refute, or mitigate the charges.

Many cases are so technical that expert witnesses are required. Both parties in a technical case typically use expert witnesses. Expert testimony is expensive to obtain and to refute. Even the cost of reproducing pertinent documents or obtaining witnesses can be significant. Sometimes, the amount of testimony is so extensive that computers are used by the lawyers to keep track of all the evidence.

Beyond legal fees (which may become substantial), the defendant is usually responsible for paying all costs imposed by the court. Those costs include jury fees, filing fees, and premiums on bonds required by the court.

Costs of Complying With Injunctions and Orders for Specific Performance

As a legal remedy in a civil action, a court might order a wrongdoer to do or refrain from a doing a particular activity. For example, a construction firm might have breached a contract by failing to erect a structure because of unforeseen difficulties. This firm might also have committed the tort of nuisance against owners of neighboring properties, for example, by burning construction wastes that spread noxious fumes to adjoining properties and made their occupants ill. Courts hearing suits against this construction firm might order it to complete the structure specified in the contract (**specific performance**) while prohibiting it from burning its rubbish at the construction site (**injunction**).

Both remedies will probably increase the contractor's costs. First, completing the building at the contracted price despite the unforeseen difficulties will increase the contractor's costs without any comparable increase in its anticipated revenue from this project. Similarly, complying with the injunction against burning rubbish will force the contractor to find alternative and perhaps more expensive ways of disposing of the wastes. Both increases in costs represent liability losses to the contractor.

Money for Settlements, Verdicts, or Fines

A wrongdoer in a civil action might have to pay compensatory, or even punitive, damages awarded by a court. Alternatively, before a court verdict is reached, the wrongdoer and the claimant might have reached an out-of-court settlement. Correspondingly, a wrongdoer convicted of a crime might have to pay a fine. The money to pay for these verdicts, settlements, or fines represents financial loss to the wrongdoer.

Compensatory damages repay those who incurred losses due to securing needed medical care, repairing damaged property, and restoring lost income. Compensatory damages also provide compensation for physical and/or psychological pain and suffering. **Punitive damages** are assessed against the wrongdoer as a punishment and paid to the victim.

Liability Risk Control

As defined above, a liability loss is an expenditure in response to a specific legal claim. Some expenditures made in anticipation of future legal claims include the costs to perform a task safely or in the legally prescribed manner, to compile records documenting proper conduct, or to pay a retainer to legal counsel. These expenditures are the costs of liability risk control, which is designed to reduce the frequency and/or severity of future liability losses and to prepare future responses to unknown claims.

Expenditures for liability risk control, like expenditures to reduce the frequency or severity of any kind of loss, are justified financially only if they can be expected to reduce losses more than they increase the costs of risk control. Unless done for humanitarian reasons or to meet legal requirements, spending vast sums to forestall only minor future losses is not justified. Doing so would tend to decrease, rather than increase, an organization's profitability or operating efficiency.

Legally Protected Interests of Others and Legal Wrongs

The law recognizes that every entity, including every person and every organization, has certain legal interests that are protected by civil and criminal laws. By infringing on one of those interests, an entity can make a liability claim. Those legal interests and the associated civil and criminal wrongs create legal responsibility for the wrongdoer, as follows:

- *Performance of promises* is an interest that is created by a legally enforceable contract. That interest can be infringed on by the promisor's failure to perform or by fraud, duress, or other wrongful conduct. Consequently, the failure to perform or the wrongful conduct negates the genuine consent and legality underlying the contracts.

- *Physical safety of one's person* is an interest that can be jeopardized by intentional torts such as assault or battery, by tortious negligence in injuring others, and by crimes that inflict violence on others.

- *Personal freedom of movement* is an interest vulnerable to the intentional tort of false imprisonment and such crimes as kidnapping and extortion.

- *Protection of property* is an interest that can be infringed on by intentional torts such as trespass, nuisance, and conversion; by negligent damage of others' property; and by crimes such as burglary, robbery, and fraud.

- *Security of reputation* is an interest that can be infringed on by the intentional torts of defamation, either by libel or slander.

- *Personal privacy* is an interest that can be infringed on by the intentional tort of giving unwarranted publicity to a person's private dealings.

- *Economic freedom* is an interest that can be infringed on by such intentional torts as false advertising, harassing or intimidating competitors or their customers, and any other action that a court determines exceeds the limits of fair competition.

- *Safety from criminal conduct* is an interest of peace and order for society as a whole rather than for any one person.

The legal responsibility for infringing on these interests can fall equally on organizations and individuals. An organization is legally responsible for the actions of its agents, which can include employees, officers, anyone using the organization's property with its permission, and, in some situations, volunteers acting on the organization's behalf. When its agents commit legal wrongs, an organization is generally subject to the same tort, contractual, or criminal liability as are the individual agents. Under criminal law, the wrongful act is a violation of a municipal, state, or federal penal code. Under contract law, the wrongful act is the failure to fulfill a contractual promise. The wrongful acts that constitute torts generally fall into the following three categories, according to the nature of the conduct of the wrongdoer:

1. Intentional—intending the reasonable consequences of one's actions, without necessarily having malice toward those harmed

2. Negligence—exposing others to unreasonable danger by failing to exercise the degree of care the law requires under the circumstances

3. Strict liability—engaging in inherently dangerous acts for which the law imposes liability without regard to intent or negligence (for example, blasting, manufacturing or selling certain products, or harboring wild animals)

Liability Risk Control Techniques, Control Points, and Control Measures

Exhibit 8-1 shows the overall plan of this chapter. The exhibit illustrates the relationships among risk management techniques, control points, and control measures as they relate to liability exposures. As indicated at the left of the exhibit, two basic risk management techniques that apply to liability losses are loss prevention and loss reduction. As with all losses, liability loss prevention is appropriate before a peril occurs, that is, before a claim has been filed. Liability loss reduction is appropriate after the peril has occurred, that is, after a claim has been filed.

Exhibit 8-1
Liability Risk Control Points and Measures

Risk Management Techniques	Control Points	Measures
Loss Prevention (reducing frequency)	Act or omission generating responsibility	Removing or limiting obligation Preventing invasion of others' interests Establishing affirmative justifications
	Harm to others	Volunteering to restore losses Limiting kinds of harm
	Form of legal action	Negotiating settlements Agreeing on alternatives to litigation
Loss Reduction (reducing severity)	Jurisdiction	Gaining contractual agreement Challenging jurisdiction Initiating preemptive countersuits Changing laws
	Resolution	Negotiating
	Severity of harm	Mitigating harm Negotiating
	Degree of culpability	Avoiding intentional harm Treating claimants fairly
	Legal defense	Preserving defenses Selecting and cooperating with legal counsel Negotiating settlements

The center column in Exhibit 8-1 lists control points in the development of a legal claim, ranging from an act or omission generating liability to the courtroom legal defense of such a claim. These points offer opportunities for applying specific liability risk control measures (listed down the right side of Exhibit 8-1). A liability risk control program should be built from these measures, which are described throughout this chapter. The exhibit helps to design such a program by providing an overview of the options that can be applied, alone or in combination, at the various stages of a liability claim.

As in risk control for any exposure to loss, the underlying financial objective in liability risk control is to reduce the combined total of accidental losses and the costs of risk control. Liability risk control costs can mount rapidly, especially costs for investigation and defense. Therefore, an organization might sometimes prefer to settle a claim for a relatively modest amount rather than contest it and run the risk of incurring a large, adverse verdict by allowing the claim to proceed to trial.

At other times, discretion might suggest avoiding the expense of creating and keeping extensive and expensive files to document proper conduct when it is highly unlikely that such documentation will be needed. Risk management professionals should use judgment and intuition to evaluate the relative costs and benefits of alternative liability risk control measures. In many situations, the best way to reduce the sum of liability risk control costs and of liability losses is to settle claims as efficiently as possible.

In evaluating all the alternatives, risk management professionals should remember that the goal of liability risk control is to reduce the expected present value of the sum of an organization's liability losses and its liability risk control expenditures. As expected values, those losses and expenditures must be weighted by the probabilities of various outcomes: whether the organization's actions (or failures to act) cause harm, whether those who have been harmed bring suit, whether the suit is settled before reaching a final verdict, and whether the verdict is favorable to the organization. As present values, liability losses and risk control costs must be discounted to reflect their timing, that is, the interval between the present and the future dates when the organization will have to pay claims. Thus, the decision guidelines emphasized in this chapter focus on the financial considerations that should underlie all liability risk control programs.

This chapter intentionally ignores nonfinancial criteria such as concern for the welfare of society and for the image and reputation of the organization. For some organizations, those nonfinancial considerations are paramount, influencing liability risk control decisions with little regard to financial considerations. In other organizations, those nonfinancial factors have some (but not overriding) importance, and in still others, only financial factors influence the decision.

Control of Events Creating a Liability Loss

What acts or omissions create legal responsibility?

How can you prevent the invasion of others' interests?

How can you remove or limit your organization's legal obligations to others?

What are the legal justifications for invading the interests of others?

What risk control measures reduce the harm suffered by others because of an organization's acts or omissions?

How can you help prevent the filing of a liability claim?

Although almost anyone can file a legal claim against an organization at any time, three events must generally occur in sequence to create a liability loss for an organization:

- An act or omission creates legal responsibility for an organization.
- Harm occurs to some other entity as a direct result of that act or omission.
- A legal claim is brought by the harmed entity.

By preventing any one of these three events, a liability risk control program can lower the frequency of liability losses. Each of these three events is a control point at which various liability risk control measures for loss prevention can be applied.

Act or Omission Generating Legal Responsibility

The best strategy for controlling liability losses is to respect others' rights—that is, to avoid acts or omissions that generate legal responsibility. An act or omission creating legal responsibility has three elements: (1) a legally protected interest of another, (2) an invasion of that interest, and (3) the lack of a legal justification for that invasion. From these three elements, the specific liability risk control measures that can be applied to an act or omission generating legal responsibility are as follows:

- Removing or limiting an organization's legal obligations to others
- Preventing invasions by the organization of others' protected interests
- Establishing legal justifications for invading those protected interests

Removing or Limiting an Organization's Legal Obligations to Others

Under certain circumstances, an organization can rely on the wording of notices, warranties, and other contracts to remove or limit its liability to potential claimants. If this wording forestalls the filing of a legal claim against the organization, no liability loss occurs; if such wording provides the organization with an effective, full response to a claim, the organization's cost of responding (its liability loss) is greatly reduced.

The ways an organization can limit its legal obligations to others vary according to whether its obligations arise under contract, tort, or criminal law and whether the liable conduct arises out of intentional acts, negligent acts, or strict liability.

Opportunities for Limiting Legal Obligations

An organization can try to limit its liability by posting public notices, such as, "Not Responsible for Articles Stolen from Vehicles" or "No Trespassing." A written product warranty might attempt to limit the seller's or the manufacturer's warranty to a specified period or might state that "No warranties, express or implied, other than those stated above attach to this product." A contract between two firms might contain a waiver of one firm's right to sue the other for specified kinds of losses or legal damages. For example, to win a construction contract, a builder might waive its right to sue the landowner for damage to the builder's equipment while the equipment is on the landowner's property. Similarly, the builder might require that the contract limit the builder's liability for lateness to a $1,000-per-day penalty if the contracted building is not completed by a specified date.

Each of these methods tries to anticipate legal claims and to limit an organization's legal responsibility from them. Posted public notices try to limit the duties the owner might have under tort law. Product warranties are designed to restrict a manufacturer's or seller's obligations for a product defect. The building contractor's waiver of the right to sue the landowner for equipment damage contractually limits the obligations the landowner might otherwise have under tort law for damage to the equipment. Because this waiver effectively excuses or exculpates the landowner from responsibility for such damage, the provision is often called an **exculpatory clause**.

A **liquidated damages** provision, which could limit the amount for which the contractor might be liable for each day's delay, limits only the amount of the contractor's potential liability. Limiting liability to, say, $1,000 a day can protect the contractor from having to pay enormous financial damages to the landowner. For example, if the building is a private school and construction is delayed, the landowner/school operator would be unable to collect an entire year's tuition income.

These opportunities for limiting legal obligations to others and rights to sue typically apply to contract or tort law, not criminal law. For the most part, the rights of a government to act in the name of all the people cannot be limited. Only a governmental entity having jurisdiction to prosecute has the power to waive liability for criminal misconduct and, then, only for past (not future) criminal activity. Except in the rare case when a prosecutor waives criminal proceedings against a particular organization to gain that organization's cooperation in prosecuting others, limiting the right of the state to bring criminal charges is not an effective liability risk control measure.

Restrictions on Opportunities for Limiting Legal Obligations

Most states allow considerable contractual freedom in defining how organizations choose to do business. Legally competent parties are generally free to bargain as equals as long as their bargain does not unduly interfere with the interests of others. Their bargain could even alter the common law rules affecting their financial or legal responsibility. However, courts will usually uphold contractual transfer provisions unless they unreasonably interfere with the interests of others (are against public policy) or could not have been bargained fairly (are unconscionable).

Because the exact boundaries of public policy and of unconscionability are nearly impossible to define, legal enforceability of many contractual provisions dealing with responsibility for accidental losses can be doubtful. An example of a public policy that restricts an organization's opportunities to limit its legal obligations is state legislation obligating employers to provide workers compensation benefits. One of the objectives of this legislation is to relieve the state, and ultimately its taxpayers, of financing the medical care and income replacement needs of disabled workers or their families. This public policy dictates how losses from work-related injuries and illnesses should be financed. Therefore, any agreement between an employer and an employee waiving that employee's statutory rights to workers compensation benefits would probably not be honored by the courts. Such an agreement might also be disallowed as unconscionable, based on the assumption that no employee would agree to waive workers compensation benefits unless he or she was misled or coerced. Mutual consent of the parties is essential to enforcing a contract provision.

A lack of mutual consent, or absence of a freely bargained exchange of values, also limits the legal effectiveness of unilateral statements such as signs posted on walls, notices on backs of ticket stubs, or limitations on product warranties. To limit the liability of the party making those statements, the notices must not only be physically apparent, expressed in clear language, and reasonable in extent, but they must also be a subject of direct bargaining. For example, the federal Interstate Commerce Act makes a rail or truck common carrier liable for the full amount of all damage to goods while in the carrier's custody, except for specified causes. However, a common carrier can reduce the dollar amount of its liability for damage to particular cargo by offering a reduced rate to a shipper who agrees to a "released bill of lading." This bill is generally enforced by the courts because something of value, a lower cost of transport for the shipper, has been bargained for in exchange.

In addition to these judicially imposed requirements that limitations on legal obligations to others be consistent with public policy and not unconscionable, the legislatures of approximately half the states have enacted statutes that disallow certain specific contractual provisions. Those statutes generally pertain to contracts regarding the design, construction, alteration, repair, or maintenance of buildings. Legislatures have found the wording of contracts to be subject to abuse and difficult to control. Therefore, those statutes direct that such contractual provisions will be completely disregarded in interpreting any contract containing them.

Because of the complexity and diversity of limitations of liability, risk management professionals should not try to become experts in contractual liability. Legal counsel should be consulted. Nonetheless, risk management professionals should know when a lawyer's expertise is not needed and, instead, when to develop a procedure for carefully studying all the organization's contracts.

Preventing Invasions of Others' Interests

Those who believe that an organization's actions have invaded their interests as protected by contract, tort, or criminal law are likely to bring a legal claim against that organization. This legal claim causes some liability loss even if the claim proves to be unfounded. Preventing invasions of others' legally protected interests substantially reduces the likelihood of such claims and greatly lowers liability loss frequency. Most legal texts and many risk management texts assume that the best way to control liability losses is to avoid committing legal wrongs. This is sound liability loss prevention. However, since unfounded claims are still possible, even if an organization complies with the law and prevents all invasions of others' interests, liability loss prevention cannot be expected to reduce liability loss frequency to zero.

Fulfilling contractual promises and avoiding tortious or criminal behavior prevent invasions of others' legally protected interests. One approach to determining how best to prevent invasions of others' interests is to list every action an organization must take to fulfill all of its legal obligations. However, such a list would be either extremely long (describing what every employee in every department should do every day) or almost too generalized to be practical (admonishing all employees to avoid all negligence). Risk management professionals have neither the time nor the ability to direct all of the organization's activities to be certain that they invade no one's interests.

To reduce an organization's wrongful invasion of others' interests, risk management professionals should help managers establish programs to determine their departments', employees', and other agents' legal obligations and to identify the actions necessary to fulfill those obligations. This is known as a **compliance management system** and consists of procedures for managers to do the following:

- Identify all legal obligations relating to the activities of their departments
- Determine the actions the departments should take to fulfill each of these legal obligations
- Instruct employees and other agents on how they should perform their assigned tasks to fulfill these legal obligations
- Monitor employees' and others' actions to ensure that they perform their tasks according to the law

Identifying Legal Obligations

In setting up a compliance management system, managers should first identify legal obligations. These consist of broad definitions of the organization's obligations under contract, tort, and criminal law and specific descriptions of each department's obligations as they relate to the organization's obligations.

At the organizational level, risk management professionals should confer with legal counsel to identify the organization's major contractual obligations, potential torts (whether based on intentional conduct, negligence, or strict liability), and possible criminal conduct due to foreseeable misdeeds relating to its operations. The following are examples:

- A clothing manufacturer might face these liabilities:
  - **Contractual liability** to retailers for not meeting delivery schedules or to retail customers for not meeting the flammability standards for clothing
  - **Tort liability** for negligence because of the careless driving of its vehicle operators
  - **Liability for the intentional tort** of purposely defaming a competitor during a marketing campaign
  - **Strict liability** for releasing a highly toxic cleaning fumigant into the air or water
  - **Criminal liability** for exceeding Interstate Commerce Commission truck weight regulations or conspiring to evade federal or state income tax

- A veterinarian might face these liabilities:

  - Contractual liability for allowing a pedigreed dog to escape its cage
  - Negligence for giving improper care to an injured or diseased animal of a customer
  - Strict liability for letting an inherently dangerous wild animal escape and harm others
  - Criminal liability for fraudulently billing customers for veterinary procedures not performed

In short, risk management professionals and legal counsel should develop a catalog of the organization's legal liability exposures. Exhibit 8-2 classifies the examples just given according to the class of legal wrong, specified wrongful act, potential claimants, and wrongdoer's legal consequences in each case.

Exhibit 8-2
Format for Cataloging Liability Exposures

Class of Legal Wrong by Organization	Wrongful Act	Party Wronged	Legal Consequences
Clothing Manufacturer			
Breach of contract	Failure to deliver	Customers	Payment of damages
Negligence	Defective clothing	Customers	Payment of damages
Intentional tort	Defamation	Competitor	Payment of damages
Strict liability in tort	Environmental pollution	Persons injured	Fines, imprisonment, damages
Criminal liability	Overloading vehicle, speeding	Community at large (represented by Interstate Commerce Commission)	Fines
Veterinarian			
Breach of contract	Loss of dog	Dog owner	Payment of damages
Negligence	Improper care	Dog owner	Payment of damages
Strict liability in tort	Escape of dangerous animal	Persons harmed	Payment of damages
Criminal liability	Fraudulent billing	Community at large (represented by prosecutor)	Fines, imprisonment, damages

Legal obligations must also be identified at the department level. For example, referring to Exhibit 8-2, the liability of the clothing manufacturer for defective clothing can be more specifically expressed as an obligation of the clothing manufacturer's production department. Similarly, the liability of the veterinarian for improper care is more specifically expressed as an obligation of the veterinary technicians to regularly check and evaluate each animal.

Relating organizational objectives to specific departments helps the department determine how it can help the organization fulfill its legal duties. For example, how can a department help the organization deliver its products according to contractual commitments, avoid tortious harm to others, and prevent criminal conduct? The organization's risk management professional and legal counsel should explore these and comparable questions as part of planning and organizing a compliance management program.

Determining How To Fulfill Obligations

The second step in a compliance management program is determining how each department can fulfill its obligations so that the organization as a whole does not invade others' interests. For example, the clothing manufacturer's production department can ask what it can do to eliminate or reduce the clothing manufacturer's liability for defective output. The veterinarian's technicians can ask what they can do to minimize or eliminate the veterinarian's liability for improper care. Using questions like these, the risk management professional can help the managers of each department (perhaps in conjunction with legal counsel) define the departmental procedures necessary to prevent invasions of others' legally protected interests. The risk management professional and the managers should specify how departmental personnel can fulfill the department's portion of the organization's legal obligations to others.

One objective of this process is to make compliance with legal obligations an essential part of each employee's job. To illustrate (again from Exhibit 8-2), the risk management professional and legal counsel for a veterinarian determine that strict physical controls are necessary when boarding a valuable animal. The risk management professional should confer with those responsible for admitting, feeding, medicating, and transporting animals to develop specific safeguards against any potential injury, theft, or other mishap.

Instructing Employees and Other Agents

The third step in a compliance management program is instructing employees and others who might be agents of the organization in the procedures that help the organization and department fulfill its obligations. Such instruction is typically a responsibility of the department manager, reinforced as necessary by the risk management professional. Senior managers can also emphasize to front-line employees the importance of performing their duties as the law requires. In a compliance management program, these front-line employees are important because they act on behalf of the organization. Their actions hold the organization legally accountable. Therefore, they must understand the purpose and requirements of the law. If employees understand the reason(s) underlying the law and their supervisors' instructions for carrying out the law, they are more likely to accept these instructions.

For example, to control its liability for automobile accidents, a moving and storage company might want only its qualified drivers to operate its vans. The company's risk management professional, legal counsel, and the manager in charge of fleet operations agree that under no circumstances can any other company employee, family member of an employee, or even any automobile mechanic or parking lot attendant drive a company van for even a short distance.

Consequently, the fleet manager must tell drivers that no one but a qualified driver should operate a van and explain how to effectively and diplomatically handle requests from others to drive the company's vans. Without instruction in politely restricting others from using the van, an overzealous driver trying to carry out the rule might commit some legal wrongs for which the company could face liability. Furthermore, exceptions to this rule could be permitted, for example, when a police or fire official needs a van for an emergency. Drivers need instructions or guidelines for dealing with those exceptions.

Monitoring Activities of Employees and Other Agents

The fourth step in a compliance management program is monitoring whether and how well employees and other agents are adhering to the risk controls. The risk management professional can use a number of techniques to document information about employee compliance. Sometimes, documentation can be a byproduct of the organization's routine operations. The following examples of documentation are routine but also indicate compliance with instructions:

- Regular vehicle or machinery maintenance and safety inspection reports
- Product quality control reports showing that percentages of defective output are below pre-established limits
- Inventory records showing that drugs or other hazardous substances are being dispensed properly

The risk management professional only needs copies of these reports and records for documentation purposes.

In other cases, accident and incident reports, customer complaints, and reports from state or federal inspectors can indicate noncompliance. The risk management professional needs access to those reports to help managers correct employees' violations of procedures or to change illegal procedures. Risk management department personnel can also personally observe whether employees are following procedures. This monitoring activity can provide documentation useful in the organization's legal defense. For example, a claimant might charge an organization with negligence because one of the organization's automobiles injured the claimant. A series of detailed vehicle maintenance reports can demonstrate that the organization used reasonable care in maintaining the vehicle, proving that the organization was not negligent.

Similarly, documenting that employees adhered to inventory control procedures for a pharmaceutical firm can negate charges that the firm was at fault in permitting narcotic drugs to be abused by employees. While such evidence is rarely conclusive, it can be of some value in court and of even greater value in dissuading potential claimants from bringing or aggressively pursuing legal claims. Such documentation can also be damaging because it gives evidence of poor maintenance or inventory control. It has therefore been suggested that such records not be kept or that they be destroyed whenever the possibility of a lawsuit arises. However, the claimant's contention that the organization never kept records or destroyed incriminating records (which is powerful circumstantial evidence of the organization's lack of concern or even guilt) can be even more damaging.

Establishing Legal Justifications for Any Invasions of Others' Interests

A third means of risk control for liability is to justify the invasion of others' interests. In certain situations, an organization can have a special legal status that authorizes it to act with legal impunity. That is, the organization's actions do invade others' legally protected interests and do cause harm, but those actions are legally excused because the organization has legal justification for its conduct.

Nature of Legal Justifications

Legal justifications can be established on the basis of legal privilege or legal immunity. A **legal privilege** is the right to invade another's interests to promote or protect one's own, greater interests. In resolving conflicts, the English legal tradition established priorities among competing rights, particularly regarding actions that would otherwise constitute torts. For example, the law generally places more importance on protecting persons than on protecting property and more importance on preserving peace and order than on protecting privacy.

To illustrate, a department store employee giving needed emergency first aid to an injured customer happens to damage that customer's clothing or other possessions. The employee and the department store generally cannot be held liable for any damage to the customer's property that is incidental to providing first aid. Protecting life and health would take precedence over safeguarding property, creating a legal justification for any resulting but unintended property damage.

As another illustration, a bank security officer following a suspected bank robber immediately after the robber leaves the bank can continue the pursuit into another's premises without becoming liable for trespass. If the security officer pursued the bank robber into a physician's waiting room, the security officer and the bank probably would not be liable for trespass into the physician's office or for any unintended damage to the office furnishings incidental to apprehending the suspect. Legally, catching bank robbers is more important than disrupting a doctor's office or damaging some office furniture. The common law of contracts, torts, and crimes often views the invasion of legal interests as a privilege when those invasions safeguard higher priority interests.

The second basis for legal justifications is **immunity.** Certain entities such as governments and governmental officials, charities, young children, and the insane have traditionally not been subject to lawsuits arising out of contract and tort law. Generally, children and the insane are incapable of the intent or mental powers that legal liability usually presumes. Governments and their officials have immunity when conducting their regulatory activities so that the agents of the state can act without fear of legal retribution. Charities are usually immune from suit so that their resources, largely donated for humanitarian purposes, will not be drained.

As stated, governmental or charitable organizations have traditionally been immune from liability loss. Today, however, this immunity has been eroded by courts and legislatures that have found, in practice, little difference exists between businesses and governmental or charitable entities. (For business risk management purposes, the immunity of young children and the insane is rarely relevant.) The growth of social and judicial concern for compensating victims has eroded the traditional legal protections for governmental entities and charities. Consequently, when the interests of the two conflict, governmental immunity and charitable immunity have been revoked to compensate claimants more adequately.

Although immunity can still be valuable in establishing legal justification, sound risk control should not rely on blanket immunity. Risk management professionals of charitable or governmental entities must be aware of the scope of any remaining immunity and, if cost-effective and consistent with the organization's goals, tailor the organization's operations to stay within the bounds of any remaining immunity.

Using Legal Justifications

Most legal justifications, whether based on privilege or immunity, arise from technical legal considerations. Therefore, early in the development of a compliance management program, an organization's risk management professional should consult with legal counsel to determine how much protection privilege and immunity to provide the organization. With counsel, the risk management professional can identify and describe those situations in which the organization and its employees might invade others' interests and be legally protected.

To continue a previous example, the bank guard in immediate pursuit of a thief has the privilege of damaging others' property as an incident to the pursuit, but not to cause others bodily injury (the safety of persons generally having legal priority over the protection of property). Rather than ask a bank guard to weigh these potentially conflicting interests while pursuing a robbery suspect, the bank's risk management professional and legal counsel should develop instructions for guards on how much force they can use when chasing a suspect. This example highlights the risk management professional's central role as facilitator and motivator in developing and implementing a compliance management program.

Another important responsibility of the risk management professional is to encourage others throughout the organization to view their responsibilities from a risk management perspective. All employees should consider how their daily activities can contribute to the organization's cost-effective risk management activities. To illustrate, an organization might have a processing operation that generates considerable noise, fumes, or waste. Owners of neighboring properties might object and perhaps threaten legal action. To forestall any such claims, the risk management professional can work with legal counsel to obtain a special license or zoning variance, permitting the organization to continue its potentially objectionable manufacturing or processing operations. Receiving such special permission or variance would strengthen the organization's negotiating position in resisting or defending neighbors' claims.

Resulting Harm to Others

To prevent liability loss, organizations should try to eliminate the harm suffered by a potential claimant. To bring a legally valid claim, a person or an entity whose legally protected interests have been wrongfully invaded must show harm as a direct consequence of that wrongful invasion. Therefore, even if an organization's activities have invaded the legally protected interests of others, the organization can still prevent claims by eliminating any harm to potential claimants.

The two basic liability risk control measures applicable at this second control point are voluntarily restoring any loss or damage to potential claimants and limiting the kinds of harm potential claimants suffer. This discussion deals with how to reduce liability loss *frequency*. Later in this chapter, similar control measures will be applied differently to show how to reduce the *severity* of liability losses.

Voluntarily Restoring Claimants' Losses

When an organization's activities have clearly caused loss to another, volunteering to restore the damage (repairing or replacing property, paying medical bills, or replacing lost income) can maintain the goodwill of those harmed and reduce the likelihood of a suit. Making voluntary payments to forestall legal action can save a great deal of investigative, legal, and related expenses. Also, should the claimant press for a trial, a judge or jury might award the claimant substantial general damages for pain and suffering. Voluntarily compensating a potential claimant can be a good investment, particularly for small claims. The organization could save a significant amount in settlements and legal expenses, especially if the claimant is likely to win the court case.

Before deciding to volunteer compensation, an organization should carefully analyze the alternatives. Although situations vary, an organization should generally volunteer to compensate a potential claimant when the expected present value of the payments it volunteers is less than the expected present value of the payments of the alternatives, such as (1) defending the suit and letting the case go to a final court verdict or (2) waiting for a claim to be brought and negotiating a settlement before a final court verdict. (This settlement option is really a series of options because settlement can be negotiated at any time before the case reaches a final verdict.) One procedure for evaluating and selecting an alternative is presented at the end of this chapter in the section "Liability Claims Management."

Limiting Kinds of Harm to Potential Claimants

When an organization's wrongful act causes harm, the claimant might be willing to negotiate a voluntary settlement on an amicable basis without filing a legal claim. If, however, the harm to the potential claimant goes unchecked or generates other kinds of harm, the aggravated loss might prompt the potential claimant to file an actual claim. Therefore, the organization should cooperate with a potential claimant to mitigate the initial loss or at least to forestall other kinds of losses from developing.

To illustrate how an organization can help limit harm, assume that a van operated by a moving company backed out of a customer's driveway and damaged the front of a restaurant. If the circumstances suggest that the van driver was negligent, the moving company should help the restaurant repair the property damage, allowing the restaurant to remain open or to reopen promptly with as little loss of business revenue as possible.

On the other hand, if a delay in repairs caused the restaurant to lose substantial income, the restaurant owner might become hostile to the moving company. The restaurateur, once willing to negotiate a friendly settlement, might bring suit to recover the once preventable net income loss. Had the moving company promptly cooperated in confining the loss to the building itself, a suit probably could have been avoided.

An organization should treat potential and actual claimants politely and respectfully whether or not the organization's liability clearly exists. Polite, respectful dealings with potential claimants are essential to avoid liability for harassment, bad faith, or humiliation. Poor conduct can provide new grounds for lawsuits against the organization as well as grounds for punitive damages.

Form of Legal Action

A third control point for liability loss prevention is to attempt to control the legal process. The objective is to dissuade potential claimants from filing a legal claim, or if that is not possible, to limit their legal options.

At least two measures to prevent the filing of a claim are available: (1) negotiating a settlement or (2) agreeing to an alternative to litigation. If an organization has not prevented a claim at the two earlier control points (that is, by preventing invasions of others' interests or by eliminating harm to others), either of these measures might be more cost-effective than waiting for a legal claim to be filed.

Negotiating a Settlement

Even though potential claimants are hostile to the organization, they might be persuaded not to file a claim for a variety of reasons, including the following:

- If the probability is very small that the potential claimants can win in court (perhaps because they have little evidence and the organization intends a vigorous defense). The potential claimants' costs of bringing their legal action could be substantial, and a percentage of the amount awarded the claimant must be paid to the claimant's attorneys.

- If the organization volunteers to pay the potential claimants' compensation and expected present value approximates what could be won in court.

- If the defendant might countersue if the potential claimants bring suit, causing the potential claimants greater financial loss than if they lost in court.

The appropriateness of these strategies varies with the circumstances. Countersuing a defendant, for example, is not always feasible or appropriate. As parties on both sides contemplate the possibility of a formal suit, they should weigh the probabilities of possible outcomes, the effects of other strategies, and the associated expected present values.

Successfully negotiating a settlement at this stage usually requires each party to have at least one set of settlement terms that has a higher expected present value than going to court has. If this set of settlement terms can be identified and cogently presented by one of the parties, a settlement is likely.

To attain a mutually agreeable settlement, the organization must negotiate honorably and not take advantage of a distressed, uninformed, or misled potential claimant. Any lesser standard of negotiating fairness could expose the organization to further liability in tort for bad faith, deceit, intentional infliction of mental distress, or other legal wrongs. Those torts can generate additional adverse court awards (often including punitive damages) against those who have negotiated unfairly. Moreover, a reputation of being overly harsh or unfair to potential claimants can harm an organization's long-term ability to negotiate with future claimants and can jeopardize the organization's public image.

An organization should also avoid the image of being an easy mark, ready to offer a financial settlement to any potential claimant. An organization should strike a balance between fairness and empathy in negotiating settlements, regardless of whether negotiation occurs before or after a formal claim has been filed.

Agreeing on Alternatives to Litigation

Because a lawsuit is usually fraught with delay, court and legal expenses, and uncertainty, many potential litigants favor faster, less expensive, and more predictable mechanisms for resolving their disputes. Parties to a contract usually have broad powers to include in the contract terms for resolving contractual disputes.

The parties might, for example, agree to a nonbinding **mediation** or an **arbitration** procedure to reduce the likelihood of going to court. If the parties are in different states or if the court of jurisdiction is in question, the parties can agree to resolve conflicts according to the law of a particular state. Parties can also agree on liquidated damages, which are sums agreed on in advance as adequate compensation for particular kinds of harm. Such before-the-fact arrangements reduce the likelihood of litigation; they serve as liability loss prevention for at least the defendant and probably save costs for both parties. If some litigation is necessary, before-the-fact arrangements simplify and shorten legal proceedings.

Even in tort cases, which do not typically have preexisting contractual relationships, negotiation or arbitration often discourages claimants from litigation. In many cases, even if negotiation or arbitration does not fully resolve a
claim, it can provide a basis for negotiating an out-of-court agreement on the
remaining disputed items.

To summarize, when all parties to a potential legal claim recognize the advantages of alternatives to litigation, litigation might not be necessary. By ex-
plaining the advantages of litigation alternatives to potential claimants, an
organization can help prevent a liability loss for itself.

Control of Events Increasing Liability Losses

**What factors influence the
size of liability losses?**

**How can you control those
factors and thereby
reduce liability losses?**

The remainder of this chapter deals with
liability loss reduction, which involves
controlling events that occur after a legal
claim has been filed. Loss reduction affects
the amount the organization must pay not
only in a verdict or settlement but also in
investigation, defense, court, and other
litigation-generated costs.

The events that tend to increase the amount (or severity) of a liability loss
are the following:

1.   The plaintiff's choice of a jurisdiction unfavorable to the defendant orga-
     nization
2.   The absence of an amicable resolution of the suit
3.   Severe harm to the plaintiff
4.   A high degree of culpability by the organization
5.   The absence of a strong legal defense by the organization

(Note that when a suit is filed against the organization, the person or other
entity who was a claimant in the earlier discussions in this chapter becomes a
plaintiff, and the organization becomes a defendant.)

Liability loss reduction involves countering one or more of these five events,
each of which offers another liability risk control point. Those five control
points influence liability loss severity rather than loss frequency. The following sections discuss the five control points and their corresponding loss reduction measures.

Selection of Jurisdiction

From a defendant's standpoint, some state or federal district jurisdictions are more favorable than others. The plaintiff, however, usually has the most direct control over the jurisdiction in which a case is heard. The plaintiff typically has the right to bring suit in any jurisdiction that has an interest in the case either because of where the alleged wrongful act occurred or where one of the parties resides, is headquartered, or does business. Therefore, a claimant seeking to file a suit often looks for a jurisdiction that is likely to find for the plaintiff and/or grant a larger verdict. (No such options apply in criminal cases because the location of the government entity bringing the criminal charges determines the jurisdiction.)

Nonetheless, a defendant can use several measures to influence and perhaps limit the plaintiff's choice of jurisdictions to one more favorable to the defendant. First, the defendant can specify in the contract the jurisdiction(s) in which any disputes between the contracting parties would be resolved. This contractual agreement binds both parties, provided the specified jurisdiction has some reasonable contact or concern with the matters in litigation.

Second, once a plaintiff has filed a claim, a defendant can challenge the court's jurisdiction and have the case moved to another jurisdiction. The challenge must be based on conflicts of law, principles that are complicated and often the subject of extensive litigation.

Challenging a court's jurisdiction is a defensive, delaying measure that can generate substantial legal and court costs for the defendant. Nonetheless, if a challenge lowers the expected present value of the defendant's ultimate liability loss by postponing compensation or increasing the likelihood that the plaintiff will settle on terms more favorable to the defendant, this measure might be warranted.

Third, the defendant can countersue in a jurisdiction whose laws or legal procedures are favorable to the defendant. In effect, the defendant can put the shoe on the other foot by filing what amounts to a counterclaim against the threatened suit. Properly filing any aspect of a dispute in a particular jurisdiction generally ensures that, unless a conflict of laws arises, all other suits regarding that dispute will be heard in the same jurisdiction. This measure might be applicable only to contractual claims, which have greater possibilities for valid counterclaims than do tort claims. However, even in some tort cases in which both parties are arguably at fault, a preemptive suit can offer opportunities to obtain a favorable jurisdiction.

Fourth, an organization can undertake a long-term effort to modify the laws of the jurisdiction, slowly making them more favorable. Such a measure is really liability loss prevention for future claims and is not applicable after filing a claim, which will usually be adjudicated on the basis of the laws in effect when the alleged wrongful act occurred. For example, many organizations work with legislative, executive, and other government bodies to modify the unfavorable terms of products liability, workplace safety, and environmental pollution statutes or court precedents. Organizations believe that changing the laws ensures that future claims will be adjudicated in jurisdictions with laws more favorable to them.

Resolution of Claims

Reaching an amicable, out-of-court claim settlement, even after it has become a formal lawsuit, typically reduces a defendant's liability losses. The settlement is at least reasonably acceptable to the defendant, and the defendant's cost of litigation and uncertainty are reduced. Thus, negotiating a settlement can be cost-effective liability loss reduction just as amicably resolving a dispute before it becomes a legal claim can be sound liability loss prevention.

The same negotiating and claims administration measures for pre-lawsuit liability loss prevention are also valid for post-suit liability loss reduction any time before a final verdict. For example, negotiations can lead to a settlement that offers both parties a financial outcome whose expected present value is greater than that of continuing the litigation. To foster such productive negotiations, a defendant should avoid aggravating the plaintiff or increasing original harm. Rather, the defendant should seek areas of cooperation and agreement to reduce its liability losses.

Severity of Harm

Preventing harm to potential claimants is the best liability loss prevention. After a claim has been filed, however, reducing the severity of the plaintiff's harm remains a valid measure for decreasing, or at least not increasing, a defendant's liability loss.

Once a suit has been filed, the defendant can ask the court having jurisdiction to require the plaintiff to mitigate its own loss. To illustrate, in the previous example of the restaurant damaged by the moving van, the moving company can emphasize in court the restaurant's duty to remain open (or reopen as soon as possible) to reduce both its own revenue loss and the amount the defendant would otherwise have to pay to compensate the defendant.

Again, the defendant can invoke the court to protect or salvage damaged property or rehabilitate injured persons as part of a negotiated settlement or final court verdict. The court might be an ally of the defendant, encouraging or forcing the plaintiff to reduce the harm for which the defendant is required to pay.

As discussed earlier, the defendant's negotiations play an important role in liability loss reduction by controlling the severity of harm to the plaintiff. The defendant must not commit further wrongful conduct (harassment, bad faith, or deceit) while negotiating a settlement. Once a claim has been filed, the court can help maintain a constructive climate for negotiations. The parties and their legal counsels can ask the court as a mediator and referee to overcome any seemingly unreasonable positions of either party. Faced with congested court dockets and aware of the public expense involved in protracted courtroom proceedings, many judges can facilitate negotiated settlements.

Degree of Organization's Culpability

The degree of a defendant's culpability or guilt often affects the court decision and size of the verdict or severity of the punishment. A defendant who acts with clear intent to harm, who wantonly disregards others' safety, or who acts wrongfully with knowledge of the consequences generally deserves more blame and a higher legal penalty than someone who is careless and inadvertently harms others.

Because a low degree of culpability tends to lower the number of court verdicts (or sometimes a judgment favoring the defendant), an organization can reduce its liability losses by acting responsibly and ethically toward actual and potential plaintiffs. Once a legal claim has been filed, ethically responsible conduct toward the plaintiff requires the same equitable negotiating conduct described earlier for liability loss prevention. A plaintiff should be treated fairly. Any attempt to secure a settlement through abusive tactics could seal a defendant's guilt or add to the plaintiff's court award.

Carefully instructing all employees and other agents in proper conduct at the scene of an accident or other event that might be expected to generate a legal claim is another means for controlling the degree of an organization's culpability. An employee's conduct and attitude can greatly influence how a potential claimant views the organization.

Moreover, the failure of an organization's employee to secure first aid for an injured person or to safeguard another's property from further harm can be an act of negligence. Thus, employees and other agents should be trained to deal with accident victims, complaining customers, visitors, and others when an accident or other event creates circumstances that might lead to a legal claim. Supervised role playing can be useful in such training.

Legal Defense

When an organization wrongfully invades another's legally protected interest, causing harm, and when those who have been harmed will not agree to a negotiated settlement, the remaining liability risk control measure is a strong legal defense. The goal of this defense is to convince the judge and jury that legal liability does not exist or is minimal for the defendant.

Controlling the courtroom legal defenses is an essential risk management responsibility. This responsibility includes (1) preserving the organization's legal defenses, (2) selecting and cooperating with legal counsel defending the claim, and (3) participating in negotiation decisions.

Preserving Legal Defenses

Preserving legal defenses means documenting the facts related to a loss-causing event and protecting the organization's rights. Preserving legal defenses is often a result of actions taken long before the event that generates liability. All employees who might become involved in liability-generating events should be trained not only in the procedures described in the preceding section but also in those listed below:

- Obtaining the names and addresses of persons involved in or witnessing the events that can produce a claim

- Collecting (or photographing, if possible) physical evidence of the accident or occurrence, especially in the case of an allegedly defective product

- Avoiding statements that could be interpreted as admissions of responsibility

- Notifying the appropriate person within the organization

In addition to these general guidelines, documentation should indicate the organization's commitment to proper, safe, and legally mandated conduct. This is especially true for particular activities such as manufacturing a safe product, maintaining premises in acceptably safe condition, operating and maintaining vehicles properly, complying with pollution regulations, and paying taxes when due. In addition, training, inspection, and maintenance activities should be documented to ensure that personnel are carrying out their responsibilities as instructed. Records should also indicate steps taken to achieve legal compliance and measures to prevent the recurrence of unsafe activities.

Regular documentation can be valuable evidence in defending future lawsuits. Because it is impossible to predict the timing or the circumstances of a claim, documentation must be maintained for substantial, even indefinite, periods and should include information likely to be needed in defense against particular types of claims. For example, against products liability suits, an organization needs to document the following:

- The organization's commitment, as a matter of policy, to the safety and the quality of the product
- Product design procedures and prototype testing
- Compliance with applicable regulatory standards for initial design and marketing and for subsequent product changes
- Care in selecting and purchasing the raw materials or other components of the product and independent organizations that distribute, market, or install the product
- Regular quality control testing of output
- Procedures for identifying particular items, batches, or models of products and tracing their specific manufacture and distribution to allow recall of potentially defective output
- Procedures for promptly and courteously handling customer complaints and appropriate actions to correct any potential product defects suggested by those complaints

Selecting and Cooperating With Legal Counsel

Many organizations do not use legal counsel until after an accident or incident (or perhaps until after an actual claim has been filed). In doing so, those organizations forfeit the contributions that legal counsel can make to many phases of a liability risk control program, thus significantly weakening a legal defense when a case goes to trial.

In contrast, if an organization retains an attorney to prepare for potential future liability claims, the attorney can (1) design a documentation system to help defend particular kinds of claims, (2) develop warranties, sales literature procedures, exculpatory agreements, and claims-handling procedures, and (3) help employees and other agents acquire the attitudes and basic legal knowledge that can prevent invasions of others' interests.

An organization can employ an in-house attorney, retain independent counsel, or rely on an insurer's pool of legal talent or the organization's risk management professional. However, regardless of which type of counsel is used, the organization should select counsel who has experience and demonstrated expertise in defending the kinds of contract, tort, or criminal claims likely to be brought against the organization. The organization should be honest with this attorney within the privileged context of the attorney/client relationship and be willing to follow the advice of counsel in the strategic planning and execution of specific legal claims.

Participating in Settlement Negotiations

An organization's risk management professional (and perhaps, for major claims, its senior management) should take an active interest in lawsuit negotiations. Before a final verdict, the negotiations might offer opportunities to resolve the suit more favorably than would the court. Therefore, regardless of whether any negotiations are handled by the organization's or by the insurer's legal counsel, the organization's risk management professional or other responsible executive should advise the lawyers in designing or appraising the acceptability of various settlement offers. Without such guidance, the attorneys might fail to recognize or might reject a possibly advantageous settlement offer.

The key words describing the organization's role in these settlement negotiations are "participate in," "advise," and "guide." However, the attorneys should direct the settlement negotiations. If the suit is not covered by insurance, the organization's own legal counsel should direct the negotiations. If an insurance policy applies, this policy will almost always give the insurer the right to control the litigation, including settlement negotiations. In either case, however, the organization's risk management professional and/or senior management should ensure that counsel is aware of the organization's goals in any settlement and should be available to assist in settlement negotiations.

Liability Claims Management

> **What strategies can help you manage liability claims effectively?**
>
> **How can those strategies be applied to particular situations?**

Exhibit 8-1 summarized risk control strategies for liability losses. Effectively managing potential or actual liability claims often combines these strategies or uses different strategies at different times. The options available throughout a liability case and the need to estimate the expected value of each of these options provide the opportunity to use the decision tree analysis (presented in Chapter 3) to choose the best option or options.

The logic of the decision tree is illustrated in Exhibit 8-3, which portrays a simplified decision tree that the risk manager of the hypothetical Sheltering Arms Hospital might construct in deciding whether the hospital should contest a specific medical malpractice claim. If Sheltering Arms decides to legally defend the claim, the hospital faces the second choice of whether to offer the claimant advance payments. Sheltering Arms would hope that voluntary payments, made without admission of liability, would speed the claimant's recovery and reduce hostility toward Sheltering Arms.

Exhibit 8-3
Defendant's Decision Tree for Liability Claim

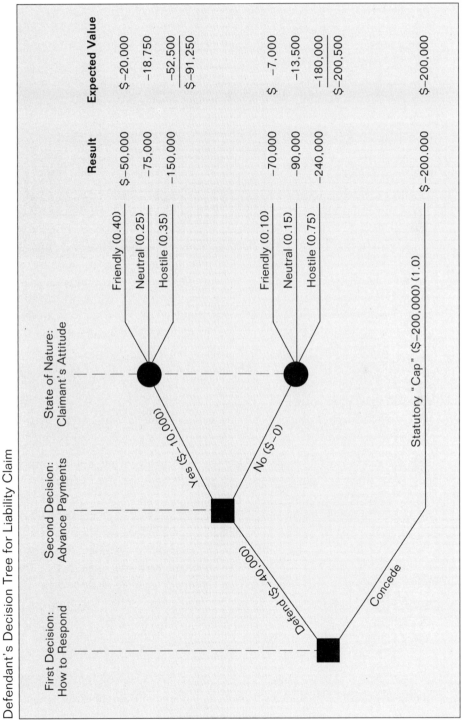

First Decision: How to Respond	Second Decision: Advance Payments	State of Nature: Claimant's Attitude	Result	Expected Value
		Friendly (0.40)	$-50,000	$-20,000
		Neutral (0.25)	-75,000	-18,750
		Hostile (0.35)	-150,000	-52,500
				$-91,250
	Yes ($-10,000)			
	No ($-0)	Friendly (0.10)	-70,000	$ -7,000
		Neutral (0.15)	-90,000	-13,500
		Hostile (0.75)	-240,000	-180,000
				$-200,500
Defend ($-40,000)				
Concede	Statutory "Cap" ($-200,000) (1.0)		$-200,000	$-200,000

Assume that the hospital's risk management professional estimates that a legal defense would cost Sheltering Arms approximately $40,000. On the other hand, conceding fault allows the claimant to collect the maximum amount permitted by the applicable state statute, which places a $200,000 cap on medical malpractice claims. Furthermore, if Sheltering Arms presents a legal defense and offers the claimant advance payments, these voluntary payments would probably amount to another $10,000.

As Exhibit 8-3 suggests, the expected outcome of conceding fault is a certain $200,000 loss. In contrast, the likely outcomes of presenting a defense for $40,000 and then either offering or not offering an estimated $10,000 of advance payment depend heavily on the claimant's attitudes. If, as depicted in the upper branches of the exhibit, Sheltering Arms presents a $40,000 legal defense and the claimant is satisfied with the $10,000 volunteered advance payment, the total cost to the hospital will be $50,000. If the claimant is not fully satisfied with the advance payment but adopts a neutral attitude toward the hospital, the claimant might be willing to settle for an additional $25,000, making the hospital's total cost $75,000. Alternatively, if the claimant is hostile despite receiving $10,000 in advance payment, the risk management professional estimates that the claimant might be able to collect an additional $100,000 in court, bringing the hospital's whole cost to $150,000 ($40,000 + $10,000 + $100,000). Having discussed this case with the hospital's medical personnel and its legal counsel, the risk management professional estimates that, under these conditions, there is a 40 percent chance that the claimant will be friendly, a 25 percent chance that he will be neutral, and a 35 percent chance that he will be hostile despite receiving an advance payment.

If Sheltering Arms spends $40,000 for legal defense but offers no advance payment, the risk management professional believes the claimant is much more likely to be hostile. Under the conditions indicated in the center portion of Exhibit 8-3, assume a 10 percent chance the claimant will be friendly, a 15 percent chance his attitude will be neutral, and a 75 percent chance he will be hostile. A friendly claimant might settle for only $30,000, bringing the hospital's total cost to $70,000 (defense costs plus the settlement). In contrast, if the claimant is neutral, he might demand $50,000, bringing the hospital's total cost to $90,000 (the same $40,000 for defense plus the higher settlement). Under the worst circumstances, a hostile claimant unwilling to settle could probably collect the full $200,000 statutory cap on the claim, making the hospital's total cost $240,000 ($40,000 + $200,000).

The expected values of each of the three basic strategies (conceding the claim, defending and offering advance payments, and defending while offering no advance payment) are shown in the right side of the exhibit. Those expected values are computed by multiplying each result by its associated probability and then summing the results for each strategy. Conceding the claim can therefore be expected to result in a $200,000 loss; presenting a defense but offering no advance payment appears to be a slightly worse strategy, resulting in an expected loss of $200,500. Among those three strategies, the best choice appears to be defending the claim while offering advance payment. This strategy can be expected to lead to a loss of only $91,250.

This example of decision making in managing liability claims has been simplified by (1) assuming a statutory cap that places a limit on the maximum potential loss, (2) considering only two decision points (the first being to defend/concede and the second to offer/not offer advance payment), and (3) assuming the probabilities of the alternative results can be estimated with some accuracy. A more realistic decision tree would contain more rectangular boxes for additional decision points and more circles for outcomes of chance events. Nonetheless, Exhibit 8-3 illustrates the logic of the decision-making sequence that should underlie the proper management of liability claims.

Summary

Liability losses are the expenses an organization incurs to investigate, defend, settle, or fulfill court verdicts from specific legal claims against the organization. The organization's risk control program must reduce the expected present value of the sum of these liability losses plus expenditures to prevent potential claimants from bringing suit. Controlling the costs of preventing the peril (here, liability claims) from occurring and the costs of the losses to the organization when the peril does strike is crucial for controlling all kinds of property, liability, personnel, and net income losses. For liability losses, however, the expenditures to prevent losses deserve particular attention because the most cost-effective opportunities for liability risk control arise long before an actual legal claim occurs.

This chapter has traced the stages in the development of a claim and of the claim's potential development into an adverse court verdict. At each of these stages, an organization can take a number of specific measures to control its losses. At the control points that occur before an actual claim is filed, liability loss prevention measures are applicable. After such a claim is filed, the remaining control points provide opportunities for liability loss reduction. Those loss prevention and reduction measures as well as the control points at which they can be applied most effectively were illustrated in Exhibit 8-1.

A risk management professional should act as a catalyst, an initiator, and a coordinator of others' actions to control or ideally to reduce the expected present value of liability losses and liability risk control costs. He or she needs to actively work with others to (1) develop a compliance management system to forestall wrongful invasions of others' interests; (2) confer with legal counsel to limit obligations to others, reach settlements with potential or actual claimants on relatively favorable terms, and provide the organization with a strong defense where appropriate; and (3) work with senior executives, middle managers, and front-line employees to make liability risk control an essential element of every employee's job.

Chapter 9

Controlling Environmental Losses

Outline, continued

Environmental Risk Assessment
Review Components

Conducting an Environmental Risk
Assessment

Applying Risk Control to Environmental Loss Situations

Loss Control and Regulatory
Noncompliance

Loss Control and the Discovery of
Contamination

Loss Control and the Sudden or
Accidental Event

Loss Control in Ongoing
Organizational Practice

Role of Risk Management Professionals in Environmental Risk Management Programs

Risk Assessment and Evaluation

Review and Management of
Environmental Risk Financing

Comparative Risk Evaluation

External Risk Communication

Internal Risk Communication

Acquisition and Litigation Support

Summary

Controlling Environmental Losses

Over the past twenty years, few issues have generated as much public attention, scientific research, and government regulation as environmental protection. Environmental concerns seem endless. Smog in cities, unsafe drinking water, the threat of cancer from pesticides or other toxic materials, abandoned landfills, and wildlife habitat destruction are just a few examples of the issues society is addressing. The public is deluged with information about potential hazards to human and environmental health, and science continues to provide insights into cause-and-effect relationships never before imagined or understood. All of this prompts even more attention and concern about the effect human activity and development has on the environment.

The concept of **environmental risk management** is central to societal debate and discussion concerning environmental issues. However, this concept has two possible interpretations. For risk management professionals, environmental risk management means protecting organizational assets and resources from losses pertaining to the natural environment and from losses pertaining to environmental protection. Like other exposure areas, the physical environment and the laws designed to protect it are a potential source of net income, personnel, liability, and property losses that must be identified, evaluated, and managed. But within public agencies and other organizations with environmental protection responsibilities, the concept of environmental risk management is different. Within these circles, the values at risk are environmental values such as clean air, clean water, productive land, and wildlife. The source of hazards are human and organizational activity, and the objective of risk control is to manage these activities to protect environmental values at risk. The challenge of reconciling both perspectives of environmental risk control—protecting environmental values while safeguarding the economic interests of organizations—makes environmental risk management one of the most technically demanding and complex risk management areas. This chapter presents both perspectives.

Adding to the challenge of environmental risk management are the many ways an organization interacts with its environment. Environmental exposures permeate every aspect of an organization and its activities. A facility's site might threaten a rare plant or animal. Constructing this facility might cause runoff and sedimentation in a nearby lake or river. Operating the facility might create many exposures pertaining to the materials used, their transportation and storage, the waste and releases created in the process, and treatment and disposal practices. Using and disposing of the products might create the potential for environmental harm. Even office activities might create loss exposures due to indoor air pollution, especially for employees who are particularly sensitive to specific chemicals. Smokestacks, storage tanks, and landfills are just a few of the traditional exposures associated with environmental loss control.

It is not possible or even desirable for risk management professionals to attain a scientist's or an ecologist's understanding of environmental issues. The complexity of environmental loss exposures requires an organization to tap information, skills, and expertise from many areas of the firm. People from many disciplines—including risk management professionals—should be included. This chapter provides risk management professionals with basic knowledge of environmental risk control. First, it provides an overview of key environmental definitions and concepts. The chapter then explores major types and sources of environmental loss exposures, discusses procedures to identify and evaluate them, and applies the loss control process to common environmental decision-making situations. The chapter concludes by discussing the roles and contributions of risk management professionals in controlling environmental losses. Specifically, after reading this chapter, risk management professionals should be able to do the following:

- Recognize primary types of environmental loss exposures and their sources
- Apply a hierarchical framework for reducing environmental exposures and controlling environmental losses
- Describe essential elements of an environmental risk assessment
- Communicate more effectively with environmental risk management specialists and other managers in planning and implementing an environmental risk management strategy
- Develop and implement an environmental risk management program
- Contribute to the development and functioning of an environmental risk management program

Environmental Risk Management Concepts

This chapter presents concepts important in identifying, evaluating, and reducing environmental exposures. Several concepts and issues make environmental loss control unique and are presented here as an introduction for risk management professionals.

> **What are the environmental liability concepts of pollution, cross media transfer, life cycle impact, nonpoint sources, and environmental risk management hierarchy?**
>
> **What are your special challenges in environmental loss control?**

Fundamental Concepts

Like any other field of study, environmental risk control contains specialized concepts and terms. Risk management professionals need not be proficient in all fields of study, but they should understand several key concepts in order to help environmental risk control professionals develop and implement effective environmental loss control strategies.

Pollution

The **environment** is a complex, interconnected set of relationships and systems involving all living things and their surroundings. These relationships and systems provide many values essential to all life, including clean air, clean water, food, raw materials, energy, and the ability to process wastes. **Pollution** means introducing physical or chemical properties that negatively affect the ability of environmental systems to provide these values. This broad definition is subjective, and determining what is and what is not pollution remains a subject of tremendous societal debate. Risk management professionals should understand the key characteristics of pollution, which have implications for identifying and evaluating risks.

First, pollution has a **qualitative dimension**. As stated, pollution can result from introducing materials or substances into the environment that are not naturally found in that environment. This introduction, or contamination, may present a direct hazard to the health and welfare of plants, animals, or people, or it may prevent natural systems from providing environmental values as effectively or efficiently as before contamination. The qualitative dimension of pollution includes properties as well as physical materials or substances. Consider a facility that discharges waste water into a local river or lake. Although this waste water contains no contaminants, it is discharged at a significantly higher temperature than the receiving body of water. Over time, the temperature of the receiving body of water is raised, triggering algae growth near the facility. This growth reduces the oxygen available in the water, killing fish and other aquatic life. This is one example of how pollution can also result from introducing physical or chemical conditions, such as light, noise, or higher acidity, into the environment.

Pollution also has a **quantitative dimension**. All natural systems, as well as the populations in these systems (plants, animals, and people), have limited abilities to process wastes, withstand contamination, and adapt to changes without harmful effects. Pollution occurs when these natural thresholds are exceeded, resulting in harm or damage. Quantitative risk assessments attempt to determine the natural thresholds for various populations. These assessments examine the levels of exposures that, if exceeded, adversely affect populations and systems. Much of environmental regulation is based on risk-based quantitative standards that limit the amount or concentration of substances that can be released into the environment. For example, permissible levels for releases of heavy metals in the environment are typically measured in concentrations of parts per million. These standards will change as a result of new scientific understanding and political pressure. In the eyes of regulatory agencies, once these standards or thresholds have been exceeded, "pollution" occurs.

Cross-Media Transfer

Pollution enters the environment through one of three media—air, water, or land. Efforts to protect one medium from harm (and reduce the associated risk to the organization) frequently create new threats and risks in another medium. This phenomenon is called **cross-media transfer**, and it is a special challenge for environmental and risk management professionals. For example, consider a painting operation that needs to control paint particles escaping from the facility as air pollution. Management purchases a water-wash spray booth to capture these paint particles in water. Although the air pollution problem has been solved, a potential water pollution problem now exists. To address this new concern, management installs a water treatment system to treat the water so that it can legally be discharged into the environment. However, the paint particles must now be distilled into a sludge, creating a potential land disposal problem. If after many years the landfill leaks, the ground water may become contaminated, resulting in a new water pollution problem.

Cross-media transfer often forces managers to find optimal ways to manage pollutants. Using control equipment to capture pollutants and using treatment systems to reduce pollutants' environmental effects are standard risk reduction practices. However, use of these practices may create a potential new set of environmental exposures in another medium. Risk management professionals should recognize that once pollutants or wastes are created, environmental exposures can seldom be completely eliminated.

Life Cycle Impact

Materials and substances may pose different types and degrees of risk to the environment and to the organization at different times. **Life cycle impact** is the cumulative review and assessment of the environmental effect a product or substance has at different stages of its existence. For example, a car battery, which contains heavy metals and acids, has environmental exposures associated with its manufacture. New environmental risks arise once the battery's useful life has expired and the heavy metals and acids must be disposed of. Another example is the class of chemical compounds known as chlorofluorocarbons, or "CFCs." For many years, CFCs were considered the ideal refrigerant and propellant because they were nontoxic, noncorrosive, and nonflammable. CFCs were considered "environmentally friendly," and once their useful life was complete, they were simply released into the atmosphere. However, new evidence suggested that once released into the atmosphere, CFCs degraded the earth's protective ozone layer. Consequently, use of these compounds in many applications is now illegal, and the substances are being phased out internationally.

Increasingly, organizations must assess "cradle to grave" environmental exposure—environmental risks posed during research, design, manufacture, transportation, use, and disposal of the product. Identifying potential environmental concerns before they exist may allow organizations to reduce or even eliminate certain exposures by changing the design of the product, the materials used, and the manufacturing processes. Strategic approaches, such as life cycle impact assessments, are becoming important tools for risk management professionals.

Nonpoint Sources

Pollution is often attributed to an individual source or discharge point—such as an individual manufacturing plant. However, much of what is considered pollution is the cumulative result of activities spread over large geographic areas. The resultant pollution is called "nonpoint source" pollution because it is difficult to identify its point of origin. Examples of nonpoint source pollution include pesticide contamination of a river from farms extending for hundreds of miles along the banks or sedimentation of a lake from large-scale logging and construction practices. Historically, nonpoint sources have been difficult to regulate because of the challenge of tracing the origins of pollutants and applying specific controls to them.

Environmental Risk Management Hierarchy

Environmental risk management is the process of managing the materials, wastes, and releases of an organization to lessen their effects on environmental values and to ensure compliance with all applicable laws and regulations. The **environmental risk management program** is the set of policies, structures, strategies, and procedures created to implement this process. A successful environmental risk management program is integrally connected to the risk management program, and most environmental risk management decisions should be made within the context of this program. The relationship between risk control and organizational environmental risk management is discussed later in this chapter.

An organization may have many strategies to reduce or eliminate its environmental loss exposures. These strategies can be grouped into five general environmental risk management approaches:

1. Source reduction
2. Reuse
3. Recycling
4. Control and treatment
5. Disposal

Source reduction, or pollution prevention, is any action taken at the source to reduce or eliminate the actual creation of pollutants or wastes. In this management approach, the organization investigates and identifies the reasons the pollutants, wastes, and releases exist. Changes are subsequently made in processes, materials, or equipment to reduce or eliminate waste creation and increase process efficiency. In the painting example, switching to a more efficient paint gun, which applies more of the paint to the part (and therefore releases less into the air), is an example of a source reduction strategy.

Reuse is a management approach that uses the product or material again without physically or chemically treating it. For example, a solvent that has been used to clean machinery might be collected and used in another manufacturing area where a dirty solvent wash is acceptable. **Recycling** is reusing the material or substance after it has gone through some physical or chemical process to restore its functional properties. In the solvent example, after several uses, the solvent might be too dirty for use in any application. Rather than dispose of the material, it might be collected, distilled to remove contaminants, and used again.

Control and treatment encompass many activities to handle wastes after they have been created. **Pollution control** is capturing pollutants before their discharge or release into the environment. **Pollution treatment** is physically or chemically altering pollutants or wastes to reduce their volume, toxicity, or overall environmental effect. Many sophisticated treatment technologies exist, including physical treatment, chemical treatment, biological treatment, thermal treatment, and immobilization. These control and treatment technologies are often regulated by law. **Disposal** is depositing or discharging waste directly onto the land, into landfills, or into bodies of water. Disposal is carefully regulated, and materials typically require extensive treatment before this strategy is permissible.

A company will commonly employ all of these strategies in its overall environmental risk management effort. From the standpoint of environmental risk control, risk management professionals typically view these strategies in a hierarchical manner; the strategies, in descending order of preference, are source reduction, reuse, recycling, control and treatment, and disposal. Source reduction is the preferred option in this hierarchy because exposures are avoided completely or reduced without creating new exposures in other areas. In the painting example, the new, more efficient paint gun reduces air emissions without creating new liability exposures due to water or land pollution. Reuse and recycling contain elements of both loss prevention and loss reduction. By reusing and recycling the spent solvent, the organization may prevent and reduce exposures because it decreases inventory and storage needs and reduces the frequency and volume of shipments of dirty solvent. Control and treatment approaches decrease the potential environmental effect and are the most common strategy used because they provide the highest degree of predictability and simplicity in dealing with environmental regulations. However, because those approaches manage but do not avoid pollutants, some risks and exposures might remain or new ones may be created. For example, although hazardous waste incineration may be an effective loss control option for an organization, environmental risks will not be completely eliminated because the incineration process creates air emissions and ash residue that must still be managed. Disposal is the least desirable risk management option for two reasons. First, introducing pollutants directly to environmental media implicitly entails the greatest risk. Second, environmental law dictates that liability for environmental harm will remain with the organization—even if the firm contracts with another organization for this service.

In reviewing management options, risk management professionals must consider other factors besides risk. Employee safety, cost, technical feasibility, disruption to operations, and regulatory demands are other key factors risk management professionals must consider in selecting and implementing a strategy. Although the hierarchy can provide general guidance for managing environmental risks, specific management decisions also require evaluating these other factors.

Special Challenges of Environmental Loss Control

The previous discussion of basic environmental concepts suggests some of the difficulties of environmental risk management. Environmental risk management has several distinguishing characteristics that place considerable demands on the organization.

More Than Just Accidental Events

Risk management professionals typically focus on sudden or accidental occurrences. Many environmental losses do originate from events such as spills, leaks, or equipment failures that result in unplanned discharges. However, the majority of environmental loss exposures have a very strong element of predictability and planning associated with them. Organizations consciously release certain types and amounts of pollutants into the air, water, and land and will make carefully calculated decisions about the technologies, techniques, and procedures with which this is done.

These "planned" releases still create exposures because environmental compliance does not protect an organization from suits pertaining to third-party or natural resources damages resulting from legal emissions or discharges. Moreover, many environmental losses are based on past practices rather than present conditions or future events. Many of the high-profile and most expensive environmental losses are for waste disposal practices undertaken over past decades when environmental awareness was low and safeguards were nonexistent. Similarly, standard operating practices may gradually contaminate property. In many ways, these loss exposures are the opposite of sudden and accidental occurrences—they are time bombs that have existed for years. The concept of accidental loss remains essential to effective environmental risk management, but "accidental events" are just one of many possible types of environmental loss exposures.

Technical Demands

Environmental loss control is also marked by very steep technical learning curves. A variety of technical specialists need to be part of the risk control team. These specialists include toxicologists to understand the behavior of materials, biologists to evaluate the effects of pollution on environmental relationships, and industrial hygienists to evaluate the risks of pollution to human health. A high degree of coordination among these professionals is also needed for effective loss control decisions. Because the technical demands placed on environmental risk management experts are great, it has been preferable to take specialists in environmental risk management and teach them risk management principles rather than to transform risk management professionals into environmental risk management experts.

Event/Loss Relationship

A lag time of months, years, or even decades can exist between an environmental occurrence and a claim or financial loss. Materials deposited in a landfill may slowly leach into ground water supplies and require cleanup twenty-five years later. A worker in a manufacturing facility may be exposed to a toxic chemical that results in chronic health problems a decade after the initial exposure. Time lags such as these are common in environmental risk management and are a continuing challenge for risk management professionals.

Regulatory Change and Complexity

Risk management professionals also face the challenges created by complex and changing environmental regulations. One of the most significant perils accompanying environmental risk management is regulatory change. New standards, new regulated substances, and new technology or permitting requirements can dramatically increase liability exposures. Changing environmental standards may render an organization's past investments in pollution control insufficient. Moreover, land use regulations and requirements and a growing body of international environmental agreements add to the regulatory challenge and possibility of loss. The regulatory framework for environmental loss control decisions can be very complex.

Difficulty in Evaluating Environmental Risk

Evaluating environmental risk and assigning expected values to potential exposures is often as much art as science. In the environmental area, more information on risk does not necessarily result in an increased ability to evaluate risk. For example, an organization may know it shares responsibility with other organizations for cleaning up a contaminated site. Detailed information may exist on the types and amounts of contamination and its threat to off-site areas. However, identifying expected values of losses will likely be complicated because the organization is uncertain about its degree of responsibility and the final remediation costs, which may extend for years following the start of the cleanup. Further complicating the financial analysis of loss exposures are historical inconsistencies in legal rulings regarding damages and the difficulty of assigning economic values to ecological values that do not readily lend themselves to economic analysis. Debates commonly occur over assigning economic values to clean air, clean water, an old growth forest, or a particular plant or animal. Creating expected values for natural resource damages can be especially problematic. For example, in a famous oil spill accident, extensive debate arose over the appropriate dollar value ascribed to sea otters.

Limited Risk Financing Options

The number of available environmental risk management options may be limited, making risk control the only economically feasible management option available. Contractual transfer of environmental risk financing is difficult, if not impossible, to attain for most organizations that generate pollutants. Estimates are that the steep technical and regulatory learning curves create start-up costs two to three times higher than nonenvironmental insurance offerings and are 8 percent to 12 percent more expensive to maintain. The high cost of claims, lack of historical data, inconsistencies in legal rulings, pace of regulatory change, and time lags between occurrence and loss all contribute to an uncertain base for policy creation. Although specialty markets exist in environmental risk financing for organizations that specialize in waste transport or cleanup or deal with particular substances, "pollution insurance" is rare or prohibitively expensive for most organizations. This places even greater demands on the environmental risk management effort.

Implications for Environmental Risk Management Efforts

These special challenges are shifting the emphasis and strategy of many environmental risk management programs. Some organizations may control certain environmental risks by contractual transfer. If it is compatible with other business and economic needs, the organization will outsource to other firms the operations with significant exposures. However, for organizations that must control risks internally, a shift to a pre-loss program orientation and an aggressively preventive approach to loss control are increasingly necessary. The technical and financial realities of environmental damages are such that organizations focusing on managing pollutants after they have been created face an uphill and often costly struggle.

Many organizations see source reduction (or pollution prevention) as a cornerstone of a new risk management approach. Chapter 1 observed that the objective of the risk control manager is to reduce both the cost of risk control measures and the costs of losses those measures aim to control. For environmental pollution losses, only source reduction accomplishes both of these objectives simultaneously. Control and treatment will remain popular and effective risk control measures because they reduce the severity and frequency of potential losses and often facilitate compliance with existing regulations. However, these risk control measures are also typically expensive, do not add value to the organization, and are open to the peril of changing regulatory standards. Understanding cause-and-effect relationships (the reasons wastes and releases exist in the first place) and undertaking preventive measures at the source to eliminate or reduce pollutants have become the preferred risk control strategies for many organizations.

Sources and Types of Environmental Loss Exposures

What is the relationship between the Environmental Protection Agency and the states concerning environmental protection?

What loss exposures can arise from the major environmental liability statutes?

What loss exposures arise from actual harm to the environment?

Environmental loss exposures pervade many organizations. The types of products made, the raw materials used, the equipment used, the inventory storage and handling procedures, the types of waste generated, and the location of the facility are potential contributors to an organization's environmental loss profile. Generally, an organization's environmental loss exposures can be broadly grouped into two classes. The first class is liability exposures arising out of environmental regulations and consisting of penalties, fines, injunctions, and even criminal indictments for violating environmental protection laws. Such liability exposures exist regardless of whether actual harm to the environment occurs. The second class of exposures is based on actual physical or functional harm done to the environment that results in losses either for the organization itself or for third parties who have experienced property, net income, or personnel losses as a result of the organization's activities.

Loss Exposures Arising Out of Environmental Liability

Until a quarter century ago, releasing pollutants into the environment went largely unchecked. Today, a complex set of federal, state, and local laws regulates the activities of organizations that generate, use, transport, treat, or dispose of potential environmental pollutants. Much of this regulation concerns materials and substances that are either carcinogenic to humans or deemed "hazardous," that is, having properties that are either toxic, corrosive, flammable, or reactive with other substances. However, given less and less space for landfills, regulatory interest in solid wastes and other materials that do not exhibit any of these properties has grown. In short, most manufacturing or service organizations involved in transforming or using substances and materials are likely to have some environmental liability exposure. To understand the challenges of controlling liability losses, an overview of the environmental regulatory system is appropriate.

EPA and the Federal/State Relationship

Established in 1970, the Environmental Protection Agency (EPA) is the primary government agency responsible for protecting land, air, and water resources. As the nation's largest administrative rule-making agency, the EPA establishes specific environmental protection standards and policies that comply with the intent of national law and also oversees the enforcement of the laws themselves. The relationship between the EPA and individual state regulatory agencies can be defined by the concept of "federal standards, state implementation." Under this arrangement, which pertains to most areas of environmental protection, the EPA establishes the environmental protection standards and policies but delegates implementation and enforcement authority to states that have demonstrated that their plans and programs meet the standards and requirements of national law. Under this relationship, state programs may not weaken EPA standards but may set more stringent standards and requirements. To make standards and enforcement more responsive to local environmental conditions and concerns, many states subsequently delegate implementation and enforcement to local or regional government authorities. For example, regulatory authorities are often created in metropolitan areas to better address the air, water, and other environmental concerns unique to large urban centers. Such authorities may implement policies and standards that are more comprehensive and stringent than those in out-of-state areas. State and local implementation produce various bodies of environmental law and regulation that often differ in their environmental standards and legal requirements. Such differences may even drive organizations to relocate to other states. Risk management professionals should be aware that the scope and degree of liability exposures will often vary significantly from one area to another.

Major Environmental Statutes

Several pieces of major environmental legislation form the foundation for environmental protection in the United States and define standards of care and practice by which organizations must abide. Many of these laws have been amended by Congress since their creation, and each reauthorization has typically resulted in more comprehensive and stringent requirements. Exhibit 9-1 is a summary of the important elements of this regulatory framework and includes a synopsis of what these federal statutes cover, a description of the mechanisms used to implement these laws, and a description of key legal requirements that are the sources of liability exposures. This table is not meant to be an all-encompassing review of environmental protection laws; a comprehensive list of all potentially applicable state and federal laws is beyond the scope of this text. However, the exhibit should give risk management professionals an overview of the primary sources of liability exposures for businesses.

Exhibit 9-1
Federal Legislation Protecting the Environment

Legislation	Focus	Primary Mechanisms	Primary Requirements

Clean Air Act and Amendments	• Ambient air quality
	• Releases of over 200 substances
		• Air permit that
		  — establishes the maximum volumes of pollutants a facility can emit
		  — prescribes the use of pollution control equipment
		  — binds organization to abide by certain operating practices
		• On-site inspection
			• Complying with all permit conditions
			• Obtaining new permit before changing processes or expanding operations
			• Record keeping of amounts of substance emitted, product produced, maintenance practices

Clean Water Act and Amendments	• Waste-water discharges
	• Nonpoint sources
	• Wetland protection
		• NPDES permit for direct discharge (or POTW permit for discharge to a treatment facility) that
		  — establishes permissible concentrations for discharges
		  — binds organization to abide by certain operating practices
		• On-site inspection
			• Complying with all permit conditions
			• Waste-water monitoring
			• Waste-water testing
			• Record keeping

Resources Conservation and Recovery Act (RCRA)	• Treatment, storage, transportation, and disposal of hazardous waste • Nonhazardous waste	• Permit for treatment, storage, and disposal facilities • Waste manifesting—cradle to grave documentation • On-site inspection	• Waste testing • Labeling • Storage practices and procedures • Record keeping • "Program in place"
"Superfund" (CERCLA)	• Cleanup of contaminated sites/disposal sites • Accidental releases	• National and State Priorities Lists	• Site cleanup • Spill reporting

Superfund Amendments and Reauthorization Act (SARA)	• Use, storage, and release of over 300 toxic substances
	• Community access to this information
		• Toxic Release Inventory (TRI) Forms—documentation of storage use and release of recordable quantities
		• Local Emergency Response Plans
			• TRI form completion
			  — complete
			  — accurate
			  — on time
			• Pay fees

Toxic Substances Control Act (TSCA)	• Introduction of new chemicals • Import of new substances	Pre-Manufacturing Notice (PMN)	• Obtaining PMN • Testing for toxic, flammable, reactive, and corrosive properties
Land Use and Species Protection Laws (Endangered Species Act, Coastal Zone Management, etc.)	• Protection of threatened or endangered species • Protection of habitat and sensitive areas	• Environmental impact studies • Variety of permits	• Mitigation • Land use restrictions

Clean Air Act

The Clean Air Act (CAA) and subsequent amendments are the foundation for protecting air quality in the United States. The act requires that air quality standards be established for a wide variety of substances associated with industrial emissions, automobile exhaust, and other sources. States are typically responsible for implementing these standards and writing the specific rules and regulations in a way responsive to their own air quality needs and consistent with federal intent.

Much of the environmental liability exposure in this area is based on the air permits an organization holds to conduct its operations legally. Air permits typically prescribe the type and amount of contaminants that can legally enter into the environment, commit the organization to abide by certain operating practices, and mandate the use of certain types of control equipment to capture air releases. Not all organizations with emissions need permits, but reporting thresholds continue to decrease, which brings more facilities under the umbrella of air regulations. Many conditions are included in the permit, and each condition is a potential liability exposure if violated. Many of these conditions, such as monitoring and testing air releases and using specific types of control equipment to capture pollutants, are mandated by the regulatory agency. Other conditions may be the result of a negotiated process between the public agency and the organization as the firm seeks to meet responsibilities more flexibly. For example, to reduce the reporting requirements, a company may promise to stop using a certain chemical, operate only a certain number of shifts, or use an environmentally preferable substance in its operations. Such agreements can be written into the conditions of the operating permit and are fully enforceable. Risk management professionals should recognize the small amount of flexibility within the permitting process and recognize that this negotiation process may affect loss exposures.

In addition to complying with all permit conditions, organizations must also obtain a new permit before operating a new emission source or modifying an existing one. All facilities above reporting thresholds are required to keep accurate records of emissions, products produced, and maintenance practices to enable inspectors to evaluate whether permit conditions are being met. Penalties can be considerable for failing to comply with permit conditions, for operating without a permit or with an invalid permit, or for inaccurately or incompletely documenting operations. Perhaps most important, risk management professionals should also understand that air permits do not release an organization from all liabilities associated with their air emissions. An organization can completely comply with its air permit but still be open to civil suits from citizens' groups or other organizations as a result of its air pollution.

Clean Water Act

The Clean Water Act (CWA) protects surface water quality by regulating discharges and waste-water treatment. It also regulates nonpoint sources of water pollution and dredging and filling operations in wetlands. As with air regulations, much of the implementation and enforcement of the CWA is delegated to the states, which rely on permitting processes to accomplish the legislative objectives. Every source that directly discharges waste water into a lake, river, or other body of surface water is required to have a National Pollutant Discharge Elimination System (NPDES) permit. Other sources must discharge to publicly owned treatment works, or POTWs, which treat the effluent before discharging it into surface waters. Although these sources are not required to have NPDES permits, they must have permits from the POTW. As with air permits, many operating conditions, technology uses, and specific materials discharge standards are written into the permit and form the basis for liability exposures. Violating any of these permit conditions can result in severe penalties. Extensive monitoring, testing, and record keeping are also required to document discharges, and inspectors are likely to review this documentation closely. Should the waste water of a NPDES-permitted facility fail one of several mandated environmental impact tests, a new permit may be required. As with air permits, the waste-water permit does not release the organization from other liabilities created by its discharges.

Resources Conservation and Recovery Act (RCRA)

The RCRA addresses the treatment, storage, transportation, and disposal of hazardous wastes. One of the more influential pieces of environmental regulation, the RCRA has five main purposes:

- To define hazardous waste
- To set up a system in which the flow of hazardous waste from "cradle to grave" is known and regulated
- To require that all hazardous waste be treated, stored, or disposed of in special facilities for which permits have been issued
- To impose specific hazardous waste management requirements on generators and disposal facilities
- To regulate the disposal of nonhazardous solid waste

The heart of the RCRA is the waste manifesting system that provides comprehensive documentation for generating and disposing of hazardous wastes. Precise records must be kept on the types of wastes, their volumes, on-site treatment activities, transportation, and disposal. The RCRA manifesting system acts as an accounting system to make sure all hazardous wastes that are generated have been accounted for. The specific hazardous-waste handling and storage practices and procedures mandated by the RCRA are also areas of concern. If on-site inspections uncover violations of labeling requirements or storage practices or if manifests are missing or incomplete, the facility is subject to significant fines. The RCRA also requires proof of the existence of a waste minimization program to reduce the toxicity or volume of hazardous wastes generated. Compliance with this "program in place" provision has seldom been enforced but is now receiving greater attention.

To address a nationwide problem of leaking underground storage tanks, the 1984 RCRA amendments established a leak prevention, detection, and cleanup program. These amendments regulate underground storage tanks to limit corrosion and structural defects and thus decrease future tank leaks. Specific requirements now exist for tank design and operation, leak detection, reporting, corrective action, and tank closure.

Comprehensive Environmental Response, Compensation and Liability Act ("Superfund")

One of the largest and most controversial regulatory programs is Superfund, which provides funding and technical direction for responding to the cleanup of hazardous spills or contaminated sites that pose a significant threat to human and environmental health. Under Superfund, organizations must notify officials at the EPA and the state of a spill or other type of release of hazardous material. It is the site cleanup provisions of the law, however, that make Superfund one of the most recognizable, and potentially most costly, sources of liability exposure.

The Superfund law led to national and state priorities lists, which prioritized areas for cleanup based on the seriousness of the human and environmental health concerns. Superfund sites need not be waste disposal sites; operating facility sites, which have had long manufacturing histories, may have sufficient contamination to be put on state or national priorities lists for cleanup. Two fundamental ideas incorporated into Superfund cleanup make it an area of primary concern to environmental professionals and risk managers. The first is that the generator is always responsible for wastes and always remains liable for any contamination that might occur. Although many organizations will contract with other firms to treat, store, or dispose of wastes, the environmental risk exposure cannot be transferred; instead, it is shared by that contracted party. Thus, an organization may have abided by all regulations, never managed the site, and still be held liable for cleanup.

The other key principle is the concept of joint and several liability. If property has been contaminated by the waste disposal activities of many organizations, each organization may be individually liable for the entire cost of cleanup, regardless of its respective contribution to the contamination.

The purpose of joint and several liability was to ensure that cleanup could be completed even if all of the parties responsible for the contamination could not be identified. Cleanup had often been delayed because several parties shared financial responsibility for the damage. In addition, since waste disposal practices were largely unregulated for many years, contaminated sites typically featured a very large number of potentially responsible parties, or PRPs (organizations whose wastes were disposed of on the site). Many organizations whose wastes were "mixed" with other organizations' hazardous wastes during disposal now have liability exposures, even though they might not have contributed to the contamination. The cost of full or partial site cleanup can easily run into the millions of dollars, and organizations aggressively pursue other PRPs for cost-sharing.

Superfund Amendments and Reauthorization Act (SARA)

In 1986, amendments to the Superfund law were passed. These amendments created a new set of liability exposures pertaining to the availability of information on toxic releases and hazardous materials used on site. These amendments have significantly improved the ability of citizens to file civil suits. Title III of the Superfund Amendments and Reauthorization Act (SARA), also known as the Emergency Planning and Community Right to Know Act, requires state and local governments to adopt response plans for emergency situations and to communicate to the public information about potentially significant environmental pollutants. To accomplish this, companies that produce or use designated hazardous materials above a certain reporting threshold are required to provide information to local committees and government. This includes information on the amounts and storage practices of hazardous materials, accidental risks involved, and any spills or releases. Companies covered by this law must also file an annual report for over 330 substances. The report must describe how much of the hazardous materials was used and stored by the company. Under the Community Right to Know provisions of Title III, facilities must also report how much toxic material entered the environment annually. These Toxic Release Inventory (TRI) forms must be filled out accurately, completely, and in a timely manner. Failure to submit the form by the due date results in a fine of $1,000 per day per substance. The availability of these inventories to the public causes many organizations to go beyond compliance to address the heightened health and welfare concerns of local communities.

In many ways, TRI information has fundamentally changed the landscape for environmental loss control. The appearance of large numbers and quantities on the TRI is likely to trigger public interest and action, regardless of the actual environmental health and safety risks involved. The outside user groups of these data often have little or no technical expertise to analyze the information from an environmental risk perspective. However, they do use the information to generate public attention and force organizational change.

Toxic Substances and Control Act (TSCA)

TSCA covers the development and use of new chemical substances and the import of new substances from other countries. The act is also designed to facilitate information gathering by the EPA to identify and evaluate potential chemical hazards. The act requires each new or newly imported chemical to undergo a process called premanufacture notification. This process uses a variety of tests to determine potential environmental and health effects from developing and using a new chemical substance. The EPA then has the authority to approve, limit, or prohibit the use and development of the chemical.

Land Use and Species Protection Laws

Laws also exist to protect the health and welfare of the environment from activities other than pollution. Many federal, state, and local land-use laws create another class of environmental liability exposures for organizations. These laws are designed to protect specific wildlife and ecological values. Examples include the Endangered Species Act, established to protect rare plants and animals, and the Coastal Zone Management Act, passed to protect barrier islands and their associated wetlands. Some form of environmental impact study or assessment is typically required before land development efforts can proceed. Based on the results of the study, an organization may be required to mitigate harm in some way (such as create a new wetland area to replace one to be filled in) or abide by particular land use restrictions or monitoring activities. Violating the conditions of a permit can result in significant penalties, including injunctions against further development.

Financial Responsibility Requirements

Certain environmental laws, especially those addressing the cleanup, treatment, or transportation of hazardous wastes, may require organizations to demonstrate a specified minimum ability to pay for cleanup or harm for which they are responsible. Financial responsibility requirements vary for different types of organizations. The RCRA requires owners and operators of treatments storage and disposal facilities to demonstrate the ability to pay for the harm caused by sudden and nonsudden accidental occurrences. Financial responsibility must also be demonstrated for closing a TSDF and for thirty years of post-closure care. Such financing covers many ongoing monitoring and maintenance activities. Transporters of hazardous materials are another major class of businesses that must show financial responsibility for any bodily injury, property damage, and environmental restoration stemming from an accidental event. Petroleum producers and marketers are also required to demonstrate financial responsibility for their underground storage tanks. Allowable financing mechanisms will vary but typically include insurance, surety bonds, letters of credit, guarantees, or trust funds. Specialty risk financing instruments have been developed to cover these very specific markets.

Loss Exposures Arising From Actual Harm to the Environment

The second class of exposures are the net income, property, liability, and personnel losses resulting from actual harm to the environment or environmental values. Generally, an organization causes harm to the environment either through its discharges, wastes, and releases or by physically altering the environment in a way that negatively affects the environment. Following are the primary sources of this class of loss exposures:

- Spills and leaks
- Legal emissions, discharges, and waste disposal
- Materials uses and applications
- Remediation activity
- Physical degradation

A review of each source reveals how loss exposures permeate every aspect of an organization.

Spills and Leaks

Harmful substances commonly contaminate soils, surface water, ground water, and air through spills and leaks. Spills and leaks can occur anywhere raw materials and wastes are transported, used, or stored. In industrial organizations, the areas of greatest concern are manufacturing and production areas, inventory storage, finished goods storage, waste storage, underground storage tanks, and raw materials or waste transportation. Spills and leaks can be either one-time accidental events or chronic occurrences resulting from poor manufacturing processes, maintenance, and operating practices. Major events stemming from catastrophic failures like chemical releases or a major oil spill generate significant public attention and can result in expenditures in the millions of dollars. However, chronic spills and leaks from faulty pipe connections, improper handling practices, corroding drums, and poor storage facilities can have a cumulative effect that creates a significant loss exposure for the organization.

To avoid site contamination, many organizations install spill collection systems. They will also separate storm sewers from manufacturing sewers to prevent unplanned discharges into municipal water works or public treatment facilities. However, the subtle and cumulative nature of many environmental exposures demands reviews of standard operating practices for effective loss control. Diligent maintenance practices, manufacturing procedures, and process reviews effectively prevent leaks and spills from occurring in the first place.

Legal Emissions, Discharges, and Waste Disposal

As mentioned, compliance with environmental regulations does not release the organization from other liabilities stemming from its uses and releases of materials. Any air emission, water discharge, and land disposal activity, past or present, can expose the organization to potential loss exposures, even if the activity is perfectly legal or currently unregulated.

An example of this is found in exposures pertaining to site cleanup. Many contaminated areas are a result of waste disposal and discharge practices that occurred before regulations prescribing strict management practices were enacted. Before environmental protection legislation, organizations routinely dumped process materials and other wastes on-site, contaminating the property. Hazardous materials were disposed of in ordinary landfills without special protection measures, resulting in large-scale contamination problems at industrial sites and at landfills across the nation. These contaminants have often penetrated into the ground water and traveled off-site to other properties, including residential areas. Although these practices were legal at the time, organizations responsible for these wastes are liable for their cleanup and any resulting damages. Compounding the risk is that any organization with current title to the property may be responsible for cleanup and damages—even if its activities had nothing to do with the actual cause of pollution. History suggests that future scientific studies will expose new health and environmental dangers, which will result in new regulations, tighter standards, and litigation and damage claims for currently acceptable practices.

Even under today's strict laws governing emissions, discharges, and disposal activities, claims will arise over permissible practices. The advent of community "right-to-know" laws and concerns over health effects on local communities living near facilities have resulted in a significant increase in citizens' suits regarding "legal" air and water pollution. Legal emissions can also result in third-party damage claims for income and property losses. For example, air emissions from a manufacturing facility in a rural area may result in crop damages or nuisance odors or negatively affect aesthetic and recreational values on which a number of local businesses are based. All of this suggests that risk management professionals should consider any discharge, emission, or release containing contaminants as a potential exposure source, even if the organization fully complies with all existing laws and permit conditions.

Materials Uses and Applications

Environmental harm need not be created by disposing of materials; in many situations, the use of materials creates an exposure for the organization. Ground water or surface water contamination from applying pesticides and herbicides is an example of use-based loss exposures. Asbestos and dichlorodiphenyltrichloroethane (DDT) are examples of how the threat of harm to the environment and human health may result in limiting, phasing out, or even banning the use of particular substances. Many organizations are currently working to reduce or eliminate the use of chlorofluorocarbons (CFCs), chlorinated solvents, and other pollutants from their operations because of environmental and human health concerns and legal requirements. Risk management professionals should think of uses as well as wastes in identifying and evaluating environmental exposures.

Remediation Activity

Pollution problems and environmental damage can also occur when attempting to clean up a contamination problem. **Remediation** is the process of cleaning and restoring a contaminated site to a level of cleanliness demanded by or negotiated with the regulatory agency. Although only undertaken by highly trained and proficient engineering organizations, the process of moving large amounts of earth, contaminated soils, and toxic materials might aggravate a contamination problem. If the contamination problem is made worse by remediation activity, the generator may sue the contractor for any damages that result. However, as with waste disposal, the generator always remains liable.

Physical Degradation

Physical changes to the environment are also a significant source of loss exposures to organizations. Construction and development activities are likely to result in the need to physically change land features, contours, and even water flows. Poor or insufficient planning can result in liability exposures for violating environmental protection laws and open the organization to many government suits and third-party damage claims. For example, a hydroelectric dam or a timbering operation may cause harm to the water quality of a river and result in damage suits from the local commercial fishing industry. Associations of affected businesses, community interests, and local or national environmental organizations could seek compensation for income and recreational losses or sue to restore lands to preexisting conditions.

Before an organization begins construction and development, it must perform a careful planning study to identify such potential adverse effects and respond appropriately if necessary. Many development projects have encountered substantial expense and delay as a result of poor environmental planning.

Common Examples of Environmental Contamination

Improperly planning and managing any of these source areas can lead to significant environmental pollution exposures for organizations. Thousands of regulated substances and pollutants may form the basis for a specific exposure. Following are a few of the more notable types of contaminants that risk management professionals may encounter.

Metals and Metal Compounds

Metal-bearing wastes are a growing area of concern among regulatory agencies and environmental health specialists. Metals exist naturally in trace amounts; however, mining, purifying, using, and incinerating metals concentrate their presence in the environment. Exhibit 9-2 describes some metals of particular concern to environmental health specialists, their primary sources and characteristics, and common control strategies.

As the exhibit indicates, metals contamination includes nonindustrial sources such as leaking landfills, fuel combustion, and household waste disposal. Risk management professionals should be aware that metals can never be destroyed, only managed in ways to reduce risks to human health and the environment. As a result, if source reduction is not feasible, loss control strategies should strive to recover metals from the waste, treating them in various ways to reduce toxicity and/or mobility through a variety of techniques, including solidification and stabilization.

Solvents

Solvent is a generic term for many chemical compounds that have versatile applications in industrial and commercial processes. Solvents include alcohols, aromatic hydrocarbons (for example, benzene), and chlorinated hydrocarbons (for example, the dry cleaning solvent perchloroethylene). Solvents are used to dissolve another substance to create a uniformly dispersed mixture; have valuable cleaning and degreasing properties; are used as propellants for inks, paints, and adhesives; and are used in producing the coatings for pharmaceuticals.

Exhibit 9-2
Some Metals That Pollute the Environment

Metal	Sources	Characteristics	Controls
Mercury and mercury compounds	Industrial chemical manufacturing primary metals plastics manufacturing electrical industries Other natural outgassing coal combustion application of fertilizers and fungicides landfill disposal of electrical switches, thermometers, and fluorescent bulbs	In air: months to years Highly mobile Stable Bio-magnification in food chains Highly toxic	Precipitate out of solution Recovery Treatment through chemical reduction Encapsulation
Chromium and chromium compounds	Industrial chemical manufacturing metal finishing photography tanning metal production textile manufacturing Other oil, gas, and coal combustion	In air: less than ten days In water and soil: several years Carcinogenic Highly toxic to aquatic life	Precipitation and recovery from solution Chemical reduction to reduce toxicity Encapsulation and disposal
Lead and lead compounds	Industrial steel and iron making copper refining electronics metal finishing rubber and plastics Other fuel combustion leachate from plumbing fixtures paint chips leachate from landfills	Highly toxic to humans and wildlife Leads to nervous system and developmental disorders Persistent	Precipitation and recovery Chemical reduction to reduce toxicity Removal from soil through solvent extraction
Nickel	Industrial metal finishing steel manufacturing circuit manufacturing used as industrial catalysts	Dust and particulates remain aloft from weeks to months Remain in water for years Carcinogenic and toxic	Precipitation and recovery from solution Chemical reduction to reduce toxicity Encapsulation and disposal

Because of the diverse number of applications and uses, solvents are perhaps the most pervasive class of chemicals used in society. As a result, they are also a primary concern to environmental health professionals.

The environmental effects of solvents are almost as diverse as the uses of the product. Some are photochemically reactive, reacting with sunlight to produce smog. Many are highly carcinogenic and toxic. Some are highly reactive with other materials. Solvents typically vaporize quickly, leading to air pollution, and have the ability to travel quickly through the ground, contaminating soils and ground water. The combination of mobility and a high degree of application makes solvents a concern for environmental loss control in many organizations.

PCBs

PCBs, or polychlorinated biphenyls, are a family of over 200 substances that, until the late 1970s, were used in many industrial and commercial applications. Their chemical properties made them desirable for several diverse applications, including heat transfer fluids, hydraulic fluids, compressor lubricants, waterproofing aids, inks, carbon paper, adhesives, and coatings. Because of their outstanding electric insulating properties, the greatest application of PCBs was in the manufacture of electrical equipment such as transformers and capacitors. However, because PCBs can persist and accumulate in the environment, producing toxic effects, their production and use were banned in the United States.

Because of their widespread use before the late 1970s, their resistance to breaking down, and their ability to accumulate in biological systems, PCBs are still a primary and pervasive environmental and health concern. Exposure to some level of these materials through ambient air, water, and food appears to be unavoidable. The processes of treating and disposing of PCBs at concentrations greater than fifty parts per million through incineration or physical and chemical methods are stringently regulated. However, PCBs can still be indirectly released into the environment through a number of sources, including leaking landfills or spills, explosions, and accidental releases of in-service electrical equipment. As a result, PCB contamination is a problem that is likely to persist for many years. Being aware of the potential sources of PCBs and preventing their release through appropriate disposal or containment procedures help to reduce the risks they pose to human health and the environment.

Asbestos

Asbestos is another material that was widely used in commerce until environmental studies revealed its threat to the environment—a threat that resulted in significant limitations on its manufacture and use. Asbestos was widely used in commercial and industrial applications because of its non-combustible, nonconducting, and chemically resistant properties. In fact, it might still be present in such products as thermal insulation, cement products, brake linings, heating and air supply systems, electrical appliances, and surfacing materials.

Asbestos is a recognized carcinogen to humans if it is inhaled as airborne asbestos fibers. A noncarcinogenic health hazard associated with asbestos is asbestosis—a chronic lung disease leading to functional disabilities and early mortality. Asbestosis is associated with exposure to high asbestos concentrations in occupational settings, such as in mining asbestos or manufacturing asbestos-related materials. However, the ease with which asbestos is readily transported through the air creates a number of other exposure sources. Deteriorating building insulation and materials are major exposure sources. The EPA has estimated that more than 500,000 commercial and public buildings contain damaged asbestos insulation materials that threaten the occupants of those buildings. This estimate does not include schools, houses, apartment buildings, and state and local government buildings.

Dioxins

Dioxins are a large family of substances that are the byproducts of certain chemical manufacturing and combustion processes. Unlike metals and other materials, dioxins are not known to be constituents of any natural environment. The amounts of dioxins produced as byproducts of manufacturing processes are quite low, but once formed, these dioxins are difficult to eliminate. Dioxins were widely produced in the 1960s and 1970s for domestic herbicides and defense. They are currently produced by manufacturing pulp and paper, incinerating municipal and medical waste, and refining petroleum. Nonindustrial sources include disposing of materials treated with certain wood preservatives and unused pesticides and herbicides.

One particular dioxin compound of concern is 2,3,7,8—TCDD, which is generally recognized worldwide as one of the most toxic manufactured compounds known to exist. Its biodegradation rate is very slow, and the compound adheres tightly to soil particles, which prevents migration into ground water or surface water unless contaminated soils themselves migrate through erosion. Thus, wastes and soils contaminated with 2,3,7,8—TCDD tend to pose long-lived, persistent environmental problems with few simple remedies. Incineration at temperatures exceeding 1,000 degrees centigrade is generally recognized by the EPA as the only technology that has been sufficiently demonstrated to achieve the 99.9999 percent destruction and removal efficiency demanded by treatment standards.

In addition to these chemical families commonly associated with industrial sources, indoor air pollution is receiving greater attention as a hazard source. Office workers are not insulated from exposure to potentially hazardous substances in the workplace. They can be exposed to biological hazards such as fungi and bacteria that grow in dirty or inadequate ventilation systems; chemicals, such as formaldehyde that may be emitted from carpeting and room furnishings; and ozone and hydrocarbons released from copying machines, lead from old plumbing fixtures, and cigarette smoke. Many of these problems are associated with new energy-efficient buildings. If adequate fresh air is not provided, these pollutants can be recycled and concentrated, causing irritation and general discomfort. Particularly sensitive workers may suffer more serious effects.

Values Exposed to Loss From Environmental Contamination and Degradation

The sheer magnitude, complexity, and changing nature of environmental regulations make liability exposures the predominant concern in environmental risk management. However, risk management professionals should also be aware of the primary property, personnel, and net income loss exposures that can arise from environmental pollution.

Property Values

Environmental contamination and degradation create many risks to real, personal, and intangible property values. Environmental contamination often prevents an organization from selling a piece of property. Prompted by their banks and by fears of assuming environmental liabilities, potential real estate buyers will undertake detailed and exhaustive environmental studies to identify any potential environmental liability they might be assuming through the property transaction. In some states, this review is required before a sale can be made. Without prior cleanup and remediation, the organization will not be able to sell the property. Contaminated property may appear as an asset on an organization's balance sheet, but the inability to sell the property combined with the legal and financial consequences of cleanup can turn this asset into a liability.

Personal property is also at risk. Spills and leaks may result in substantial inventory losses for the organization. Exposure of process equipment or other tangible assets to adverse substances or materials may reduce useful life and salvage value. Moreover, after an environmental loss, functional or reproduction costs are likely to increase to ensure that such activities are not repeated. A leaking underground storage tank may trigger a review of other storage facilities and may result in modifying or even removing all such tanks on a site. Following a major oil spill, one firm decided to retrofit its tanker fleet from single to double hulls.

Intangible property, such as an organization's reputation and community goodwill, are especially susceptible to loss through environmental events and are perhaps the most difficult to repair. No post-event actions easily reduce the loss of trust, negative public opinion, and stigma of poor citizenship. When emotions and public interest run high, loss events are likely to trigger a series of reactions within government and among the public that create additional perils for real, personal, and intangible property values.

Personnel Values

A survey on environmental management of many senior business executives from Europe, Canada, and the United States identified worker health and safety as the issue of greatest concern. This issue surpassed those of clean air, waste disposal, and clean water. Employee concerns are a primary focus for developing and implementing environmental risk management strategies. Chronic exposures to carcinogenic, toxic, or odorous substances may cause key manufacturing personnel to miss work days or even resign from the organization.

The clear link between environmental protection and worker health and safety has caused many organizations to combine these two risk management areas into an "environmental health and safety" function. On the management side, courts are more willing to imprison executives if repeated violations or gross negligence in failing to address environmental concerns can be proved. Thus, liability under the Occupational Safety and Health Act (OSHA) and other worker protection laws is only one dimension of the personnel values at risk created by inattention to environmental protection needs.

Net Income Values

Any environmental event is likely to result in some degree of business interruption and revenue reduction. A spill or leak within a facility may shut down a manufacturing line or area for repairs and cleanup. Small events may disrupt business activity only slightly, and they are likely to produce little if any financial consequence. However, if raw materials or equipment needed for production are affected, the organization may miss production deadlines and lose business. In higher profile events, negative press may result in consumer boycotts. Under extreme circumstances, the environmental liabilities may cause the enterprise to cease operation. Injunctions on business operations or development activities are not uncommon in certain business sectors like timber and oil development, which are based on extracting or processing natural resources or involve substantial land development activities.

Significant expenses are also incurred in environmental cleanup. Legal and technical consulting services are a staple of environmental events and consume significant funds otherwise available to maintain or expand the business. The financial consequences of environmental losses are likely to be felt by customers, suppliers, and perhaps even local communities when the organization provides a primary source of employment for the area.

Identifying and Evaluating Environmental Loss Exposures

What types of assessments can you use to evaluate environmental loss exposures?

What factors should you consider in evaluating environmental hazards?

How can you use risk assessments?

What are the components of an environmental risk assessment review?

How do you conduct an environmental risk assessment?

Almost all organizations face some type of potential environmental loss or hazard as a result of ongoing operations. The first step in the risk control process is to identify and evaluate these loss exposures. This is accomplished through a process called an environmental risk assessment. Once an uncommon practice, an environmental risk assessment is now a powerful and essential tool for identifying existing and potential exposures.

Types of Risk Assessments

Risk assessments can be either quantitative or qualitative. A quantitative characterization of risk identifies numerical relationships between an exposure to a hazard and the actual occurrence of adverse effects to human health or the environment (that is, it determines cause and effect). In determining this relationship, quantitative risk assessors must study the relationship between an adverse effect and the exposure type, amount, frequency, and duration. The risk may be characterized by its probability of harm (for example, 1 in 10,000 risks of cancer) or by an exposure standard above which adverse effects would be expected to occur (for example, concentrations not to exceed .05 parts per million). Quantitative risk assessments are highly technical and extremely expensive to conduct.

Many quantitative risk assessments are conducted by the government and are expressed in environmental and occupational health and safety statutes in terms of allowable concentrations and exposure levels. Private firms commonly conduct quantitative assessments for new product development. Government agencies, such as the Food and Drug Administration and the EPA, carefully review assessments conducted by organizations before permitting use of a product. Examples include assessments associated with soaps, cosmetics, and other consumer products that humans ingest or come into direct contact with.

Far more common in environmental risk management are qualitative assessments. These are used to identify and evaluate environmental hazards rather than to establish scientific cause-and-effect relationships. Two general types of hazard assessments are those undertaken to identify and evaluate existing environmental hazards and those designed to identify and evaluate potential hazards. Although the term "risk assessment" connotes forward thinking, many assessments are oriented towards evaluating and remediating preexisting conditions. Those assessments are used to determine how much human health risk a particular contaminated site might pose, what controls should be implemented, and how the cleanup activities should proceed. Such qualitative risk assessments require considerable scientific and technical expertise and are different from a "preventive" assessment geared toward avoiding potential exposures and losses. A preventive assessment requires investigating many ongoing practices, programs, and operations. Its purpose is to implement changes so that environmental losses do not occur.

The knowledge base and skills of risk management professionals are likely to be more valuable in identifying and avoiding potential exposures than in assessing risks associated with existing environmental problems. Once contamination has occurred, risk assessments are performed by engineering specialists. The remainder of this section emphasizes the preventive aspects of the environmental risk management process.

Factors in Evaluating Environmental Hazards

A qualitative hazard assessment can be organized into four primary risk factor categories: (1) characteristics and behavior of materials, (2) pathways, (3) populations at risk, and (4) management practices. These factors provide a general picture of the overall environmental risk of a particular site.

Characteristics and Behavior of Materials

Evaluating the properties and behavior of substances is an integral part of the environmental risk assessment process. Materials that would need to be investigated include any wastes, releases, or discharges; process inputs such as raw materials or catalysts; and any byproducts from past, present, or future operations. Materials can be evaluated for their toxicity or other threat to human health, the amount and degree of exposure, movement in environmental media (air, water, and land), biodegradability, stability, bioaccumulation, and other characteristics. Evaluating materials and their behavior is a technically demanding process requiring assistance and input from other professional disciplines, including biology, industrial hygiene, chemistry, geology, and engineering.

Pathways

A second area of evaluation is the routes, or pathways, through which pollutants and contamination can travel from their sources at a facility. Different pathways—ambient air, soils, surface water, and ground water—pose different challenges and issues for environmental risk management, and assessors must be aware of the unique characteristics of the pathways at a particular site. For example, a facility's overall environmental risk may be affected by the distance from the facility to the underground water table, the types of soils on which the facility is built, the distance from the facility to the nearest body of surface water, and the general direction of prevailing winds at the site. Pathway analysis allows risk management professionals to judge the movement and rate of potential contamination that will improve the quality of risk control decision making.

Populations at Risk

Risk management professionals must also examine the populations at risk to determine possible harm to populations living within the existing or potential areas of contamination. Five characteristics of a **population at risk** need to be evaluated:

1. The amount and extent of potential harm
2. The numbers of populations affected
3. The population concentration
4. The vulnerability of each population to the exposure
5. The values of the population placed at risk by the exposure

Population characteristics affect the nature of exposures. For example, a facility with 10,000 families will have significantly different loss exposures than an industrial facility with 5,000 workers. Risk management professionals should also remember that populations at risk can be plants and animals as well as people. They should identify wildlife values and "sensitive receptors" (species that can be adversely affected by even small amounts of contamination) and incorporate that information into the assessment.

Management Practices

Finally, risk management professionals must evaluate how the personnel of an organization—line operators and management—decrease or increase environmental risks. Organizational attitudes, commitment, and understanding, as well as compliance with state-of-the-art environmental protection practices, are part of this evaluation. Risk management professionals should also consider policies, procedures, equipment, and programs directly pertaining to environmental risk management at the facility. They should examine management practices in "nonenvironmental" areas like housekeeping, maintenance practices, manufacturing processes, and inventory control and storage. Although these examples are not typically thought of as environmental risk management areas, they affect the environmental risk an organization faces.

To obtain an accurate picture of the degree of risk to the organization and the environment, assessments should evaluate all four factors. Quantitative risk studies may occasionally be incorporated into the hazard assessment to improve the quality of the overall assessment process. More likely, existing human health and ecological risk-based standards set by the government are used in conjunction with qualitative reviews.

Uses of Environmental Risk Assessments

Environmental risk assessments have many different uses, and many types of organizations undertake them. A manufacturing facility may use an environmental risk assessment as a planning tool to improve the overall quality of the environmental risk management program. This assessment identifies and evaluates hazards, targets areas of primary concern, prioritizes issues for management, and identifies preventive strategies. Organizations acquiring property or making foreclosures use risk assessments to identify environmental liabilities assumed when property is transferred. Organizations doing site cleanup use risk assessments to determine the nature and extent of contamination and to identify the best management and control practices to prevent further contamination. Risk assessments conducted for insurance underwriting may be the most complex of all, since they probably need to address both site contamination issues (existing problems) and company business and management practices (future problems).

Environmental Risk Assessment Review Components

No "standard" environmental risk assessment methodology exists. Professionals in environmental risk assessment have created a generally accepted assessment protocol based on three assessment phases. A *Phase 1* risk assessment is a comprehensive review and analysis of existing conditions at the site and includes an investigation of all four hazard factors—materials, pathways, populations, and management practices. A Phase 1 assessment yields information on both the existence and extent of environmental concerns and contamination. Depending on the results, a *Phase 2* assessment may be initiated. This includes monitoring, testing, and sampling studies to supply missing data and generate other relevant technical information. *Phase 3* is the actual remediation, control, and cleanup undertaken based on information supplied by the first two assessment phases. This assessment has wide application for property transfer and site cleanup activities. However, for risk financing organizations or internal environmental program managers concerned with potential exposures as well as existing problems, other models and approaches may be more appropriate.

An alternative approach commonly used by underwriting organizations divides the assessment process into three general review areas—site review, compliance review, and operations and management review. Depending on the needs of the organization and the purpose of the assessment, any one of these three review areas may be the primary area of investigation for the risk assessment. Organizations may also take elements of each review area to create a tailored assessment approach. Together, these three reviews can help an organization identify present and future exposures, prioritize issues, and generate sound risk modification options.

Site Review

Site reviews determine the existence of environmental contamination and degradation at a particular site and the threat of migration and harm to off-site areas. Specifically, a site review includes an investigation of preexisting environmental hazards, site characteristics, routes of environmental exposure, and the ecological values and human health and safety concerns placed at risk on site and off site.

Site reviews are often highly technical, featuring detailed reports on hydrology, geology, and other scientific areas. Monitoring, sampling, and testing studies of air, water, and land may be included to determine contamination levels and evaluate their associated risks. Special site concerns, such as the age and condition of the facility, historical practices, natural hazards, and nature of surrounding populations, are also investigated.

The risk assessor may also conduct a title search to determine past uses of the site, potential liabilities, and other parties that may be responsible for cleanup and remediation. Through the site review, the organization gains an understanding of the nature and extent of existing environmental problems. It also provides information to help prevent further contamination and to aid cleanup or remediation work. Although many professionals may participate in a site review, technical specialists must be employed to gather data and interpret and evaluate risks.

Compliance Review

The second component of an environmental risk assessment is a compliance review. This chapter previously described how many environmental loss exposures are in fact liability exposures and exist regardless of whether damage to the environment actually occurs. Therefore, a careful review of an organization's regulatory compliance status is an essential part of the overall risk assessment effort.

The heart of the compliance review is the **compliance audit**—a procedure to identify and evaluate existing and potential compliance problems. Although strongly encouraged by the EPA and other regulatory organizations, compliance audits are voluntary activities for organizations. These audits determine an organization's regulatory status and can help an organization to reduce its environmental liabilities by systematically identifying the corrective actions needed to achieve compliance. Audits can be comprehensive, addressing all environmental health and safety regulations at a facility, or they can focus on a particular area. Depending on the scope of the audit and the size and complexity of the facility, an audit may take from one to five days and involve up to ten people. Audit procedures will vary from organization to organization, but the following general tasks are common to all compliance efforts:

- Information review—Facility records on emissions, discharges from all sources, and other environmental concerns provide the data for the analysis and are reviewed. These records may be monitored, sampled, and tested to confirm the accuracy of facility reports.

- Regulatory status review—The audit should identify any applicable environmental regulations pertaining to the facility and determine the specific requirements facility operations must fulfill.

- Compliance and loss history review—Past violations and loss events may identify important trends and areas of chronic concern for the facility.

- Permit review—The auditor or auditing team should carefully review any operating permit conditions that form the basis for many liability exposures.

The results of the compliance audit serve both present and future risk control needs. Facility compliance audits identify any noncompliance issues and ensure that corrective actions are taken to reduce or eliminate losses stemming from regulatory violations. Perhaps as important, compliance reviews improve plans and environmental risk management budgets and enable the organization to address future environmental liability exposures in a coordinated, systematic manner.

Operations and Management Review

The cornerstone of a preventive approach to environmental risk management is the operations and management review. This review is a systematic and comprehensive study of business practices, procedures, and policies used to determine the relationship of these three factors to environmental loss exposures and to evaluate the adequacy of existing loss control strategies. It addresses all aspects of a business operation that can contribute to environmental losses, including purchasing, shipping and receiving, transportation, manufacturing processes, inventory management, pollution control, waste treatment and management, and internal management systems.

A **materials accounting** can ensure that all releases or materials losses have been identified. Materials accounting operates much like a balance sheet. The total amount of material going into the process step should equal the mass of material coming out of the process. Engineering professionals are typically required to conduct this investigation. Other activities usually included in an operations review are the following:

- A thorough examination of all use, storage, or disposal activities pertaining to hazardous substances and waste materials
- A review and characterization of all storage tanks and materials inventory procedures
- A study of equipment maintenance and housekeeping activities
- A review of emergency response plans and measures
- A study of the adequacy of any control and treatment technologies used at the site

The management portion of the review provides insight into the overall awareness, commitment, and ability of the organization to reduce environmental risks. Specifically, the management review explores the quality of established policies, plans, and programs to reduce the environmental impact and control environmental losses. These elements are perhaps less tangible but no less important in reducing environmental loss exposures. Much of this review focuses on how the organization currently manages its environmental affairs. Among the assessment areas reviewed are the characteristics of the organization's management and commitment, the characteristics of the environmental risk management function, and the existence of special programs facilitating loss control.

Characteristics of Organization's Management and Commitment

The success of any environmental risk management program begins with a commitment to the effort by senior officials. An organization can demonstrate a commitment to environmental risk management by having formal environmental policies. These policies are a visible statement of the intentions and objectives of the organization and its employees regarding environmental protection and describe the basic principles under which the company operates. Policies can gauge how progressive an organization is with regard to its environmental affairs. Organizational goals and quantifiable objectives regarding the environment indicate that the organization is actively involved in risk reduction practices. These goals and objectives may be short-term environmental initiatives, such as eliminating a certain chemical from operations in a current operating year, or more strategic, such as reducing 90 percent of toxic air emissions over five years. An important indicator of the overall quality of the environmental risk management effort is senior management's clear and tangible commitment to it.

Characteristics of Environmental Risk Management Function

Another factor influencing an organization's environmental risk is the quality and capabilities of the environmental risk management function. An assessment should include some investigation into how well this function is performed. Key indicators are the human and financial resources invested in the environmental risk management program and how well the program is controlled.

Human Resources   Answers to the following questions help evaluate the human resources of an environmental risk management program. Is the number of persons assigned to the facility's environmental risk management program adequate? Is there a strong reliance on outside consultants for basic environmental risk management activities? Does the environmental risk management staff have the skills and knowledge to accomplish their jobs? Are other employees aware of their contributions to environmental exposures and environmental protection? The quality and availability of human resources to track and manage environmental issues are significant contributors to the organization's environmental risk management profile.

Financial Resources   Does the environmental risk management function have access to working capital and long-term funding sources? Organizations will probably not hesitate to fund environmental projects needed to keep the facility in compliance with environmental protection requirements. However, effective risk control also requires a budget to track and monitor progress and to fund special activities that can lead to environmental risk reduction. Such programs might include research and development, participation and membership in trade groups, training programs, and outside consulting services.

Organization and Control   Do the personnel responsible for environmental risk management have access to senior management within the organization? Is there a clear delineation of responsibility, accountability, and authority? The assessment should also determine how well the organization is complying with the reporting, record keeping, monitoring, and other procedural requirements of environmental protection laws. Signing and tracking the hazardous waste manifests, maintaining the material safety data sheets, labeling and storing hazardous waste drums, and computing the toxics release information are examples of routine environmental risk management activities. Despite the mundane nature of these responsibilities, quality control of these processes is an essential part of environmental risk management.

Existence of Special Programs Facilitating Loss Control

Special programs indicate an organization's awareness of its environmental risks, its progressiveness and dedication to environmental risk management and loss control, and its willingness to go beyond compliance. Four programs of particular value are pollution prevention, environmental auditing, training, and regulatory surveillance. Pollution prevention programs are organized internal efforts that identify opportunities to reduce the wastes and releases of a facility by making changes at the source. Environmental auditing programs determine compliance status and the effects the organization's activities have on surrounding communities. Training programs ensure that the knowledge and skills of the employees are continually updated so that the staff complies with all government regulations and conducts its activities in a way that reduces the company's environmental risks. Finally, regulatory surveillance programs ensure that the organization is aware of upcoming and impending regulations and is able to incorporate "future regulatory perils" into its planning and decision-making activities. An organization should demonstrate some ability to track and monitor these developments and have them reflected in business planning. Tracking environmental case law and practicing effective management also contribute to the quality of environmental loss control.

Risk management professionals should recognize the complementary nature of compliance reviews and operations and management reviews. For example, state law may mandate specific practices and activities regarding on-site hazardous waste management that will be the subject of a compliance review. However, the company may have established policies and procedures that expand or supplement these requirements. In essence, compliance reviews ensure that the organization addresses and abides by all applicable regulations but does nothing to evaluate the effectiveness or efficiency by which this is accomplished. An operations and management review, which addresses both efficiency and effectiveness concerns, can help an organization to make the best choices from both a risk control and financial management standpoint.

Conducting an Environmental Risk Assessment

Regardless of the methodology used, any assessment effort needs to follow a general set of procedures to accomplish its objectives. Following are the major steps involved in conducting an assessment:

1. Create an assessment plan
2. Assemble the team
3. Gather information and identify risks
4. Evaluate environmental risks

Create an Assessment Plan

Environmental risk assessments can be time-consuming and expensive for an organization. The first step in conducting the assessment is to establish a set of objectives and goals for the assessment effort and to identify the "territory" the assessment will cover. By carefully defining the scope of the assessment and specific information needs, the organization can conduct the assessment more efficiently and effectively and reduce disruption to the firm's operations.

As part of this preliminary planning, a company should examine how the organization can preserve the confidentiality of the assessment process. Maintaining confidentiality encourages the flow of information. However, the organization should recognize that no assessment is likely to possess an absolute degree of confidentiality. Information uncovered during government investigation and third-party litigation may be disclosed. This creates a disincentive for some organizations. By knowing about the problem, organizations fear they will become liable to solve it.

One strategy an organization may consider is to give its counsel the authority and responsibility to initiate the assessment, analyze the data, and provide advice. Such involvement may allow the organization to take advantage of attorney/client privilege. Although the risk assessment process itself has an inherent element of risk, most organizations believe that the cost of ignorance is likely to outweigh the risks of disclosure.

Assemble the Team

In addition to legal staff, other technical experts may be needed, including engineers, production managers, biologists, environmental scientists, geologists, chemists, industrial hygienists, toxicologists, and regulatory affairs specialists. A major issue facing organizations is how to obtain and maintain the technical expertise required to identify and evaluate all exposures associated with environmental impairment. Large organizations with sophisticated environmental risk management programs may be able to assemble this team internally. Smaller organizations may need to supplement internal staff with external consultants. A growing body of environmental risk management specialists is available to assist organizations. The risk assessor should also recognize the value of including line personnel and management on the assessment team. Those employees work closest to the sources of environmental risks and can provide valuable insights and contributions.

Gather Information and Identify Risks

Information for the risk assessment process comes from three primary sources: written documentation, site inspections, and interviews.

Written Documentation

Internal facility records are a cornerstone for risk assessments and typically provide some of the best data for analysis. As described, record keeping is an important element in the environmental regulatory system, and much documentation exists on emissions, wastes, and discharges. A systematic review of this documentation should provide a good overview of the types, amounts, and characteristics of potential pollutants and pollution safeguards at a facility. Organizations that must report toxic release inventory (TRI) data find such data especially important for risk assessments because of public interest and access to that information. Other regulatory-related documents include reports from federal, state, or local regulatory inspectors; monitoring and sampling reports of air, soil, and water quality done in accordance with permit requirements; notices of past violations; and the permits themselves. Permits should be reviewed to ensure that they are secured when required, are current, are appropriate, and comply with special conditions.

Other documentation may yield insights into the quality and performance of the existing management systems and programs. Training and testing records of personnel at each facility can help document staff knowledge and abilities for meeting environmental responsibilities. Environmental risk management, waste reduction, and emergency response plans should also be analyzed. Standard operating procedures (SOPs) are an important source of information. SOPs describe how to perform specific tasks in a step-by-step manner. They are frequently written for improving quality, performance, and worker safety in a particular task. Careful analysis may show that SOPs that overlook environmental risk management concerns may be a slow but cumulative contributor to a facility's environmental risk.

Information about raw materials, process inputs, and how materials are used in the facility is also essential. Purchasing and inventory records give information about the types of material brought on site, the amount of material kept on site at a given time, and storage practices and procedures. Operators' logs can provide insight into materials uses and management practices in the facility. The assessment team should also ask for any process flow diagrams and materials accounting studies. Often, this type of information may be obtained from quality improvement managers rather than environmental personnel. The assessment team should obtain documentation and data that reflect operations over a period of time so that the assessor can account for trends, business cycles, one-time events, or any other special circumstances that could skew the analysis.

Site Inspections

Visual site inspections give the environmental risk assessment team an opportunity to observe and evaluate the facility's current operations and validate internal documentation. A quick inspection of the entire facility should be made first with more detailed inspections of specific areas of concern done later. Multiple visits may be necessary to get an accurate picture of the facility's operations during different shifts or in different production circumstances.

The assessment team should carefully review process and process support areas where the majority of sources of environmental exposures are likely to exist. Worker practices should be cross-checked against any established operating procedures. The assessment team should carefully examine any discrepancies between facility documentation or policies and actual facility practice. The site inspection should include the grounds and land near the facility, since pathways and populations at risk are two key contributors to environmental risk. The assessment team may find photographs and other historical documentation useful to see how the site has evolved. Natural features such as creeks, ponds, and lagoons or signs of potential contamination such as discolored water, stressed vegetation, absence of vegetation, and odors should be noted.

Interviews

Interviews complement visual inspections and allow the assessment team to obtain in-depth information on practices, procedures, attitudes, and commitment. Interviews should be arranged with staff personnel in charge of specific environmental risk management activities and with senior management and line operators. During the interviews, future conditions and current business practices must be explored. If a facility is expecting a 35 percent increase in production for the coming year, all risk control strategies and technologies should be reevaluated in light of this increase. The assessment team should always document the date, time, name, and title of the persons being inter-viewed. Interviews should also be arranged with other stakeholders—those likely to be affected by the organization's environmental performance.

The team may also develop questionnaires and conduct interviews with neighboring facilities and local residents who are placed at risk by an acciden-tal event or environmental exposure. These questionnaires or "town meet-ings" serve the dual purpose of obtaining local community input as well as communicating progress on environmental improvement and risk control efforts the organization has already implemented. Local emergency response networks should be engaged to determine their capacities to respond in the case of an accidental release or event.

Risk assessment professionals should recognize that although the cooperation of facility personnel is essential to the information-gathering process, it may be difficult to obtain the necessary cooperation. Assessments undertaken in hostile circumstances, such as mergers or acquisitions, can meet significant resistance. However, even in situations where the assessment is internal and supports organizational goals, the information-gathering and review process may be hampered. For example, an assessment to identify potential environ-mental risks in a facility may seem threatening to process managers and line personnel whose established, successful, and productive operating practices are now being questioned. Likewise, facility managers may not want to know of existing risks or do not want scarce financial resources reallocated to assets or activities that can be eliminated more easily and cheaply than they can be made environmentally safe. The following tips will help to overcome these potential communication problems and facilitate the assessment process:

- Let the facility personnel know about the assessment at least two weeks in advance and provide an overview of the investigation so that the staff is able to prepare and organize the necessary data.

- Clearly communicate the goals and objectives of the assessment. Reassure staff that the purpose of the assessment is to improve operations, not to criticize.

- Develop a facility questionnaire in advance and have the results before the visit so that the assessment team can conduct the review efficiently and with few disruptions.

It is not uncommon for site inspections and interviews to identify information needs, discrepancies with facility records, or even inconsistencies between statements made at the facility. The assessment team should not make as-sumptions about these issues, but should take the necessary actions to validate the information. For example, many facilities generate solid wastes from their manufacturing processes but may not have tested the waste to determine whether it must be managed as hazardous waste. Such a situation requires sampling and analyzing the waste to determine the appropriate action. Other situations may simply require a meeting of appropriate personnel. The assessment team should recognize that, as a general rule, those closest to the operation have the most accurate information.

Following the site inspection and interviews, the team should meet with key facility personnel to clarify issues observed during the visit and to discuss preliminary findings. The team should raise any issues of special concern, such as dangerous hazards or violations the team uncovered during the visit. For example, information about hazardous wastes that are being stored unsafely or illegally should be brought immediately to management's attention. The team should also discuss other risk reduction efforts and programs, such as fire prevention and worker safety, to determine any important relationships and to help develop recommendations that meet multiple risk reduction goals concurrently.

The information gathering and inspection may directly point to observable, existing liability exposures or environmental hazards. However, like any other areas of risk assessment, unrecognized exposures may exist, and identifying them may require imagination and insight. Risk management professionals are essential partners in environmental risk assessment because they are able to visualize how particular sets of operating and management circumstances might cause routine and extraordinary losses. The "art" of risk management and the professional "toolbox," including scenario analysis, failure mode and effects analysis, and fault tree analysis, are important parts of the identification process. (These analyses will be described in Chapter 12.)

Evaluate Environmental Risks

Once all the information has been obtained and risks and loss scenarios have been identified, the assessment team can analyze and prioritize them for corrective action. Liability exposures arising from noncompliance or contamination demand the greatest attention and receive highest priority for action. Measures that can easily be remedied with little or no cost, such as environmental hazards pertaining to housekeeping, can also be priority areas because of their simplicity.

A greater challenge occurs in evaluating the significance of risks that offer only the potential for harm, are not driven by current compliance concerns, or require significant resources to control. Evaluating environmental risks is particularly challenging because, as described earlier, the accidental and sudden event is only one dimension of the organization's environmental risk. As a result, organizations create environmental hazard ranking systems that help determine the probability, frequency, and severity of accidental loss. These hazard ranking systems include considerations such as the following:

- Volume of materials generated—Priority may be given to the largest emissions or wastes. The logic of such an approach may seem faulty from a human and environmental health standpoint, but the appearance of very large numbers on TRI reports typically prompts public response and concern regardless of the actual risks involved.
- Characteristic and nature of material—Organizations evaluate environmental risks by categorizing their materials and wastes by severity of environmental impact. One company places every raw material, waste stream, and discharge into one of five chemical categories ranging from highly toxic/human carcinogen to ordinary trash.
- Reportable quantities—Companies identify the threshold levels established by the government for reporting certain materials and organize their risk management activities to avoid liability exposures.

Proper environmental risk evaluation also needs to include a study of the relationship between these risks and other exposure areas. Environmental risks are integrally connected to worker health and safety exposures, fire exposures, and natural perils. Activities to modify an environmental risk have some implication—positive or negative—for these other exposure areas.

Applying Risk Control to Environmental Loss Situations

The discussion under this heading addresses the following four general types of environmental loss control situations that most organizations are likely to encounter:

1. Regulatory noncompliance—A regulatory inspection or self-assessment identifies regulatory compliance violations.
2. Discovery of contamination—An environmental risk assessment identifies a contamination problem that might have existed for many years, or the organization is named as a potentially responsible party for site cleanup.
3. Sudden or accidental events—These are emergency situations prompted by spills, leaks, or other sudden and unplanned occurrences.
4. Ongoing organizational practice—Daily activities that are contrary to good environmental risk management.

What are the effects on an organization of not complying with environmental regulations?

What are the implications for an organization that is responsible for environmental contamination?

How should your organization deal with a sudden or accidental event that could or does damage the environment?

How do you develop site emergency and preparedness plans?

How do you make environmental loss control part of your organization's ongoing practices?

How do you compare environmental loss control results to established standards?

Loss Control and Regulatory Noncompliance

Many noncompliance violations result in straightforward, relatively minor fines and penalties. However, situations such as significant violations of permit conditions or chronic and repeated violations of other requirements cause regulatory agencies to sue organizations and pursue an enforcement settlement. The statutes describe a range of penalties for various violations, and the federal or state agencies have significant flexibility in their enforcement activities. The agency must consider many things, including history of violations, current operating practice, management practice, and willingness to supply information.

The enforcement settlement process offers opportunities for exchanging proposals and counterproposals between the organization and the regulatory agency. Like the permitting process, an organization may initiate new operating practices and procedures to reduce its financial liabilities. Equally important is demonstrating commitment and responsibility to resolve the problem. Open communication improves the relationship with the enforcement agency and improves the organization's negotiation position. Conversely, an organization's failure to communicate effectively and attempts to conceal information or to otherwise mislead environmental protection officials result in stiffer fines, punitive damages, negative publicity, and perhaps even criminal indictment.

Loss Control and the Discovery of Contamination

Potentially more serious and costly is a contamination problem for which the organization may be either solely responsible or jointly responsible with other parties. No introductory chapter can adequately address the legal and technical complexities that are part of the protracted process of corrective action.

However, understanding several key loss control principles will help risk management professionals to deal with these situations.

Technical specialists and engineering professionals bear much of the risk control responsibilities in managing a contamination exposure and cleaning up a polluted site. In nearly every case, an organization needs outside consultants to assist in the risk investigation and remediation effort. The process comprises some basic elements. A site review, or preliminary assessment, is conducted to get information on the nature and extent of the problem. This is followed by a remedial investigation to understand the degree of risk associated with the site and to develop a technical strategy for cleanup. This remedial investigation focuses on topics such as the contaminants of concern, cleanup requirements, regulatory agency requirements, and legal issues to be resolved. The remedial investigation may uncover additional data-gathering needs. As a result of this step, a technical strategy and schedule of corrective actions can be developed.

Regulatory agencies take an active interest in this process. They specify sampling and testing procedures and approve the cleanup plan and technical strategy. Extensive negotiation occurs regarding the appropriate scope and content of the investigation, cleanup demands, and degree of organizational responsibility. The final strategy is affected by legal issues, insurance considerations, community relations, and cost control. The specific strategies accomplish four goals:

1. Ensure long-term protection of human health and the environment
2. Meet all federal, state, and local environmental and public health requirements
3. Are cost-effective
4. Use permanent solutions to the greatest extent possible

Developing, selecting, implementing, and monitoring specific risk control activities in the cleanup procedure are the responsibility of the technical specialists. Despite the technical and political nature of this process, there are opportunities to actively reduce organizational exposures. Following are three important loss control considerations in site remediation.

Contracting With Consultants

Since environmental liabilities can occur as a result of the remediation work, a thorough review of the capabilities and technical expertise of the outside consulting firms is essential for environmental loss control. Client firms should require that their contractors have "contractor's pollution liability" (CPL) insurance for any damages or claims made as a result of the remediation work. The client firm may also want to be indemnified and needs to negotiate with the consulting firm to be named on the CPL policy.

Proactive Response

An organization benefits by taking an active role in the remediation process rather than reacting to the problem and relying on the findings and assessments of others. An organization should supply expertise, information, and ideas throughout the process for two reasons. First, the scope of the cleanup and post cleanup care may be shaped early in the remediation process. This makes it vital for an organization to contribute technical ideas and strategies and to avoid reacting to agency demands. Government mandates regarding cleanup activities can be two or three times more expensive than voluntary efforts undertaken with guidance from appropriate regulatory agencies. Second, the organization itself may have the best talent and capabilities to assess the situation and determine appropriate responses. In short, private cleanups are likely to be done more quickly, with better control, and more thoroughly than those done through government administration.

Prompt and Effective Communication

The quality of communication between the organization and other stakeholders, including government agencies and the public, is the third important element in loss control for site cleanup. Attempting to downplay the issue, withhold information, or delay the process may increase criminal fines and civil damages and severely jeopardize the organization's relationship with agencies. Even after the problem has been addressed to the satisfaction of all parties, a negative or hostile relationship with agencies has far-reaching implications for future business activities. Likewise, the organization must establish its presence within the population exposed to the risk and demonstrate good faith, commitment, and citizenship. Failure to communicate could result in a rumor-filled environment, polarization, and conflict, which aggravate problems. Raising public expectations and then not fulfilling them can be more damaging to the organization's credibility than making no effort at all.

Implementing these three measures can help an organization reduce the adverse financial consequences of an environmental loss. However, if an organization has been named with other organizations as a potentially responsible party, there are risks associated with "stepping forward." Joint and several liability may make the organization liable for more than its proportional share of the cleanup, and the appearance of relative wealth may make the organization an attractive target. In situations where liability is shared, the legal department must work closely with the risk control specialists and the technical team to ensure that the organization's liability exposure is not increased.

Loss Control and the Sudden or Accidental Event

Despite the best attempts to control environmental risks, sudden or accidental situations do occur—often with significant press coverage and public agency attention. Moreover, in addition to whatever actual environmental damage occurs, damage to the corporation's reputation and loss of goodwill can occur.

In dealing with sudden environmental events, risk management professionals should recognize that the quality of loss control and the protection of organizational resources and assets are directly related to how vigorously the organization deals with the exposure. As with loss control in site remediation, an active response and open communication are essential. The loss control considerations described earlier apply in this situation as well.

In environmental crisis situations, the organization must quickly and thoroughly demonstrate ownership of the problem, commitment to its correction, and responsibility to all those affected by the incident. This will improve the quality of the organization's discussions with agencies after the emergency has passed. Moreover, a quick and active response reduces the potential for lasting negative publicity. Although environmental accidents tend to be the most emotionally charged and frightening for the public, organizations that respond quickly and openly are more likely to gain the public's forgiveness. Specifically, a good risk control effort has a twenty-four-hour emergency response network and release reporting.

Twenty-Four-Hour Emergency Response Network

A rapid-response cleanup network should be in place to respond anywhere and at any time to serious contamination incidents. This network includes insurers, contractors, and local emergency planning agencies. Many professionals in the environmental risk management field believe that the ultimate financial consequences of the event are largely determined by who gets to the contamination site first—the network or the regulatory agency.

Release Reporting

The EPA has developed reportable quantities for all 725 hazardous substances regulated under Superfund. If an accidental release of amounts greater than these reportable quantities occurs, the organization must immediately notify the National Emergency Response Center. Failure to do so may result in a fine of $500,000, imprisonment of up to three years, or both.

Conveying information about accidental events may be difficult because answers about health and safety risks may not be immediately known. Good risk control demands an immediate response to answer questions and demonstrate good faith.

In an emergency situation, unlike in a discovery of contamination, the organization can immediately undertake specific measures to control urgent risks to human and environmental health and safety. After the situation has stabilized, a subsequent assessment may be done to determine long-term control and cleanup needs. The high-profile nature of the accidental event may result in political and public pressure for a hasty solution. At this stage, the value of an active approach is even more evident because of negotiations about long-term requirements, fines and penalties, and levels of "cleanliness" required.

Loss Control in Ongoing Organizational Practice

Environmental risk management should be integrated into the daily activities and decision making of an organization. This section examines environmental risk management programs and the application of the risk management decision process to ongoing environmental exposures.

Evolution and Functions of Environmental Risk Management Programs

The number of environmental risk management programs increased when environmental regulations were introduced in the 1970s. During that early period, much of the program activity was devoted to meeting new regulations and implementing control technologies to keep the organization in compliance. This "firefighting" approach defined the environmental risk management function and continues in many organizations today. However, as time progressed, many organizations took a more enlightened and active approach to managing their environmental affairs. Such "renaissance" programs became increasingly involved in operations management and facility administration to ensure that environmental considerations became an integral part of all business planning and decision making. At present, a broad range of environmental programs exist, ranging from one person "damage control" efforts to sophisticated interdisciplinary programs that strive to integrate environmental considerations into all company operations. The sophistication with which an organization manages its risk management program is likely to be a function of the types and degree of environmental hazards posed by the following:

- The organization's operations
- Regulatory pressures
- Past events or loss history
- Available human and financial resources

Many parallels exist between the organization and the structure of the risk management and environmental risk management programs. In small organizations, environmental risk management typically consists of one or two persons whose primary responsibility is to keep the facility in compliance with applicable regulations. Many smaller organizations combine the environmental function with other related activities, including health and safety, security, energy management, or plant engineering. In the latter type of program, the environmental manager has many other duties, and environmental risk management may take up only 25 percent of his or her time. The environmental manager usually reports directly to the plant manager and serves as the primary facility contact for government agencies. On the other end of the spectrum, large multinational organizations typically have a coordinating environmental risk management group at headquarters and environmental departments devoted exclusively to environmental affairs and concerns at each operating facility. These organizations seek economies of scope by identifying related areas of loss control and merging them into one program. The Environment, Health, and Safety department has direct reporting responsibilities and access to senior management. Most organizations, regardless of site, design their environmental risk management programs as a staff function to support and enhance line management decision making. In this way, environmental managers secure the cooperation of those who are best able to identify, evaluate, and control environment-related risks.

The environmental risk management program serves several technical, administrative, and institutional functions. The ability of the environmental program to fulfill these functions has significant implications for the amount of environmental risk exposure assumed by the firm.

Compliance Assurance

Principally, environmental programs ensure that the company complies with all applicable federal, state, and local requirements. The environmental program develops and implements policies, procedures, and standards pertaining to facility operations and ensures that the organization meets all regulatory requirements and responsibilities.

Regulatory Tracking and Interpretation

Environmental programs can gather, interpret, and disseminate information about future regulatory requirements. This improves the organization's ability to assess potential effects, plan for future developments, and avoid crisis responses to situations.

Technical Consulting

Environmental programs provide an internal technical consulting service to managers, engineers, and technical personnel, enabling them to select and implement appropriate technologies that meet environmental regulatory requirements.

Education and Training

Environmental protection programs increase employees' awareness and understanding of an organization's environmental protection objectives. These programs also educate employees and executives, enhancing their abilities and willingness to meet the organization's environmental protection objectives.

External Communication

Environmental programs improve communication with local communities, regulatory agencies, industry environmental councils, and other organizations. When possible, environmental programs should assist in developing regulatory policy and influencing the content of proposed environmental legislation. The specific details of environmental risk management programs depend on how the program is organized.

Integrating Risk Control Into Environmental Risk Management

The section on environmental risk assessments discussed how environmental exposures are identified and evaluated. This section looks at how the remaining steps of risk management decision making apply to internal environmental loss control.

Developing Risk Control Alternatives

Typically, a company may have many options for controlling a particular environmental risk. For example, suppose a company is concerned about the large amounts of hazardous waste generated through a particular finishing process used in the manufacture of Products A, B, and C. After an environmental review, it discovers that 80 percent of the hazardous waste is generated when Product B is finished. The environmental risk management expense report might identify the following possible options:

1. Purchase new treatment equipment that reduces the toxicity and volume of wastes on site.

2. Install a new finishing process so that the hazardous waste is not created.

3. Install new equipment that uses the same process but operates more efficiently, thereby reducing the volume of waste generated.

4. Use a new chemical with the existing finishing process to reduce the amount of waste generated.
5. Contract with another company to finish Product B.
6. Contract with another company to finish all its products.
7. Redesign Product B to reduce the waste generated when the product is finished.
8. Make Product B from a different material so that it does not need to be finished.

Option 1 is often the first approach identified. Logic suggests that since a waste exists, something must be done with it. Good risk control, however, should identify several risk control options. Like identifying the risks themselves, generating options requires creativity. Options 7 and 8 would require the most creativity.

An organization's loss control options fall into two general categories: source controls and source reduction. **Source controls** are those techniques, technologies, and activities that reduce, modify, or eliminate the exposure source. **Source reduction** measures reduce exposures by reducing or eliminating the use of materials or by reducing or eliminating the byproducts produced. They achieve three risk control objectives—avoidance, prevention, and reduction. Following are the five basic methods of source reduction:

1. Changing or modifying equipment—improving the efficiency of production equipment so that less waste is created
2. Substituting materials—replacing an objectionable material with a safer one or substituting materials to improve process efficiency and produce less waste
3. Changing the redesigning process—improving the fundamental way an operation is accomplished
4. Redesigning the product—changing the fundamental product characteristics and features so that the manufacturing process produces less waste and emissions
5. Changing operations and management—changing human behavior or established procedures and practices (for example, maintenance and housekeeping procedures)

Management controls are techniques that control the exposure after it already exists. Rather than reduce the amount of pollution created, management reduces exposures by improving the ways they are managed. To generate management control options, risk management professionals should focus on altering the four hazard factors. The first hazard factor—characteristics and behavior of materials—is addressed by pollution treatment techniques. These techniques reduce the volume or the hazardous nature of the material. Other management control options depend on the other hazard characteristics:

- Pathways (pollution control measures)—capture pollutants (for example, smokestack "scrubbers") or reduce the mobility of pollutants (for example, spill collection systems and surface impoundments)
- Populations—decrease the effect of a loss event on populations (for example, purchasing land around the facility as a buffer zone)
- Management practices—establish policies and procedures in expectation of an event (for example, emergency response plans)

In developing options, the risk control team should attempt to generate both source reduction and management control options, since the best risk control alternative is likely to include options from both areas.

Types of Management Control Techniques

To choose the appropriate control technique, risk management professionals consider the characteristics and chemistry of the pollutant or waste, the form it is in (solid, liquid, or gas), the media contaminated or threatened, government demands, and cost. The number of alternative control technologies continues to grow as scientific understanding of the nature and behavior of materials increases. Control technologies generally fall into five categories—recovery processes, physical and chemical treatment processes, thermal processes, biological processes, and solidification/stabilization processes.

- **Recovery processes**—Certain wastes, emissions, and waste streams carry materials that can be reused. Recovery processes separate, remove, and concentrate reusable material from the waste. The reusable material is often sold or recycled back into the reusable process. When the reusable material is also the pollutant, the recovery process reduces the hazardous nature of the waste. However, in many cases, recovery processes are not an option for disposing of hazardous wastes, and additional treatment is required before the material can be safely and legally disposed of.

  The equipment, chemicals, and chemical reactions in recovery processes often create a new set of wastes, residuals, and environmental risks. Recovery processes are typically used to recover metals and solvents (two types of materials often economical to reclaim) and are commonly used with liquid waste. Examples of recovery processes include the following:
  - Activated carbon absorption used in chemical spill response and industrial waste-water treatment exchange to recover metals from waste streams.
  - Distillation often used to recover solvents from waste streams.

- **Physical and chemical treatment processes**—Many physical and chemical processes are available to reduce the volume of waste, permit more economical and effective treatment, make waste less hazardous, and destroy the toxic components of waste. The processes are not significantly different from recovery processes but are used primarily for their treatment capabilities rather than for recovering and reusing materials. Both physical and chemical processes are used to separate and segregate waste components. Chemical processes also alter the hazardous nature of the waste. Many sophisticated chemical-based technologies make physical and chemical treatment processes a fast-evolving field in waste management. However, as with recovery processes, the equipment and chemicals used and the residuals created from the treatment process create additional risk exposures. These processes may also require pretreatment to "prepare" the waste for treatment. Examples of physical and chemical processes include filtration used to treat material such as oily waste waters, chemical precipitation commonly used to treat corrosives, and dehalogenation used to treat PCBs and contaminated soils.

- **Thermal processes**—Thermal processes dissolve wastes either through combustion or pyrolysis (chemical decomposition caused by heating in the absence of oxygen). Thermal processes can, in a matter of seconds, destroy materials that would take many years to deteriorate in a landfill. Many sophisticated thermal processes exist to treat materials such as solvents, PCBs, dioxins, contaminated soils, and infectious wastes. Depending on the thermal process used, treatment temperatures can range from several hundreds to several thousands of degrees.

  Most thermal processes are managed by organizations specializing in waste management, although some wastes can be incinerated on site. Using waste as fuel, however, is carefully regulated. Many wastes, such as heavy metals, cyanides, insecticides, pesticides, PCBs, and radioactive materials, should not be incinerated because of safety considerations. Organizations using on-site incineration must also have an RCRA permit. Although typically very effective in destroying wastes, thermal processes are often expensive and have precise control needs. Many thermal processes also create wastes that need management and disposal.

- **Biological processes**—Biological processes are processes using living organisms. They include aerobic digestion (needing oxygen), anaerobic digestion (not needing oxygen), and composting (or land application). Many chemicals are degradable through biological processes using formaldehyde, acetone, and isopropyl alcohol. An ongoing challenge for using these processes is maintaining the right type of ecosystem for microbes. Temperature, moisture content, existence of other organisms, and oxygen supply are just some of the parameters that must be identified and controlled.

- **Solidification/stabilization processes**—These processes use additives to reduce the mobility of pollutants to make the waste meet land disposal requirements. These processes improve waste handling characteristics, decrease the surface area across which pollutants can transfer, or detoxify waste constituents. Solidification adds materials to the waste to produce a solid. Stabilization converts the waste to a more chemically stable form. This includes solidification, but may also include chemical reactions.

  Encapsulation completely coats or encloses the waste with a new substance, either by individual particles or as an aggregate. These processes treat residuals from previous treatment processes so that they can be disposed of legally. They are increasingly important, since land disposal restrictions are becoming more stringent.

Selecting the Best Control Alternative

In choosing risk control options, the environmental risk management team must consider several factors. First is the technical feasibility of the option. A risk control strategy must be technically viable and appropriate given the specific context. Technical viability includes determining the commercial availability of the option and performing an engineering study to determine whether the risk would actually be controlled to the extent needed. Technical appropriateness determines whether the option "makes sense" in the broader context of business operations. For example, a new piece of equipment might dramatically reduce waste volumes but substantially increase the time it takes to manufacture the product—a strategy unacceptable to management. Or a certain water treatment system might be technically ideal but unable to handle the amount of water wastes generated during peak production times. Following are some questions the risk control team should ask to determine the technical feasibility of a risk control option:

- What are the space, operation, or management requirements of this option?
- Is the option commercially available?
- Is the option compatible with current procedures, work flows, and production activities?
- Will the option negatively affect product quality or other business concerns?
- Will the option worsen other environmental risk concerns or create new ones?
- Will the option create other risk exposures such as worker health or fire?
- Will the option be sustainable for a long period of time?

- Will the option withstand market, regulatory, and property changes?
- Will new training, skills, or expertise be needed to manage the option once it is in place?

A second factor to consider is the economic feasibility of the option. This includes capital costs (equipment, installation, and start-up), operating costs (supplies, parts, utilities, and labor), and intangible costs (potential loss of community goodwill and future liability costs). Economic benefits should also be calculated, including cost savings in environmental risk management and compliance, raw materials, maintenance and operation, and insurance. Standard measures of calculating the economic feasibility of risk control options (described in ARM 54—*Essentials of Risk Management*, volume 2) also apply to environmental risk management.

The final and perhaps most important consideration is the feasibility of the option regarding environmental regulatory demands. Environmental laws are often extremely prescriptive. Many environmental risk management activities, which on the surface would appear to be effective and cost-efficient, might be illegal. For example, an organization may want to improve the ambient air quality for its factory workers by venting solvent emissions to the outside. This practice is probably illegal under state clean-air statutes. Suppose an organization wants to set up an evaporation system to reduce the total volume of spent solvent sent to an off-site hazardous waste treatment facility. This seemingly effective strategy would be considered "on-site treatment" and illegal under RCRA without an appropriate permit. In other situations, regulatory demands might mandate certain control options or technologies, making other loss control strategies moot. In short, coordination with legal departments and regulatory specialists is essential to ensure that options under consideration do not exacerbate or create new liability exposures.

Implementing Risk Control Strategy

Successfully implementing environmental risk management requires coordination and cooperation with other functional areas. Too often, the environmental risk management program and risk control serve as policing functions. In these situations, risk control faces an uphill battle, since specific environmental responsibilities rest with the various functional areas in which the environmental exposures are created. Following are some of the key integration areas for effective environmental loss control.

Production and Operations Management

Coordination with operations management lies at the heart of risk control, since the majority of environmental exposures deal with storing, using, transforming, and disposing of materials used in the production process. An effective environmental risk management program tries to identify cause-and-effect relationships between environmental exposures and areas such as the following:

- Inventory and purchasing management
- Product design
- Production scheduling
- Process design
- Process control
- Process maintenance
- Production floor layout
- Waste treatment, storage, and disposal

Organizations will commonly make changes in all these areas to reduce costs, shorten manufacturing times, and improve product quality.

Management Information Systems (MIS)

MIS play an important role in environmental risk management by providing decision makers with the necessary data on organizational environmental performance. Following are examples of what might be found in an environmental information management system:

- Hazardous waste shipping manifests
- Inspection results
- Permit conditions, violations, and corrective action plans
- Monitoring data
- Facility hazard descriptions
- Material safety data sheet information
- Sampling and testing results
- Training and maintenance records
- Calendar for reporting requirements

An environmental risk management information system provides quick and efficient access to information to spot key trends, review performance, and support organizational decision making.

Marketing

An effective environmental risk management effort is coordinated with marketing to ensure that the organization does not accept contracts for business that result in accepting unnecessary or costly environmental loss exposures. For example, many environmental consulting organizations review and decline remediation work because the activities are too risky. For example, a manufacturing firm may need to decline a special order from a customer because the organization's environmental controls are unequipped to handle or treat the wastes or discharges generated. Only through coordination can the organization become aware of "hidden" exposures.

Accounting

A common barrier to effective environmental loss control is the inability to identify the "true" costs of environmental risk management. For example, suppose the unit cost of Product B is $5. All business decision making, including pricing and capital investment, is based on this assumption. However, if the costs of shipping and disposing of Product B's hazardous wastes are segregated and calculated and are added to the administrative costs of manifesting, labeling, and record keeping for these wastes, the unit cost would be substantially higher and might dramatically affect internal business decision making. Effective environmental risk management requires cost accounting procedures that properly recognize and track environmental management and loss costs.

Legal

Since many environmental losses stem from liability exposures, an effective environmental risk management program should be integrated with the legal department. Legal staff assist in identifying environmental exposures and protect the organization from loss by doing the following:

- Incorporating appropriate loss control and indemnification provisions in contracts
- Clarifying exposures arising from past, present, and future practices
- Negotiating with regulatory agencies
- Defending the organization in court

Functional integration is essential to environmental loss control. Successful implementation also requires an organization to consider environmental risk management when planning. For example, the quality of environmental loss control might be improved if current expenses and capital investments for environmental risk control are made parts of an organization's operating and capital budgets.

Monitoring the Effectiveness of Environmental Risk Management Programs

An effective environmental risk management program must have control systems in place to ensure that the program is achieving its objectives cost-effectively and efficiently and is being responsive to changing conditions and needs. Management control aims to do the following:

- Establish performance standards
- Compare results to standards
- Implement corrective actions

Establish Performance Standards   Proper environmental risk management should record the results of environmental risk management activities and compare results with organizational objectives and goals. All facilities should aim for "full compliance" standards. Other, more numerical performance objectives might be established for the organization; however, these standards must be indexed to assess organizational performance accurately. For example, suppose a facility set a performance objective to reduce toxic air emissions by 20 percent. At the end of the year, facility records show that this objective was achieved. However, facility operating records also show a 30 percent decrease in production volume due to economic conditions. Thus, the apparent improvement in environmental performance resulted in poorer performance regarding production levels. Another reason performance standards should be developed and interpreted carefully is the complex, multiple effects of pollutants. Even if the goal to decease air emissions by 20 percent were valid, based on production indexes, the actions to accomplish this goal may have increased land disposal or water discharges and therefore increased other environmental risks.

Compare Results to Standards   The environmental auditing program indicates environmental risk management performance. A compliance audit, along with external inspection reports, reveals noncompliance concerns and provides information about how well the facility has managed its liability exposures. Environmental loss exposures not driven by regulation require performance review through an environmental effects assessment. Areas of review include the following:

- Unregulated air emissions
- Unregulated discharges to water
- Solid and other wastes—volumes, types, and composition
- Process materials and catalysts—toxic and hazardous properties
- Use of land, water, fuels, and other natural resources
- Noise, odor, dust, vibration, appearance, and other nuisance issues
- Effects on specific parts of the environment

An annual environmental effects assessment can indicate where improvements occurred and where loss control efforts should be focused.

Implement Corrective Actions   Effective environmental risk management relies on specific procedures for initiating corrective and preventive action. Such procedures should also define any specific responsibility and authority channels to ensure that this activity is pursued in a timely manner. Noncompliance issues demand prompt and rigorous action because of liability exposures, and a prescriptive approach to corrective action is needed. Corrective action for loss exposures not driven by compliance demands may be more challenging, since the environmental manager may need to prioritize concerns, make choices about resource allocation, and obtain voluntary cooperation of others in the organization. To facilitate corrective action, the hazard ranking systems should be frequently updated to reflect the latest circumstances and conditions.

Role of Risk Management Professionals in Environmental Risk Management Programs

What is the role of risk management professionals in risk assessment and evaluation?

How can you review and manage environmental risk financing?

How can you perform a comparative risk evaluation?

How should you handle external and internal communication about environmental risk control?

What kind of acquisition and litigation support can risk management professionals provide?

The skills and tools of risk management professionals add considerable value to environmental risk management. This section discusses the following areas in which risk management professionals can serve primary roles:

- Environmental risk assessment and evaluation
- Review and management of environmental risk financing
- Comparative risk evaluation
- External risk communication
- Internal risk communication
- Acquisition and litigation support

Risk Assessment and Evaluation

Risk management professionals have leadership and support roles when identifying and evaluating accidental events and losses (that is, performing a hazard evaluation). Applying the skills and tools used in risk identification, such as scenario planning, hazard mode and effects analysis, and fault tree analysis, improves the quality of the organization's environmental risk management effort.

Risk management professionals' support role involves ongoing compliance assurance tasks. Risk management professionals can encourage investigation of the sources of pollution rather than the control of pollutants. They can help to identify and evaluate cross-media transfer issues when the solution to one environmental exposure creates or exacerbates an exposure in another environmental media. In this role, risk management professionals work with appropriate environmental managers and technical specialists and perhaps serve on multidisciplinary facility review teams.

Review and Management of Environmental Risk Financing

As with any other loss exposure, organizations must choose how much of the risk they are willing to control and how much of it will be financed internally or externally. Specifically, risk management professionals have two important tasks: evaluating environmental risk financing options and managing claims.

Many companies may choose to finance losses internally, especially as the sophistication of their environmental risk management efforts increases. Risk management professionals may play an important role in evaluating the potential financial consequences of exposures and loss scenarios to identify the appropriate mix of internal financing and control measures. Risk management professionals may also review contractual transfer options for risk financing. Contractual transfers, however, are still evolving because of the erratic nature and history of environmental risk transfer markets.

As described earlier in the chapter, the development of risk transfer mechanisms is hampered by the unique features of environmental losses—most notably, the "planned" nature of many losses, the time lags between occurrence and loss, and the high costs of claims. The relative scarcity of environmental liability insurance reflects these challenges. Before society began to grapple seriously with environmental concerns, coverage for environmental liabilities was formally written under most organizations' general liability insurance, although these policies typically included a "pollution exclusion" clause. As the cost of environmental cleanup and remediation exploded under new environmental regulations like Superfund, disagreements arose between insurers and insureds about what these pollution exclusion clauses covered. Were they only meant to exclude claims for negligent and intentional damage, as the insureds argued, thus covering all liabilities from past "legal" disposal practices? Or, as the insurers maintained, were the exclusions meant to apply to all pollution-related damages except those that were sudden and accidental? The financial stakes in these coverage discussions are significant—one study estimates that 88 percent of all Superfund expenditures go to legal costs. Legal rulings have added to the confusion, and both generators and insurance companies have won suits. As a result of continuing legal battles, the availability of environmental coverage has dropped and enthusiasm for insurance companies to become involved in this complex and often unpredictable coverage has dwindled. Nevertheless, as risk control sophistication continues to grow, many companies are starting to carve out specialty niches in environmental insurance. If available and affordable, site-specific environmental impairment liability (EIL) insurance might be an option.

After careful study, risk management professionals may currently find appropriate underwriters. The key to success in risk transfer is teamwork with the insuring organization. Despite the contentious history of the insurer/insured relationship, it is in the interest of both parties to create a "no-loss" scenario when dealing with potential environmental exposures. Risk management professionals should work with insurers in identifying preventive measures to reduce or eliminate potential losses. The internal technical expertise of the generating organization combined with the additional engineering, scientific, and assessment skills of the insurer can result in a powerful and effective risk control team and the sound basis for underwriting. Risk modification options may be jointly developed to reduce the cost of premiums and provide a market incentive for implementing sound risk reduction strategies.

This partnership should extend into issues of claims management. Environmental insurance claims filed under EIL policies, and to some extent the obsolete general liability insurance policies, can generally be grouped into three classes:

1. Third-party claims for property damage, business interruption, bodily injury, and nuisance as a result of an organization's activities

2. First-party claims for property damage, replacement, or cleanup; business interruption; or bodily injury

3. Government claims for cleanup and remediation or fines and penalties from regulatory violations

The objective of environmental claims management is the same as for any other claims management control: reducing the ultimate cost of claims while treating claimants equitably and providing adequate compensation. In the case of an actual loss event, the insurer and the insured must work closely to control pollution-related claims. The insurer and the insured should work together to guarantee a quick response regardless of where the site is located. A contractor network might be jointly created to rapidly respond at all hours of the day. Claims management is further assisted by developing a database and management information system to track claims and correlate environmental parameters leading to these claims. Risk management professionals can take a leadership role in assembling this information system. Such information-gathering and information-processing capabilities not only improve claims response and decision making, but they can also be used to fine-tune the policy coverage or to negotiate policy price.

Comparative Risk Evaluation

Another valuable contribution of risk managers to environmental risk management is the ability to simultaneously compare and analyze different types of risk. As described in Chapter 1, controlling one type of exposure may increase the frequency or severity of losses from another exposure. This is an issue of special concern in environmental loss control, where public attention, emotion, and a sense of urgency may lead an organization into hasty and questionable loss control decision making. For example, consider a company that is under intense public pressure to reduce the amount of toxic raw materials in its manufacturing process. After substantial review, the organization identifies a substitute material that is nontoxic and technically feasible to use. However, this new substance must be stored in large, specially designed tanks, conveyed to the manufacturing process under high temperatures and pressures, and used only under tight process-control conditions.

Although this alternative may be "good" environmental risk management from the standpoint of environmental toxicity, it may easily result in a significant net increase in overall loss exposure—to both the organization and third parties. New exposure sources (tanks and piping) are created, human health and safety risks to workers increase because of the high temperatures and pressures of the substance, and more opportunities for accidents exist because new process controls are more demanding and detailed. Without an overall risk perspective, the organization may mistakenly address the risk issues of greatest current importance. Risk management professionals can play an important role in providing a comparative risk analysis and helping to generate risk control strategies that are best from a total risk control perspective.

External Risk Communication

Because of its proven value and importance, risk communication has evolved from an active measure into an active planning tool for a preventive risk control program. More and more organizations are asking local citizens and advocacy groups to provide information on operations and community concerns for incorporation in a master environmental and risk control plan.

External risk communication information flows from the organization to the community and from the community to the organization. Risk management professionals can serve as leaders in both these areas by sharing internal issues and progress with local citizens and interest groups and by assembling relevant information from community stakeholders. Risk management professionals are also able to reduce technical and complex information to simple, clear, and meaningful terms. Specifically, they may be needed to make risk analyses understandable to local populations and to describe how these risks are being controlled. Risk management professionals may help develop survey instruments, conduct focus groups, and perform other research activities when third-party concerns and issues are identified. In reviewing the results of the research, risk management professionals can help to prioritize issues and improve decision making within the company.

Risk communication is an expanding field, and many of the lessons about working with local populations have been learned the hard way. The primary objectives are to earn the trust of the public and local agencies, convey that the company is aware of the environmental impact of its operations and wants to be a good neighbor, and promote the actions the company is undertaking to control environmental risks. If an event occurs, a fourth objective would be added: control negative news about the incident without hindering information dissemination or otherwise appearing as an obstructionist. Risk communication professionals follow several cardinal rules in risk communication:

- Recognize the public as a legitimate partner in organizational risk control.
- Use the public input in the risk control planning and evaluation process.
- Listen to specific concerns that may provide insights into community values of special interest.
- Be honest, frank, and open. Tell people what cannot be done and why.
- Try to coordinate and collaborate with other credible sources and organizations in the community.
- Meet the needs of the media.
- Speak with compassion, clarity, and commitment to the community.
- Promise only what can be accomplished and do what has been promised.

Risk communication will continue to grow in importance within the context of the environmental risk management program, as will the role of risk management professionals in contributing to and facilitating this process.

Internal Risk Communication

Risk management professionals possess two characteristics that facilitate internal communication about environmental risk control.

The first characteristic is political access. Although the environmental risk management program continues to grow in stature and acceptance in the industry, it is still perceived in many organizations as an activity that generates no financial or other value. Risk management professionals should raise environmental issues and concerns in decision-making contexts where regulatory affairs specialists may never be able to gain a foothold.

The second characteristic is interpretation skills. Risk management is a process of assembling large amounts of potentially complex information, analyzing it, and communicating it in an understandable and practical way to decision makers. Risk management professionals can interpret this complex information for technical experts and the organization's decision makers.

Acquisition and Litigation Support

Risk management professionals also provide acquisitions and litigation support. As described earlier, the nature of environmental liability demands that organizations carefully review and study potential contamination problems and preexisting liabilities before purchasing a site or acquiring another firm's operating facilities. Risk management professionals play an important role in analyzing and interpreting these findings and in generating risk control recommendations and strategies for senior management. Likewise, when organizations are being sued by the government or third parties for environmental damages, risk management professionals may be key resources in the organizations' defense by providing the rationale behind specific risk control measures.

Disclosure that an organization was aware of a risk but did not control it sufficiently or at all may have two advantages. First, the organization retains control over how, where, and when this information is introduced in court. Second, nondisclosure says that the organization did nothing and never imagined that such an accident might happen. Such an admission may suggest even greater negligence than testifying that the risk was recognized but subordinated to other, more pressing risk control needs.

Summary

Effective environmental risk management accomplishes two objectives: it prevents or reduces an organization's effect on environmental values, and it protects the organization's resources and assets from exposures stemming from environmental protection laws and activities. Environmental loss control is unique because it must address other issues besides the accidental or sudden event. Many environmental losses originate from past organizational practices or from current regulated and controlled releases, which are in essence "permissions to pollute." Environmental risk control is also unique because of the technical complexity of the issues, the time lags between events and losses, and the difficulty in applying economic analysis to environmental values. Environmental professionals generally recognize a hierarchy of options in controlling environmental losses—source reduction, reuse, recycling, control and treatment, and disposal. Source reduction is the preferred option because it includes exposure avoidance, loss prevention, and loss reduction. Disposal is least preferred because the risks are implicitly greater when pollutants are directly introduced into the environment.

Environmental exposures can be grouped into two categories, liability exposures resulting from violating environmental protection laws and other exposures based on actual harm to the environment that results in losses for either first-party or third-party interests. Environmental liability exposures are largely concerned with pollution and contamination resulting from transporting and using materials, transforming materials through the manufacturing process, and generating wastes and releases. The second set of liability exposures addresses any physical degradation an organization may cause. Actual harm to the environment may be caused by spills and leaks, materials uses, remediation activity, physical degradation, and the legal disposal and discharge of wastes. Complying with applicable laws and regulations regarding the discharges, emissions, and releases does not indemnify the organization from suits for environmental damages or third-party claims for harm to economic, property, or personnel values. In addition, contractual arrangements for treating and disposing of wastes and releases do not protect the organization. In environmental risk management, the generator of pollutants always remains liable.

Identifying and evaluating environmental losses requires risk management professionals to assess existing site conditions and characteristics, current compliance status, and a wide variety of operations and management issues pertaining to how the facility is being run. Risk management professionals are probably members of larger assessment teams comprising specialists from many disciplines. Since much of a risk assessment focuses on current compliance or cleanup needs, risk management professionals can help to identify how particular management decisions might result in environmental losses and how such cause-and-effect events might be mitigated or eliminated. Risk assessments have become an integral part of management operations and special business decision-making situations such as acquisitions, mergers, and divestitures.

Without an environmental risk assessment, organizations may assume liabilities for which they had no responsibility. Assessments focus on past events such as previous waste disposal practices and site contamination, special events such as spills and releases, and current manufacturing operations.

This chapter presented the risk control decision-making process as it applies to various types of common environmental loss control situations. The traditional emphasis of environmental risk control has been on decreasing losses after an environmental contamination event occurs. However, more attention is now being given to integrating loss control into all applicable laws and regulations regarding discharges, emissions, and organizational decision making to prevent environmental contamination from occurring in the first place. Risk management professionals are important contributors to this integration effort and are responsible for risk assessment, comparative risk evaluation, and risk communication within and outside the organization.

Chapter 10

Controlling Net Income Losses

Educational Objectives

1. Illustrate risk control measures that prevent or reduce an organization's net income loss in given situations.

   In support of the above objective, you should be able to do the following:

   a. Describe how to determine the extent to which the severity of an organization's net income losses can be affected by length, timing, and degree of impairment; additional expenditures required; and time after reopening to rebuild pre-loss revenues.

   b. Describe and illustrate how appropriate pre-event actions and post-event actions limit the severity and frequency of an organization's net income losses.

   c. Describe and explain how to implement and monitor appropriate pre-event and

Outline

Variables Determining Net Income Losses

   Identification of Variables

   Risk Control Significance of Those Variables

Property-Related Net Income Losses

   Analysis of Property-Related Net Income Exposures

   Risk Control Measures

   Illustrative Financial Analysis of a Net Income Risk Control Measure

Liability-Related Net Income Losses

   Products Liability

   Work-Related Injuries and Illnesses

Personnel-Related Net Income Losses

   Analysis of Personnel-Related Net Income Exposures

   Risk Control Measures

Summary

post-event measures for reducing the frequency and/or severity of net income losses stemming from property, liability, and personnel losses.

2. Define or describe each of the Key Words and Phrases shown in the course guide for this assignment.

Controlling Net Income Losses

Net income losses are reductions in revenues or increases in expenses. Those losses are consequences of events that also cause property, liability, and personnel losses.

Net income losses have primarily been associated with property losses. Business interruption insurance covers property-related net income losses, while those net income losses associated with liability and personnel losses have typically not been covered by any kind of insurance. It is easy to understand, therefore, why liability and personnel losses have generally not been thought to cause net income losses. However, the sophistication of today's risk management and insurance community, as well as the pervasiveness of net income losses, demands a broader interpretation of the net income loss concept.

If a manufacturer sells a defective product, liability losses could be incurred. But the loss might expand because word of the defect can spread quickly, causing the public to lose confidence in the product. Fewer products will be purchased, and revenues will be reduced. Depending on the severity of the defect, the nature of the product, and the public's perception of the problem, the net income loss could be more serious than the liability loss.

Personnel losses are often net income losses as well. For example, if a key person dies, any death benefit paid would be a personnel loss, but the loss of that person would probably have a business effect also. After the marketing director of a firm dies, the new director might need time to regain customer confidence. In the meantime, revenues could slip, and advertising expenses might have to be increased. In that case, the personnel loss causes a net income loss.

Controlling net income losses involves three broad loss control objectives. The first is to prevent the events that cause net income losses, which are usually accompanied by other kinds of losses. If this objective can be accomplished, no other actions are needed. Indeed, many property, liability, and personnel loss prevention measures are "sold" to management out of concern for a potential net income loss rather than the property or other related loss. But loss prevention measures are not always effective. Therefore, loss reduction steps should also be taken.

The second broad objective is to reduce the severity of the net income loss if one does occur. The magnitude of either the revenue reduction or the increase in expenses must be controlled.

The third objective is to decrease the loss of market share that can result from the net income loss. If customers stop buying a product because of a publicized defect, the manufacturer loses sales in the short term, causing a loss of revenue. If customers decide to purchase products from other firms, a permanent market share could be lost, which is a long-term effect. This translates into a permanent revenue loss. The second and third objectives can be achieved by reducing the consequence of the property, liability, or personnel loss.

This chapter explores ways to achieve those three objectives of controlling net income losses. In this chapter, as in the program, the term **net income** refers to the difference between an organization's revenues and its expenses during a particular interval. The interval starts with any accidental event that disrupts the organization's normal operations and ends when normal operations and normal revenue and expense patterns are reestablished. Net income risk control, therefore, is a means of reducing the disruptions that accidents can cause in an organization's normal flow of financial resources.

Although net income is equivalent to net revenue, the discussion in this chapter is not restricted to profit-oriented organizations. Net income loss exposures exist for nonprofit organizations as well as public entities because nonprofit organizations also depend on predictable revenues and controlled levels of expenses to perform their activities. Those organizations are nonprofit, but they are not nonrevenue or non-cash flow. Every organization needs an excess of revenues over expenses (preferably in every business period and necessarily in the long run) to function. Therefore, net income risk control is vital for every organization.

Variables Determining Net Income Losses

To control net income losses effectively, the variables that govern the loss must be identified and analyzed. Alternative control measures must then be considered and the best ones implemented. Monitoring the chosen techniques is difficult in many cases because contingency planning plays a large part in net income loss control. Unless the plans are implemented, judging their effectiveness is not possible. What can be monitored, however, is how well the

What variables determine net income losses?

How do those variables influence net income losses?

What is the risk control significance of variables that influence net income losses?

organization is prepared to implement the contingency plan. Do all employees know their roles in the plan? Have drills taken place? Has the plan been reviewed and updated if necessary? Monitoring the effectiveness of loss prevention measures designed to prevent property, liability, and personnel losses is somewhat easier since loss prevention is routinely practiced as part of normal operations.

Identification of Variables

The following are the variables that determine the extent of a net income loss:

- Length of the impairment to normal operations
- Activity level at the time of the impairment
- Degree to which the organization is affected
- Potential for extra expenses and expediting expenses to reduce the degree of impairment
- Time needed to resume pre-loss levels of revenue

Length of Impairment

The impairment to normal business from a net income loss can range from a loss of customers following a liability loss to the shutdown of a plant after a fire. The longer the impairment, the worse the net income loss. Loss prevention and reduction measures should reduce the length of the impairment.

Activity Level at Time of Impairment

In many organizations, some periods are more crucial than others. Many organizations have a peak season (such as the year-end holidays for retailers or the early fall for organizations that supply those retailers). Similarly, farmers should be fully operational at harvest and marketing times. A temporary shutdown at those peak periods caused, for example, by a trucker's strike can deprive the farmers of income for an entire year. As another example, if a defense manufacturer cannot bid on a ten-year contract because of the loss of a key engineer, the manufacturer's income for the entire decade might be a fraction of what it would have been had the firm secured the contract.

Conversely, some time periods can be of little significance to some organizations. For a government agency, an accident causing a brief shutdown during the month of August, when the legislative and executive officials are often traveling, might mean little loss of revenues or increases in expenses. For a building contractor well ahead of schedule on a particular project, a few days' delay due to inclement weather probably causes little, if any, loss of net income. In short, the timing of a disruption can greatly affect the severity of a net income loss.

Degree of Impairment

A net income loss could affect only part of an organization's normal operations. Suppose a company is facing an environmental liability claim by a town because the company is polluting the town's water supply. The company obviously wants to stop the operation that is polluting the water. In the meantime, the rest of the company's operations can continue, and the process causing the pollution can be handled by an outside contractor. The additional expense of having the contractor do the work (over and above the normal processing expense) would be a net income loss. The rest of the operations continue normally, so the degree of the impairment to operations is minimal.

Identifying those parts of an operation that can shut down either all or part of a business is important. Those parts of an operation are called **bottlenecks.** Determining how badly the operation would be affected is equally important. With this information, a dual approach to loss control can be used. First, the bottleneck can be eliminated or its effects reduced. Second, those parts of an operation that would be unaffected by the loss can be kept running as efficiently as possible.

For example, Ace Baking Company bakes bread on the first floor of its heavy concrete building. On the second floor it bakes cupcakes. If the cupcake operation is shut down because an oven explodes, the bread-baking operation can still continue. Of course, Ace Baking Company could still have complete bottlenecks. If a fire in the truck garage destroys all of the company's trucks, a total shutdown would occur. That problem might be quickly alleviated by renting trucks or hiring a delivery firm; nevertheless, the problem is still a bottleneck.

Additional Expenditures

Reducing the degree of impairment by incurring extra expenses is often possible. The expenses are extra because they would not have been incurred had no impairment occurred.

Renting delivery trucks or hiring a delivery firm is one example of extra expenses. Another example is paying expediting expenses to obtain replacement equipment, supplies, or services more quickly than usual. If Ace Baking Company's oven had to be imported from Europe, having it shipped by air rather than by sea would be an expediting expense. That expense could significantly reduce the length of time the cupcake operation was down, thus reducing the loss.

Resuming Pre-Loss Revenues

The length of time to resume pre-loss levels of revenue is a major variable that determines the severity of a net income loss. Even when the cause of the net income loss is eliminated, the organization will not immediately be able to resume operations at its normal level. Time, effort, and additional expenditures are necessary to regain lost customers, for example. The faster this lost market share can be regained, the less the net income loss.

To illustrate, suppose that Beta Hospital suffers a fire, and one of its three wings is destroyed. Doctors will send their patients to other hospitals. When reconstruction is complete and Beta Hospital reopens its third wing, time and effort will probably be required to motivate doctors to resume using Beta Hospital.

Risk Control Significance of Those Variables

After studying the objectives of net income loss control and the variables that govern a net income loss, the overall approach to net income loss control should be clear:

1. The organization's operation should be studied to pinpoint those property, liability, and personnel loss exposures that can cause particularly frequent or particularly severe net income losses. Pre-loss and post-loss risk control techniques (exposure avoidance, loss prevention, loss reduction, segregation of exposure units, and contractual transfer) should be applied to those exposures.

2. The variables that govern the severity of a net income loss should be determined so that countermeasures can also be developed to reduce the potential severity of a loss.

The remainder of this chapter discusses net income losses that are a consequence of property, liability, and personnel losses and explains how to prevent them or reduce their severity.

Property-Related Net Income Losses

> **How can you analyze property-related net income exposures?**
>
> **What risk control measures can you implement to control property-related net income exposures?**
>
> **How can you financially analyze a net income risk control measure?**

Net income losses often result from property losses. Controlling property-related net income losses first requires analyzing the exposures and then evaluating, selecting, and implementing appropriate risk control measures.

Analysis of Property-Related Net Income Exposures

To analyze an organization's net income loss exposure resulting from property losses, the systems approach should be used. The risk manager must step back to see the big picture of how all parts of the business function together.

General Systems Analysis

For a typical organization, the analysis covers outside and inside entities. Outside entities include customers, suppliers, and utilities. The internal entities are the processes and operations themselves, including the raw materials and components, labor and management, and the equipment or other physical assets that are used. Any one of those entities, if impaired, could affect one or more parts of the operation and cause a net income loss.

Flowcharts are valuable tools for that analysis. They graphically display the structure of the organization, making the relationships among the parts clear. Bottlenecks or contingent net income exposures become obvious.

There are at least two kinds of flowcharts, process flowcharts and supply, marketing, and distribution flowcharts. Process flowcharts, which show the physical layout of a facility, are useful for analyzing the operations of the facility as well as the separations and concentrations of value within the facility. Since flowcharts show physical layout, they are also very useful for emergency response planning, including the development of emergency exit routes and the location of emergency medical and fire control equipment.

Supply, marketing, and distribution flowcharts display the relationship between the organization and outside entities such as suppliers, customers, and utilities. Those flowcharts also show the flow of values between each entity and between major parts of the organization. They can be used to determine the dollar value associated with each supplier or customer, thus enabling the risk management professional to estimate the effect of a contingent net income loss caused by a problem with the supplier or customer. Showing the contribution that each supplier, customer, and department makes to the values created by an organization allows the analyst to calculate the effect that a loss associated with a supplier, customer, or department will have on the organization's net income.

Analysis of Internal Subdivisions

After performing a systems analysis, the risk management professional analyzes the internal structure of the organization by assuming different points of view. At a minimum, the risk management professional should look at the organization by building, by floor and by subdivisions of floors, by process, and by product. If the risk management professional at the Ace Baking Company did not analyze the company's operation by floor, he or she might not have discovered that each floor could operate independently. Consequently, after the oven exploded, the company might not have been as well prepared to operate using only one floor. The risk management professional should have also analyzed the baking process more carefully. The risk manager should have determined that with temperature adjustments and different baking times, the first floor oven could have baked cupcakes for the other floors, thus reducing their overtime expenses. As this example illustrates, failure to look at an operation from all angles contributes to an organization's loss. The timing of the analysis is also a key factor. After an occurrence like an explosion, management often discovers ways to keep operating and to expedite repairs. However, advance analysis and planning can reduce a loss by having contingency procedures in place before an accident occurs. Consequently, time (and, by implication, money) is not lost because of confusion and a lack of appropriate action.

The objectives of a general systems analysis also include estimating the effect of a loss: the extent of the impairment, the degree of the impairment, additional expenses, expediting expenses, and time to resume normal operations.

Suppose that the Tempting Fragrance Company, located in California, consists of two one-story buildings. One houses the administrative offices and warehouses; the other is a manufacturing plant. Within the plant, fragrances are mixed in steam-heated stainless steel mixing vats. The steam is produced by a gas-fired boiler. Even on the basis of such limited facts, the analysis of the net income loss exposure from property damage (illustrated in Exhibit 10-1) can be quite complex.

Although the analysis depicted in Exhibit 10-1 is incomplete, it illustrates how to analyze a company by its internal subdivisions: by building, process, and dependence on outside utilities. Other customers, suppliers, and products could easily be added for a more complete analysis.

Exhibit 10-1
Framework for Analyzing a Net Income Exposure from Property Damage

Category	Degree of Impairment	Time	Risk Control Measure
Building	Number of buildings Importance of activities they house Full or partial shutdown	6 months to replace	Rent space Subcontract work
Process vats	Leaking	2 months to replace	Subcontract work Expedite replacement Add flexible couplings to piping
Steam	Damage to boiler	6 weeks to replace	Rent temporary boilers Expedite replacement Duplicate boilers
	Gas line break	1 week to repair	Cooperate with public utility Duplicate gas lines and include flexible couplings

Note that the risk control measure column in the exhibit does not indicate loss prevention for the building category. This is because the loss prevention measure for the building is earthquake-resistant construction, which cannot be easily added to an existing building.

One variable not considered in this chart is the time to resume normal sales and operating levels. Estimating that time involves more information than appears on the chart and probably some intuition.

For more complex organizations, analyzing internal subdivisions beyond the plant level might be necessary. The plants within a company might be interdependent. If one plant manufactures a fruit drink and then ships it to its other plant for canning and labeling, analyzing just one of the plants is insufficient. The company as a whole must be analyzed.

Risk Control Measures

A risk control program is the key to achieving net income risk control objectives: preventing a loss, reducing its magnitude, and preserving market share. The program should address the property-related net income loss exposures uncovered during the analysis and should also prepare an organization for any kind of disruption.

Risk control measures can be divided into two categories: pre-loss and post-loss. **Pre-loss measures** are steps taken before a loss occurs to prevent or reduce it. **Post-loss measures** are steps taken after a loss occurs to control its severity. Post-loss measures should be developed before a loss occurs.

Developing a risk control program and implementing it can also have educational benefits for an organization. By planning to cope with interruptions to the normal work process, people develop the ability to recognize exposures and are more willing and better able to avoid the hazards that cause them. The following are risk control measures to prevent and/or reduce property-related net income losses.

Preventing Property Loss

Pre-loss Risk Control Measures

    Preventing property loss

    Devising contingency plans

    Cross-training employees

    Planning for post-loss
       communication

The best way to prevent a net income loss after a property loss is simply to avoid the property loss in the first place. Property loss prevention measures are by definition pre-loss measures. Various aspects of property loss prevention are covered in several chapters in this text, but a review is in order.

Sophisticated systems and procedures are often installed to prevent fires and explosions. Elaborate physical protection in the form of sprinklers, alarm systems, fire-rated construction, and control measures for specific hazards is often provided. Procedural controls, such as standard operating procedures for hazardous jobs, fire extinguisher training for employees, and inspection programs, are also used. Controlling machinery breakdowns requires periodic inspections and preventive maintenance programs.

Proper building design and construction are necessary to withstand severe weather and earthquakes. Proper building maintenance, especially roof coverings and drains, is also important. Earthquake and flood losses can be avoided by careful site selection, if possible. If avoidance is not possible, earthquake-resistant building designs can be used. Mild flooding can be controlled by pumping and drainage systems, but little can be done to control severe flooding.

Devising Contingency Plans

Contingency plans address a potential impairment to normal operations by answering the question, "What would we do if . . .?" The plans should consider each possible impairment in detail and should specify procedures for emergencies such as fire, flood, storms, earthquake, machinery breakdowns, and power outages. As explained in Chapter 8, contingency plans are pre-loss measures to reduce post-loss disruption.

The duties and actions required to handle every contingency should be assigned specifically. Complete descriptions of each person's actions should be provided, along with a description of the management structure during the emergency if that structure is different from the usual chain of command.

For example, if a plant suffered a power failure, the engineering manager and the plant engineer would be required to determine the cause of the failure. The plant engineer would determine whether the problem was internal and would contact the public utility to determine whether it was also experiencing difficulties. If so, the plant engineer would want to know what could be done to expedite normal service. When the engineering manager received this information, he or she would decide what to do next.

The plant might be required to shut down all equipment to prevent an excessive power drain when power is restored. If a power drain is expected, the maintenance manager would shut down the equipment. The engineering manager would report the situation to the plant manager and the production manager because they would have to decide about sending people home, scheduling overtime, and handling products that might be spoiled because processing is incomplete. Together, they would decide what to do about restoring power. What they decide, of course, would depend on the nature of the problem. They could be faced with a damaged transformer owned by the plant or with a burned out incoming power line owned by the utility. The required actions will be different for each of those situations.

Describing the emergency tasks in detail ensures that the tasks will be carried out during the confusion of an emergency. Even if the tasks are based merely on common sense, explicitly describing them and assigning them to specific persons help eliminate the possibility that the tasks will be overlooked. In effect, the contingency plan is a standard operating procedure for emergencies.

Contingency plans should be in writing for reference and training purposes. Everybody who has an active role in the plan should be well versed in it, and drills should be held whenever feasible. Drills are very important because they give all employees a chance to practice their duties. In addition, problems or concerns not previously considered sometimes become evident during drills.

Some parts of the plan might require evacuating the employees or having them take cover during a weather emergency. Those activities should be practiced to make sure that everybody knows what to do and how to do it.

Finally, organizaitons must consider updating their plans. Organizations and their activities change, which means procedures to change the contingency plan must exist. Otherwise, the plan can quickly become outdated. The best way to make sure a plan is current is to have a coordinator ask employees who have an active role in the plan to submit changes and corrections periodically. Even if those employees believe that no changes are necessary, they should be asked to respond. That procedure forces employees and management to review the contingency plan.

Cross-Training Employees

Designating and training back-up employees for every job, or at least a variety of jobs, should be part of all contingency plans, not just liability or personnel loss contingency plans. Such broad training, known as cross-training, helps the organization keep all jobs staffed after a loss and also provides the flexibility to shift employees to temporary jobs if necessary. Cross-training enables an organization to cope with the personnel loss exposures and loss of employees who are injured in job-related accidents or in fires, explosions, and storms.

Planning for Post-Loss Communication

Good communication with employees and the public is important after a property loss, especially one serious enough to cause a net income loss.

Employees are likely to be confused immediately after a loss. They will undoubtedly realize that a loss has occurred, but they will not know exactly what happened or how it affects them. Thus, employees might rely heavily on the news media for information even though press coverage is sometimes unfair or inaccurate. The confusion creates anxiety in employees who are vital to the organization's business.

Since worried, anxious employees cannot perform well, organizations should directly inform employees when normal operations are disrupted. For a small firm, telephone calls might be feasible. For a larger organization, other arrangements, such as an all-employee meeting, can be made. Employees can also be asked to call a special telephone number for information or listen to local radio and TV stations for public service messages.

Public relations (communication with the news media, customers, suppliers, and the financial community) is essential when a net income loss occurs. Press releases are valuable because they leave less room for misinterpretation and error than do off-the-cuff spoken comments. Customers and suppliers must know whether the firm can continue its normal supply and purchasing schedule. If so, they must be reassured; if not, they must be told the extent of the problem and how it will affect them. Being less than honest at this point would jeopardize the organization's relationship with customers and suppliers. The organization should try to conduct business as normally as possible. The goal is to prevent customers from turning to other suppliers and to prevent suppliers from favoring other customers. Good communication is not a panacea, but it can help tremendously.

The business and financial communities should also be kept informed about the organization's loss and recovery from it. Their perception of how management handles the impairment is important because the people in those communities extend credit to the organization. Their willingness to continue doing so depends on their being convinced of the continued viability and profitability of the organization.

Protecting and Salvaging Property

Post-loss Risk Control Measures

Protecting and salvaging property

Protecting key equipment

Segregating facilities

Maintaining manual capacity for automated operations

Using overtime

Managing extra, expediting, and continuing expenses

Replacing utilities

Maintaining business relationships

Protecting and restoring vital records

Controlling contingent net income losses

Protecting and salvaging property, which is another element of net income risk control, is also part of normal property loss recovery procedures. After a property loss, the opportunity often arises to protect damaged property from further damage and to salvage undamaged property. Net income losses are often simultaneously reduced.

Protecting property usually involves covering openings in buildings where glass is broken, where high winds rip the roof covering off, or where firefighters cut holes to vent the fire. Protecting property could also mean posting guards to deter looting and vandalism.

Salvage operations usually involve removing or protecting the contents of a building for reuse or sale at distressed prices. However, salvage can result from any property loss. For example, salvaging a car that has been in a flood is possible. The actions involved in salvaging property depend on the circumstance. If a shirt manufacturer has shirts that have been in a flood, salvage operations require segregating the damaged shirts, drying them, and finding a buyer for them.

Salvage companies specializing in buying damaged merchandise constitute the normal market for damaged goods. However, a manufacturer could decide to wash and repackage its shirts, believing that the merchandise has not really been damaged by the flood. On the other hand, food products or drugs probably could not be reprocessed following a fire or flood loss because food and drugs are regulated by the Food and Drug Administration (FDA). The FDA would probably take a conservative position and prohibit selling such products for human consumption. In that case, the damaged goods could be sold for animal feed or veterinary use.

Machinery and equipment are also salvageable. Some items merely need to be washed, dried, cleaned, or painted. Other equipment has to be disassembled and lubricated. Because electronic components are sensitive to heat, smoke, and water, the control systems for some machinery might have to be replaced. Computer equipment exposed to fire is a good example. Some of the sensitive components would need to be replaced, and other parts would need to be dried and cleaned.

Sometimes salvage does not involve cleaning or replacing goods at all. For example, assume a restaurant's meat freezer had a refrigerant leak in the cooling system that could not be repaired. The salvage operation would involve removing the meat and quickly placing it in other freezers. The restaurant could borrow space in another restaurant's freezer or rent space in a refrigerated public warehouse. In those cases, the salvage operation is the transfer of the meat to prevent further damage.

Acting quickly in an emergency reduces property loss, but reducing the net income loss is just as important. If damaged property is protected from further damage and salvage operations are promptly started, the disruption of normal operations is lessened. The shirt manufacturer does not have to run overtime shifts to make up for the inventory that was destroyed. In the computer example, replacing the damaged parts means that the computer is quickly ready for service, thus avoiding overtime processing or buying computer time from a service bureau. And because the restaurant promptly moved its inventory of meat, it continues to operate efficiently. In each of those examples, prompt salvage action reduces the net income loss.

Exposure analysis reveals where prompt salvage action is necessary. Salvage plans should be included in contingency procedures. Actions to handle each of the problem areas should be described in detailed in the plans.

Protecting Key Equipment, Facilities, and Processes

Bottlenecks in an organization's operation deserve attention because damage or interruption at those points can create large net income losses. The classic example of a bottleneck is a single machine through which all production flows. If the machine breaks down or is destroyed, production is interrupted. Sometimes the bottleneck is not a single piece of machinery but an entire process or even a whole facility.

Suppose a manufacturer prints the labels for its finished product, and the manufacturer's printing presses, paper stock, inks, and cleaners are destroyed in a fire. The quickest way to reduce the impairment and associated net income loss is to have the printing done outside, at least temporarily. The entire printing process is a bottleneck in this case. The best protection for any bottleneck is to have some plan to continue some level of operations until normal operations are restored. One solution, segregating an organization's facilities, is described in the following section.

Segregating Facilities

The ideal solution to a bottleneck problem involves segregating, through duplication, the key element (equipment or process) so that two or more elements operate together. Thus, if one element becomes impaired, the other can still function, maybe even absorbing the full load.

Unfortunately, financial reality is such that duplication seldom, if ever, occurs solely for risk management reasons. If one machine with a five-ton capacity is needed for production, an organization would not usually purchase two five-ton machines to reduce a bottleneck. However, if eight tons of capacity are required, purchasing two five-ton machines rather than a single ten-ton machine might be considered. Management could see the risk management value of two machines and, if the cost differences are not extreme, might approve such a plan. In addition to the loss control implications, having two machines provides flexibility if production schedules vary.

A similar approach is often used when designing boiler installations. Because heating and process steam requirements vary, multiple boilers are sometimes provided. However, the number of boilers operating at any time depends on the capacity required. Risk control benefits in this case are a byproduct of other financially beneficial practices or decisions. For example, if a firm that makes clothing is just starting out and has one fabric-cutting machine, a bottleneck exists. When the firm grows and has twenty cutting machines, the loss of any one machine becomes less consequential. Again, risk control benefits are a byproduct of growth.

Spare Parts and Equipment

Duplication is widely practiced for spare parts and small pieces of equipment. Maintenance departments routinely stock replacement parts of all kinds: motors, switches, gears, cables, and so forth. If those parts are not stocked, they are available through a local supplier. Many maintenance departments also have on hand important spare parts that they know would be difficult to obtain quickly. For example, one firm has spare motors that are only available on special order; another has a spare for a very large gear that would have to be ordered specially and could require many months to get. Many manufacturers that process plastics and rubber use molds or cutting dies. Those manufacturers routinely keep duplicate molds and dies at an off-site location. In data processing, computer data and software are typically copied, and the copies are kept in a separate location, often off site. If the original is destroyed, the copy is available.

Outside Manufacturers and Suppliers

Some types of operations can purchase services from an outside organization in the event of a loss. Knowing that that option is available can eliminate the need for duplicating major processes and can provide psychological comfort if the property loss control effort is inadequate. For example, a shampoo manufacturer owns a small plant that makes plastic bottles for the shampoo. The management of that plant is told that the plant sprinkler system is inadequate to control the kind of fire that could develop in the plastic storage area. The required sprinkler system improvements are prohibitively expensive, and since the building is leased, the improvements are not made. Nevertheless, the firm feels that the net income loss potential is minimal because if the plant were destroyed, the molds for the bottles would be given to an outside plastics molding firm for manufacture.

Ideally, this situation should have been studied in depth as part of the contingency planning process. Outside manufacturers should have been contacted to determine whether they would be able to handle the workload. A list of suitable suppliers should have been drawn up and updated periodically to make sure they would be available if needed. The need for considering this issue in advance cannot be overemphasized. The time to find outside suppliers is before, not after, a loss. Notice that finding multiple suppliers is a type of duplication.

A Financial Illustration

Although having spare parts and standby equipment increases an organization's total investment, having a greater number of separate units reduces the organization's needs for funds to finance losses to any one unit. The reduced need for risk financing funds can be particularly important to an organization that plans to retain losses to one (or a few) units that might be damaged. That reduced risk financing need can free more of the organization's capital for uses in the organization's normal operations. The resulting additional earning power of the newly available funds is the main contribution made by segregating exposure units. An example of that more efficient use of funds appears in one authoritative text:

> [A]ssume that a firm has a piece of heavy equipment valued at $100,000 and that without insurance a $100,000 reserve fund is necessary since there is only one piece of equipment and no possibility of predicting average losses through the use of the law of large numbers. Assume further that the reserve fund earns interest at the rate of .04 in savings accounts and .10 if invested in the business. Assume further that insurance is available for two percent or $2,000 annually....

> Suppose, however, that a firm's equipment of $100,000 consists of 200 machines each valued at $500 and it is predicted that the average annual loss is two machines worth $1,000 with a standard deviation of $200. Assuming that losses are normally distributed, the firm would have to have a buffer fund of $600 (three standard deviations) to be 99 percent certain that its losses would not exceed $1,600.... The size of the buffer fund is reduced from $100,000 to $600....[1]

The heightened efficiency of the 200 smaller machines, in contrast to the single large one, results from segregation that reduces the buffer fund by $99,400.

The increase in operating efficiency can be compared by calculating the differential annual after-tax net cash flow from the one machine (without segregation) and from the 200 machines (with segregation). Each of those two separate streams of net cash flows can then be evaluated. Either the net present value method or the time adjusted rate of return method can be used (see the Appendix to Chapter 1).

Computing and evaluating those alternative net cash flows requires making some assumptions:

- The differential aggregate revenues in either situation is the same, $20,000.
- Actual losses to either the one large machine or the 200 smaller ones equal the expected value of $1,000 per year, segregation having no effect on overall losses.
- All machines have a twenty-year useful life and no salvage value.
- Straight-line depreciation is used on all machines.
- Income taxes are 50 percent.
- The minimum acceptable annual rate of return is 10 percent.

If the organization invests in the one large machine, the two elements to the initial investment are (1) $100,000 for the one machine and (2) $100,000 for the buffer fund to absorb losses to that machine. The resulting differential annual after-tax net cash flows are computed in the upper portion of Exhibit 10-2 and evaluated in the lower portion of the exhibit. As shown, the one-machine alternative generates an after-tax net cash flow of $14,000 per year and a time-adjusted rate of return of only 3.496 percent, substantially less than the 10 percent required by the organization.

Alternatively, if the organization invests in 200 separate machines, a buffer fund of only $600 will be required (given the assumptions in the quotation above). With this smaller buffer fund, the after-tax annual net cash flow from the machines and the fund is $12,012, as shown in the upper portion of Exhibit 10-3. However, as the lower portion of this exhibit also indicates, the investment in 200 machines generates a rate of return slightly over the 10 percent required by the organization. The investment gives the organization a positive net present value.

Maintaining Manual Capacity for Automated Operations

When an automated operation is impaired, it is sometimes more cost-effective to run the operation manually than to have the processing done by an outside firm. Manual operations should be considered as part of the contingency plan so that pre-loss provisions can be made for the additional labor that would be required after a loss.

Suppose a machinery breakdown shuts down an automated production line that puts vitamins into bottles, screws caps on the bottles, and places the finished product into cardboard boxes. That machinery is very specialized, and it would be prohibitively time-consuming and expensive to have an outside manufacturer do the work. If the machinery cannot be repaired for an extended period of time, hiring temporary employees to do the work by hand might be wise. For a short breakdown, that would probably cost less than having the work done outside.

Assuming that heavy machinery and equipment are not required, performing some work manually when normal operations are disrupted is often possible. Many times that involves reverting to the method of operating that was used before automation. A case in point is a manufacturer of custom-fitted support hose prescribed by physicians for people with circulatory problems. The patient's leg is measured at many points, and a computer-controlled printer is used to draw a smooth pattern for the garment. Management has planned to resume its old methods if its computer is destroyed: the measurements are transferred to paper so that a garment design is drawn and adjusted manually. The work would be slow and cumbersome, but the alternative would be to cease operating altogether.

Exhibit 10-2
Differential Annual After-Tax Net Cash Flows (NCF)—
One Machine and $100,000 Buffer Fund

Calculation of NCF

Differential cash revenues:	
From machine	$20,000
From buffer fund ($100,000 x 4%)	4,000
Total	$24,000
Less: Differential cash expenses (except income taxes):	
Expected value of machine damage	1,000
Before-tax NCF	$23,000

Less: Differential income taxes:		
Before-tax NCF	$23,000	
Less: Differential depreciation expense ($100,000/20 years)	5,000	
Taxable income	$18,000	
Income taxes (50%)		9,000
After-tax NCF		$14,000

Evaluation of NCF

Factors:
Initial investment—$200,000
Useful life—20 years
Differential after-tax NCF—$14,000
Minimum acceptable rate of return—10% annually

Evaluation by the Net Present Value Method:

Present value of differential NCF ($14,000 x 8.514)	$119,196
Present value of initial investment	200,000
Net present value (negative)	($ 80,804)

Evaluation by the Time-Adjusted Rate of Return Method:

$$\frac{\text{Initial investment}}{\text{Differential NCF}} = \frac{\$200,000}{\$\ 14,000} = 14.286 = \text{present value factor for project}$$

Interpolation To Find the Exact Time-Adjusted Rate of Return (r):

Rate of Return	Present Value Factor	Present Value Factor
2%	16.351	16.351
r		14.286
4%	13.590	
Differences: 2%	2.761	2.065

$$r = 2\% + \left(\frac{2.065}{2.761} \times 2\% \right) = 2\% + 1.496\% = 3.496\%$$

Exhibit 10-3
Differential Annual After-Tax Net Cash Flows (NCF)—
200 Machines and $600 Buffer Fund

Calculation of NCF

Differential cash revenues:	
From machine	$20,000
From fund ($600 x 4%)	24
Total	$20,024
Less: Differential cash expenses (except income taxes):	
Expected value of machine damage	1,000
Before-tax NCF	$19,024

Less: Differential income taxes:		
Before-tax NCF	$19,024	
Less: Differential depreciation expense ($100,000/20 years)	5,000	
Taxable income	$14,024	
Income taxes (50%)		7,012
After-tax NCF		$12,012

Evaluation of NCF

Factors:
    Initial investment—$100,600
    Useful life—20 years
    Differential after-tax NCF—$12,012
    Minimum acceptable rate of return—10% annually

Evaluation by the Net Present Value Method:

Present value of differential NCF ($12,012 x 8.514)	$102,270
Present value of initial investment	100,600
Net present value	$ 1,670

Evaluation by the Time-Adjusted Rate of Return Method:

$$\frac{\text{Initial investment}}{\text{Differential NCF}} = \frac{\$100,600}{\$\ 12,012} = 8.375 = \text{present value factor for project}$$

Interpolation To Find the Exact Time-Adjusted Rate of Return (r):

Rate of Return	Present Value Factor	Present Value Factor
10%	8.514	8.514
r		8.375
12%	7.469	
Differences: 2%	1.045	0.139

$$r = 10\% + \left(\frac{0.139}{1.045} \times 2\%\right) = 10\% + 0.266\% = 10.266\%$$

Using Overtime

If an organization has some duplicated or separated facilities, overtime work can reduce a net income loss. If operations are duplicated in several locations or if parallel operations exist within a single location, the surviving operation can run on an overtime basis to compensate for the capacity that was lost in the property loss. That, of course, presumes the availability of excess capacity.

Using overtime to make up for lost production is probably the most common way to compensate for interrupted operations and to control the net income loss. Notice that a net income loss is not prevented because a premium is paid for overtime work.

An organization often has an inventory cushion sufficient to continue normal sales while overtime replaces the inventory. Here, again, the company has a net income loss even though the firm does not cease to operate. Overtime is a way to control, not to prevent, property-related net income losses.

Managing Extra, Expediting, and Continuing Expenses

The overtime expenses previously mentioned are called **extra expenses.** Those are expenses incurred when an organization purchases labor, space, supplies, or anything else to reduce a net income loss. Paying an outside manufacturer to continue operations or renting a replacement warehouse are other examples of extra expenses. Paying extra expenses is an important post-loss measure to control a net income loss. The same is true of paying expediting expenses.

Expediting expenses can be thought of as very specialized extra expenses. They are paid to speed up the return to normal operations. If replacement parts or machinery are shipped by air instead of truck, the cost for air transportation is an expediting expense. If a raw material supplier adds rush charges to send new supplies quickly, that is also an expediting expense. Even if a firm is successful at preventing a shutdown by some expediting action, a net income loss has still occurred because of the expediting expense. The purpose of expediting expenses, as well as extra expenses, is to reduce the net income loss the organization would suffer if it did not incur those expenses. Therefore, extra and expediting expenses are justified only if they do not exceed the organization's net income loss (reduction of revenue minus increase in expenses). Extra expenses are sometimes justified even when they exceed the net income loss if operations must continue.

Continuing expenses are costs that continue even when an operation is impaired. Examples are management's salary, real estate taxes, and a minimum level of energy costs for light and heat or air conditioning. **Noncontinuing expenses** are those that do not continue, like hourly wages.

Replacing Utilities

Problems at utilities can cause net income losses for an organization. For example, a hospital would be unable to continue operating without electricity and water. Vulnerability to such a loss warrants a study of those dependencies and of actions to prevent a loss.

Some information about the utility and its performance is probably available. If problems occur frequently at the generating station, not much can probably be done by the average utility customer. Suppose, though, that power outages frequently occur along a feeder that supplies a customer and that such an outage would cause a serious loss. The customer might be successful in negotiating with the utility to make whatever improvements are necessary to ensure a reliable power source. A customer that is important to the community, like a hospital, might even be able to convince the utility to provide parallel feeders for redundancy. Even if this must be done at the customer's expense, such a measure could be a wise expenditure if there is a serious loss potential.

Certain essential functions must be supplied with electricity at all times. For example, loss of lights and air conditioning in a hospital operating room or loss of power to a computer facility could result in major losses. An emergency generator that starts automatically when a power outage occurs is a necessary safeguard against such losses.

If lack of water could cause a serious loss and maintaining a reliable water supply could be a problem with the water utility, the organization should try to resolve the problem by working with the utility and local government. If the problem is not satisfactorily resolved, however, the customer might consider independent action, like digging a well for emergency or even routine use. Again, the need for such a step depends on the loss potential to the organization and the reliability of the water supply. A company that manufactures baby formula, for example, cannot tolerate variations in water quality if it is to maintain a consistently high-quality product. Other than digging wells, a company can have water shipped from other sources, although that solution is a more extreme measure.

Net income loss exposures due to loss of natural gas supplies should be analyzed in a similar way. Risk control measures might include multiple supply lines and storage of emergency supplies (propane or butane) in tanks. In the case of boilers that can be switched from gas to oil, fuel oil can be used as an alternate.

Maintaining Business Relationships

Successfully implementing loss control measures after a loss depends on the availability of temporary labor, replacement supplies, machinery and equipment, and repair contractors. If a firm cannot make repairs quickly, if a supplier does not ship parts on time, or if a temporary labor force cannot be quickly located, the loss suffered will be greater than it should have been. Good relationships with suppliers and contractors will increase the likelihood that they can be counted on in an emergency. Having several suppliers and contractors is also prudent.

Protecting and Restoring Vital Records

Vital records like customer files, accounts receivable, accounts payable, mailing lists, and blueprints are crucial to smooth operations. Mailing lists are among the most valuable assets that some organizations own. Some organizations cannot operate without historical files or blueprints. Unfortunately, the degree of dependence on valuable records is not always recognized, and as a result, the organization's records become vulnerable to loss.

When valuable records exist, property loss control steps should be taken to prevent their destruction. But measures to prevent a net income loss should also be devised. The most effective and most common loss control technique is duplicating records and storing the duplicates offsite. A duplicate can be a full-size copy or a microfilm copy, depending on the volume to be stored and cost considerations. An off-site location can be another, physically distant facility used by the organization or a specialized storage facility like a bank vault or record retention warehouse.

If a property loss occurs and important records have been duplicated, a net income loss would be reduced or even prevented. Even if duplicates do not exist, reconstructing certain kinds of records might reduce a loss. For example, if an organization's accounts receivable records are destroyed, customers' purchase orders can help reconstruct the receivables. Reconstructing records might not work in all cases, but the possibility should be considered in the contingency plan. Reconstruction is most promising when computer processing is used because the input data are generally derived from source documents. If the computer records are destroyed and no backup records are available or if the backup records are obsolete, the source documents can be used to reconstruct the data.

Controlling Contingent Net Income Losses

When a net income loss is caused by events that occur outside of the organization, the loss is called a **contingent net income loss.** The loss of services from a utility can cause a contingent net income loss, as can disruptions in the operations of a supplier or customer. Segregation of exposures (through separation or duplication) is often an appropriate risk management technique for dealing with the contingent net income loss exposure.

Separation means having multiple regular suppliers and many regular customers. The suppliers should be chosen so that the loss of one supplier's capacity can be quickly absorbed by the remaining suppliers, thus preventing a net income loss. Absorbing capacity is not possible with customers because they cannot be forced to buy more of a product. The best that can be hoped for is that the organization has a large number of customers of similar size so that the loss of any one customer does not cause a devastating contingent net income loss. Those responsible for sales and marketing do not want the loss of a single customer to affect profitability severely. Thus, good business management and sound risk management require an organization to reduce its dependence on any single supplier or customer.

Duplication involves maintaining standby resources if the organization's normal resources become unavailable. With respect to controlling contingent net income losses, duplication entails (1) being aware of alternative suppliers and customers and (2) maintaining informal relationships with these potential suppliers and customers. Being aware of alternative suppliers and customers is good business. Maintaining some continuing relationship with alternative firms might require an organization to buy at least some portion of its supplies from, or sell some portion of its output to, these alternative suppliers or customers. Expanding a small but continuing relationship is usually easier than establishing a new relationship in an emergency.

Illustrative Financial Analysis of a Net Income Risk Control Measure

Many loss prevention measures require no capital investment. Furthermore, despite the best efforts of risk management professionals, some of the costs incurred in a net income loss are difficult to quantify. Therefore, an investment analysis to weigh the costs and benefits of a loss prevention program is often not meaningful. Still, few managers would argue against such programs. The potential loss to a firm is usually obvious and sufficient to justify action without rigorous analysis.

However, if capital expenditures are proposed, analysis might be necessary. A net present value analysis can confirm that the benefits outweigh the cost of the project. The following example illustrates such an analysis.

The Smith Steel Foundry casts steel ingots using automatic machinery that pours molten steel into molds. After the molds are filled, they are moved by conveyor belt to a holding area to cool. Both the machine that pours the molten steel and the conveyor system are driven by a large electric motor. Smith's risk management professional has determined that the motor has a 10 percent probability of breaking down and not being repaired during any given year. The risk management professional argues that a spare motor should be kept on hand at all times. The company's financial director has asked for justification of the expense because the spare motor would cost $20,000 and have a useful life of only five years even if not used regularly.

During the five weeks that the risk management professional believes it would take to replace a failed motor, the estimated losses to the foundry would be $50,000 in canceled orders, $2,000 in extra expenses to communicate and negotiate with customers about the problem, and $15,000 in overtime to return to normal operations once the motor is replaced. Those estimated losses total $67,000. When weighted by the 10 percent probability of the motor breaking down and becoming unrepairable during any given year (and the 90 percent probability of no breakdown and no net income loss), the expected value of those losses is $6,700 annually.

Based on the assumptions that (1) no more than one breakdown will occur in any given year, (2) any motor being replaced has no salvage value, and (3) the foundry's financial executives presume a 50 percent tax rate and require an annual after-tax rate of return of at least 8 percent, the risk management professional prepares calculations like those shown in Exhibit 10-4. (Tables of present values of single payments and of streams of equal annual payments, discounted at different interest rates, are presented in the Appendix to Chapter 1.)

Assuming that having a standby motor will eliminate the $6,700 annual expected net income loss, the computations in Exhibit 10-4 indicate that purchasing the motor is financially justified. A replacement motor has a net present value of $1,363 and can be expected to generate a time-adjusted rate of return of 10.57 percent.

Different numbers could produce different results: actual losses prevented could be more or less than $6,700; the replacement motor might require special periodic maintenance to ensure its readiness, necessitating a cash outlay that reduces the motor's expected annual net cash flow; or the required minimum rate of return might rise to 12 percent, making the motor an unacceptable investment. Consequently, this illustration is not intended to show that risk control is always a sound investment. It instead demonstrates the process and the assumptions for analyzing the financial effect of a proposed risk control measure.

Exhibit 10-4
Computation and Evaluation of Annual After-Tax Net Cash Flow
From Standby Motor

Calculation of NCF

Differential cash revenues (expected value of losses prevented)	$6,700
Less: Differential cash expenses (except income taxes)	0
Before-tax NCF	$6,700

Less:
Differential income taxes:

Before-tax NCF	$6,700	
Less: Differential depreciation expenses ($20,000/5 years)	4,000	
Taxable income	$2,700	
Income taxes (50%)	1,350	1,350
After-tax NCF		$5,350

Evaluation of NCF

Factors:
Initial investment—$20,000
Life of Project—5 years
Differential after-tax NCF—$5,350
Minimum acceptable rate of return—8 percent

Evaluation by the Net Present Value Method:

Present value of differential NCF ($5,350 x 3.993)	$21,363
Less: Present value of initial investment	20,000
Net present value	$ 1,363

Evaluation by the Time-Adjusted Rate of Return Method:

$$\frac{\text{Initial investment}}{\text{Differential NCF}} = \frac{\$20,000}{\$ 5,350} = 3.738 = \text{present value factor}$$

Interpolation To Find the Exact Time-Adjusted Rate of Return (r):

Rate of Return	Present Value Factor	Present Value Factor
10%	3.791	3.791
r		3.738
12%	3.605	
Differences: 2%	0.186	0.053

$$r = 10\% + \left(\frac{0.053}{0.186} \times 2\% \right) = 10\% + 0.57\% = 10.57\%$$

Liability-Related Net Income Losses

> **How can you analyze products-related net income exposures?**
>
> **What risk control measures can you apply to products-related net income exposures?**
>
> **How can you analyze work-related net income exposures?**
>
> **What risk control measures can you apply to work-related net income exposures?**

Just as net income losses often accompany property losses, net income losses frequently follow liability losses as well. The nature of the net income loss is largely independent of the particular type of liability. The net income loss is essentially the same regardless of whether the liability arises out of a products, workers compensation, automobile, premises, or other liability claim. The first step in controlling liability-related net income losses is to distinguish between the liability loss itself and the adverse effects the liability might have on an organization's net income.

An organization incurs a liability loss whenever a legal claim is brought against the organization for an alleged wrongful tort, breach of contract, or crime. The peril causing a liability loss is the claim itself, regardless of whether the claim proves justified and results in a verdict or financial settlement against the organization (defendant). The financial consequences of legal liability losses include the following:

- Legal and investigatory expenses
- Money paid for settlements, verdicts, or fines
- Costs of complying with injunctions and orders for specific performance
- Loss of reputation or market share for the organization

The legal expenses and settlements, verdicts, or fines associated with a claim, as well as the expenses of complying with an injunction or order of specific performance, are liability losses. Loss of sales from decreased market share because of adverse publicity following a legal claim (justified or not), as well as the additional expenses of legally mandated changes to the organization's production processes, are net income losses. (Notice that the expenses an organization incurs to prevent or to reduce future liability losses are not liability losses but are risk control expenses. For example, a physician might decide to keep detailed patient records supporting the physician's actions or a smelting firm might decide to install devices to remove environmental pollutants from the smelter's emissions.)

To illustrate the differences between liability losses and net income losses related to liability, consider the pollution liability claims that Smith's Foundry could face if its operations release pollutants that exceed legally permissible levels. Smith's Foundry will face liability losses consisting of (1) expenses for investigating and defending the claims, (2) money paid as fines or settlements, and (3) the conversion costs of altering its processes or purchasing special equipment to reduce emissions to legal levels. The Foundry's net income losses attributable to those claims are the reductions in net income from (1) the reduced efficiency of the environmentally cleaner production process and (2) reduced sales revenue due to adverse publicity.

Risk control for those liability-related net income losses entails reducing (1) the frequency, severity, and unpredictability of the legal claims that generate such net income losses and (2) the adverse effects that a claim might have on an organization's net income. Controlling claims was discussed in Chapter 8. To illustrate net income loss controls applicable to any kind of liability-related net income loss, the following sections focus on the net income loss effects of products liability claims and workers compensation claims.

Products Liability

An organization incurs a liability if one of its products injures people or damages the property of others. The loss that results is a liability loss.

Analysis of Products-Liability-Related Net Income Exposures

Suppose a firm's product or service is not obscure but is sold in a market where news of a problem with the product travels quickly. Counteracting bad publicity, recalling the product, and starting a new marketing effort might reduce the firm's revenue and increase its expenses. In short, the firm will suffer a net income loss as a result of a product liability loss.

Even if no liability loss actually occurs, but the firm takes defensive action to prevent a potential loss from becoming an actual loss, the costs incurred constitute a net income loss. For example, suppose a firm that sells canned vegetables discovers in its laboratory that a particular batch of string beans shows a higher level of residual insecticide than permissible by law. In addition to possible fines, the firm could be sued by people alleging that their health problems were caused by the contaminated string beans. Even though the insecticide levels were discovered in the company's own laboratory, the information would probably leak out eventually, and not reporting it to the government agencies would be illegal. So even before a claim is filed, the firm recalls the affected product from all markets based on its own investigation of the situation. Some negative publicity results, and sales drop for several months until a new marketing campaign takes hold. Even though no liability loss occurred, the *potential* for a liability claim caused the firm to take actions that reduced revenues and increased expenses. Even the threat of a liability claim can cause a net income loss.

As stated, at some point in its investigation, the firm might decide to recall all or some of the product. The recall might be necessary because the product is actually defective or because the public perceives that the product is defective. The cost to the firm would consist of the cost to communicate the recall to the affected groups, shipping costs, the cost to replace the merchandise, and the cost of follow-up communications and public relations work. The cost of a total recall can be tremendous.

After a widespread product defect problem, whether real or perceived, the firm might have to run a major public relations and advertising campaign to bolster customer confidence. This could be expensive, depending on the extent of the campaign. After a product defect incident, sales revenue could also suffer. The amount of the loss would depend on the nature of the problem and how much publicity it received. Because of the number of variables, the revenue loss is difficult to quantify.

The firm might decide that the best long-term solution is to continue marketing the product. The product could be substantially the same with different packaging and a new name, or the product could be redesigned. In either case, the cost would be the additional cost to design, manufacture, and market the new product. Since those costs would reduce the loss of future sales revenues, the additional costs would be part of the net income loss.

Once the cost factors are known, the firm is in a good position to assess the potential severity of the problem and to decide how much of a loss control effort is justified. Because of the tremendous number of variables involved in projecting costs and the difficulty in quantifying them,cost projections are not completely accurate, Nevertheless, cost projections are valuable for anyone involved in making financial decisions about a product.

Risk Control Measures

Risk control measures for products liability-related net income losses should have two main thrusts. First, a pre-loss effort should be directed at preventing product defects in the first place. Prevention is the best way to reduce the frequency of net income losses related to products liability. Second, for products liability claims that do arise, a post-loss effort should be directed at controlling the severity of a related net income loss. Reducing severity thus focuses on loss reduction and requires contingency planning, the ability to recall defective products, customer notification, and sound public relations. The next five sections describe loss prevention and reduction efforts for a products liability-related net income loss.

Preventing Products Liability Losses

Although this chapter is not about products liability loss prevention per se, net income losses can and do accompany products liability losses or threats of loss. Defect prevention is, therefore, very important. The basis for loss prevention is a good product design program coupled with proper production methods and strong quality control.

Products liability loss prevention programs are pre-loss programs. Consequently, these programs should be instituted before a problem arises to detect product defects in products that have already been purchased. Any reports of unusual service or reliability problems, product misuse, or customer dissatisfaction should be brought to management's attention. Management, in turn, must quickly act on that information.

Because product defects and losses can have many causes, including poor design, production problems, and inadequate product instructions, loss prevention is a multidisciplinary function. Therefore, many companies use a team approach for products liability loss prevention. The team might consist of design engineers, production managers, quality control managers, marketing managers, attorneys, and the risk management professional. This team can have broad duties, including risk analysis and contingency planning.

Contingency Planning

Contingency planning is a pre-loss control measure designed to coordinate post-loss measures and is aimed at reducing the severity of product liability losses and net income losses. Responsibility for reacting to a product liability loss and specifying the actions to be followed should be specifically assigned. A contingency plan should guide responsible persons from the initial notification of a problem through the recall process and a public relations program if necessary.

When an organization is informed of a product defect, the appropriate managers must be notified. That notification might be communicated through a committee that decides on the action required or through an executive who has the authority to take the necessary actions. Those options exist for all aspects of the plan.

If the reported problem appears to be widespread, stopping production and/or the shipment of goods might be prudent. That stoppage will provide time to study the problem in detail and decide what to do. A problem might be less serious then it first appears, or a defective batch of the product might still be in inventory. In the worst case, products currently being made might contain a defect that could require halting all operations for an extended period of time. Once the firm defines the problem, it can implement corrective action.

Ability To Recall Products

When complete information about the problem is available, the firm can decide whether a recall is necessary. A recall depends on many factors, including the nature of the product, the potential injury or damage it could cause, the type of defect, the cost of a recall, and the effect that a recall would have on future sales.

Management might determine that the injury potential is not serious and that a recall is not necessary. Under those circumstances, a recall would be ill-advised because of the cost and possible negative publicity. On the other hand, the injury potential could be great, as in food products or drugs. Recalls in such cases are a business (and perhaps a health) necessity and are often required by regulatory authorities.

Before a recall is instituted, corrective actions must be determined so that the customer can be informed. In some cases, possible corrective actions can be explored and the best option chosen before a product problem develops. For example, if a certain model car contains a defective component, the car will be recalled and repaired. If a toy is defective, the toy will be recalled and replaced. When blanket statements like those are possible, they should be included in the contingency plan. If not, the firm will have to decide defect problems on a case-by-case basis.

Customer Notification

The system for notifying customers of a recall should be specified in the contingency plan. For large, expensive purchases, like cars, customer lists are readily available. For most retail purchases, however, customer lists are not available. In those cases, recall announcements are made through newspapers and news broadcasts. If customers return their warranty registration cards, the manufacturer can use the cards to establish a partial customer list, but contacting customers directly can still be a problem. Contacting wholesalers and distributors is easier because businesses usually keep current records of customers.

Effective Public Relations

An intensive public relations campaign might be advisable if the product defect receives widespread publicity or if the recall is publicized. By handling the publicity properly, the company can make the public understand the nature of the defect and the reason for the recall and can convince the public that the company is acting responsibly. The importance of this behavior cannot be overemphasized because a company's future hinges on its reputation. If customers believe that the company will correct the problem, the firm and its product have a good chance of surviving a major recall.

Brand names can also suffer from recalls. In those cases, increased advertising expenditures and perhaps even a new marketing campaign would be needed. In extreme cases, an organization might consider selling a modified product under a new brand name. Although these actions are very expensive, they reduce the future loss of revenue and therefore reduce the net income loss.

Work-Related Injuries and Illnesses

When an employee is injured or becomes ill on the job, the organization suffers a liability loss, usually in the form of a workers compensation claim. From every such loss also results a net income loss. The net income loss could be very small, almost immeasurable, or it could be significant, depending on the seriousness of the injury or illness and the employee's job function.

Analysis of Work-Related Net Income Exposures

The net income loss from a work-related injury or illness results from expenses connected with morale problems with other employees, losses in productive time as a result of accident investigation, a temporary replacement for the employee while he or she is unable to work, and reduced efficiency resulting from training a replacement employee. Those expenses include many of the indirect losses traditionally associated with work-related injuries and illnesses. Indirect losses are frequently estimated to be several times the amount of the direct workers compensation claim. Indirect loss expenses should be measured like any other net income loss, by reduced revenues or increased expenses. Indirect loss expenses, in addition to other losses related to a net income loss, are discussed in the paragraphs that follow. For a single case, the net income loss might not seem important, but if the personnel in an organization suffer many injuries during the year, the aggregate loss to the organization could be significant.

An accident is a disruptive event. People who witness a serious accident or who hear about it are often upset. They are frequently too upset to continue working at their jobs immediately after the accident or continue to work at reduced efficiency. Employees typically discuss the accident a great deal.

Discussion, of course, is a necessary emotional release, but it also results in reduced revenue (because fewer goods or services are produced) or increased expenses (because additional labor costs must be paid to compensate for the time lost because of the disruption).

In some cases, morale might be lowered, especially if employees believe that management could have prevented the accident. They might feel that additional physical protection should have been provided or that more training or warnings about hazards should have been given. Employees could also be afraid to go back to their jobs. Morale problems can also reduce efficiency, thus increasing the net income loss.

An accident must also be investigated. Investigations take time, and they can involve many people. The injured employee's supervisor must interview each witness to the accident as well as any people who adminsitered first aid. The supervisor might also need to speak with maintenance employees who repaired physical damage and made modifications to prevent similar accidents. All of this is disruptive to normal operations and generates a net income loss.

Line employees and managers who have to participate in the investigation have less time to devote to their work. This causes a loss in productive time, which adds to the net income loss.

If an injured employee does not return to work at all, somebody else will have to be trained as a replacement. That training will be an expense even if the training is not formal. For example, if the a temporary employee replaces an experienced employee, reduced efficiency will result during the training period.

After the replacement employee is trained and begins to function independently, a learning period occurs during which the employee will not be operating at full capacity. That, again, increases the net income loss. Even if the injured employee does return to work, he or she will probably need time to readjust to the old position.

If the injured employee returns to work but is assigned to another, less demanding job, he or she will have to be fully trained in the new job. This creates a chain reactin, because every time a vacancy is filled from within, another person will have to be trained. At some point, an opening will have to be filled by an outsider, who will also require training.

Recruiting and hiring replacement employees from outside (and even from within) the organization takes time and money. Advertisements must be written and paid for, or the services of an employment agency must be obtained. Candidates will have to be interviewed, and this might involve travel expenses. Recruiting and hiring tasks take people away from their normal duties and add expenses.

The severity of a net income loss that follows an employee injury or illness can vary widely. Although the foregoing discussion details many sources of additional expense and loss of revenue, all of the sources will not be involved in every net income loss. In general, the severity of the net income loss depends on the severity of the injury or illness and on the nature of the employee's job.

If an employee receives a cut, leaves work to see a doctor, and returns the next day fully able to work, the net income loss will be small. Perhaps only a few hours of overtime will be necessary. On the other hand, an injury such as a back injury that causes an employee to be in extended traction will likely result in significant additional expenses and lost revenues.

The employee's job is also a factor. Unskilled labor is much easier to replace than highly skilled labor. That is, recruiting, hiring, and training a cafeteria worker is easier and less costly than replacing a skilled machinist. As the job skills increase, the potential effect on the organization increases, although it also becomes harder to quantify that effect.

Much of this discussion is most applicable to production operations. Although the analysis is easiest to apply to a manufacturing situation, the principles apply to all other operations as well. Suppose a member of a computer programming team trips on loose carpeting in the office and is temporarily disabled. The project that the team is working on would undoubtedly suffer, and a long-term negative effect on the organization would result. Many of the same costs incurred in a manufacturing environment could also be incurred in that case.

An employee's injury or illness always results in a net income loss, whether large or insignificant. The loss might be impossible to measure or it might be measurable. And although any given case might not seem that significant by itself, in the aggregate, most exposures become significant. The next section discusses pre-injury and post-injury (or illness) measures to reduce net income loss.

Risk Control Measures

Controlling work-related net income losses requires pre-injury and post-injury (or illness) measures, just as other kinds of losses require pre-loss and post-loss measures. Pre-injury actions are loss prevention measures, while post-injury actions are loss reduction measures.

Safety Program

A strong safety and industrial hygiene program is the most important pre-injury loss control measure. If accidents are prevented and health hazards controlled, few injuries and illnesses will occur to cause net income losses.

Contingency Planning

A contingency plan is an essential pre-injury risk control measure. The plan defines, before any accident or injury occurs, how best to coordinate important post-injury controls, such as medical assistance, communication, backup employees, and the replacement of disabled employees.

Medical Assistance

Providing prompt medical assistance to employees who become injured or ill on the job should reduce the severity and duration of work-related disabilities. Medical assistance not only reduces workers compensation liability costs, but it also hastens employees' return to work and, therefore, restores productivity.

Two kinds of medical assistance should be provided: emergency and routine care. Emergency medical care must be available to anybody who is seriously injured or ill. In most communities, an ambulance is readily available either through a hospital or an independent agency. The ambulance might be staffed by paramedics, who can diagnose and treat the employee immediately. Hospital emergency room services must also be available.

Routine care is provided for injuries that are not life threatening. Examples of routine injuries are foreign objects in employees' eyes, cuts, sprains, and minor burns. Sometimes a company doctor or nurse will either treat the injury or refer the employee elsewhere for treatment. Because some apparently minor injuries could be serious, common sense and caution must be exercised.

Many organizations arrange for a group of employees to receive training in first aid and CPR (cardiopulmonary resuscitation). Those employees are responsible for acting in medical emergencies until medical professionals arrive.

Medical assistance varies widely from organization to organization, depending on injury potential, employee population, community resources, and organizational resources. Every organization must assess its own needs and plan accordingly. Every employee in the organization must know what to do during a medical emergency. They should know whom to call for help, both internally and externally, which means training employees and posting telephone numbers. Some organizations hold medical emergency drills in which an employee plays the role of an injury victim.

Effective Communication Throughout the Organization

Communication throughout an organization is always important, but when an employee is injured, an organization must directly, honestly, and promptly notify its work force. After an injury, employees are likely to be concerned about the accident and somewhat distracted from their jobs. Management's failure to communicate about the accident can only increase employee distraction, as employees become concerned about their colleagues' and their own welfare, as well as management's failure to let them know what has happened. The result is an environment of confusion and distrust, which interferes with productive time. The ultimate result is a net income loss. With effective communication, however, management can allay employees' fears, thus allowing them to focus on their work, not on the accident.

Accident Investigation

An established accident investigation program (commonly called an injury or illness investigation program) enables a post-injury investigation to proceed with as little disruption as possible. If the supervisor who conducts the investigation is well trained, he or she will be able to interview the necessary parties quickly and efficiently. The actual causes of the injury or illness will therefore be determined promptly. Determining the cause of an injury or illness helps reduce the net income loss. Employees' questions are answered, and they can return to their normal routines and frame of mind. Management can also take corrective action.

Providing Competent Temporary Replacement

Every employee who has a job that requires special knowledge or skills should have at least one backup who can take over if necessary. That post-injury measure has tremendous potential for reducing a net income loss by quickly restoring normal work flow. Providing backup or fill-in employees is pre-injury planning; actually using them is a post-injury measure. Such a backup network requires pre-loss planning and effort and is also valuable when employees are absent. For jobs that do not require special skills, access to temporary employees through an agency or other source should suffice. Standard operating procedures, which should already exist for general training and safety purposes, will be helpful in training backup employees and outside temporary employees.

Personnel-Related Net Income Losses

How can you analyze personnel-related net income exposures?

What risk control measures can you apply to personnel-related net income exposures?

Many businesses depend on certain key employees. Those people make major contributions to their organization's income because of their sales ability, vital business contacts, technical knowledge, or artistic ability. Almost every organization suffers some key employee personnel losses because the perils that cause those losses—death, disability, retirement, and unemployment—eventually occur. Furthermore, some percentage of an organization's work force is almost certain to be absent on a given day, and some departments' activities will be disrupted and less productive because of understaffing caused by death, disability, resignations, or retirement. For personnel-related net income exposures, the focus should be on reducing work-flow disruptions, especially disruptions involving key employees.

Analysis of Personnel-Related Net Income Exposures

Personnel losses and related net income losses do not often occur. The potential severity of those losses, rather than their frequency, is the main concern. The potential severity depends on the value of the work that the key employee performs; how much income the employee generates; and the size, organization, and ownership of the business.

For example, Able Trading Company, a very small import-export firm, is organized as a sole proprietorship. Sam, the owner, is the "brains behind the operation." He personally establishes and maintains all of the business contacts and buys and sells all merchandise. Although he has an office manager, a warehouse manager, and an accountant, they perform support or staff functions. Sam is the only line employee. If Sam dies, his heirs would probably liquidate the business because none of them would be able to manage it.

The net income loss resulting from Sam's death would be the present value of Able Trading's income for the remaining years that Sam was expected to live, according to life expectancy tables. That is, if Sam dies prematurely at age sixty (and his life expectancy is seventy-two), the loss to his company is the present value of Sam's expected income over the next twelve years. However, the present value of Sam's expected future income is not the only net income loss, although it is the easiest to measure. In the short term,

Sam's employees will probably suffer income losses as the company winds down and eventually dissolves. In the long term, Sam's employees could continue to suffer income losses, depending on their abilities to obtain comparable employment. The net income losses for Sam's employees would be difficult to project. And although those losses are related to the employees and not the organization, the potential for those losses provides another reason to control personnel-related net income exposures.

The difficulty in quantifying a potential loss can be illustrated by considering Software, Inc., a closely held corporation that writes and markets computer software. Each software package is written by a team of three or four designers because Software believes that its people are more creative when working in groups. Group X is working on a state-of-the-art product when one of the three team members is permanently disabled after being injured at home. The work of Group X is seriously disrupted because the other group members are upset, and their creativity is impaired. Even if a replacement is recruited from outside the firm, there is no guarantee the replacement would be productive quickly or ever achieve the right chemistry with the two other team members. The new product is delayed, but the length of delay is difficult to measure. Equally difficult to measure is what market share will be lost to competitors who are working on similar products.

The Software, Inc., example shows that the loss of a creative person can cause a net income loss, even though that person does not have a business interest in the firm or perform a sales function. The types of personnel loss exposures vary from organization to organization. In all cases, the starting point for analyzing and controlling the loss is determining the function of the key employee (or employees) and the resulting loss severity. The following risk control measures are applicable to the work force in general as well as to key employees.

Risk Control Measures

As with other kinds of net income losses, pre-loss and post-loss measures control personnel-related net income losses. The nature and size of the business determine what control measures are applicable. The pre-loss objectives should be to prevent death, disabilities, and unanticipated retirements or unemployment. The post-loss objective should be to replace or return the affected employee to work, if possible, and to resume normal operations.

As described below, the pre-loss objective should be accomplished by employee safety and health programs. The post-loss objective should be accomplished by contingency plans for replacing employees. For the death, disability, or retirement of a business owner, plans should include how to transfer control of the business to others without a substantial loss of income to departing or remaining employees.

Safety and Health Programs

Programs to help prevent injuries and illnesses, both on and off the job, help control deaths and disabilities and related net income losses. Programs to control work-related injuries and illnesses were discussed in Chapter 5 and in the preceding section. Off-the-job safety and health programs address injury and illness exposures that people face when they are away from work.

Safety and health programs are pre-loss measures for controlling personnel-related net income losses. They are similar to controls for work-related net income losses but are largely unrelated to work activities. For example, many organizations give their employees educational material about controlling fire and other hazards or perils at home. Safety procedures for lawnmowers, tools, slipping and tripping hazards, and loud noise, for example, might be included. Some companies distribute magazines devoted to family safety and health; others publish their own newsletters. Some firms blend off-the-job safety into their job safety programs. Other companies combine these approaches.

Employees are generally receptive to family safety programs because those programs address personal concerns. The employees' families are usually interested for the same reason. In fact, the educational material is sometimes sent to employees' homes to make sure the whole family sees it.

Health and fitness programs that encourage proper diet, exercise, and medical care are becoming increasingly popular. People realize that maintaining good health requires effort, but the effort pays off in how good they feel and look. People in good health are less likely to suffer premature death or disability. Organizations use delivery systems for fitness programs similar to those used for safety. Some firms have spent a great deal of money on such programs because they believe that exercise can reduce personnel-related net income losses. Some large companies have on-site health and recreational facilities staffed with physicians, nurses, and exercise physiologists. Other firms are subsidizing employee memberships to health clubs. Even if special facilities are not provided, some firms are encouraging stretching and warm-up exercises every morning because of perceived benefits both on and off the job.

Contingency Plans for Replacing Employees

To limit the severity of a loss, a contingency plan should be developed to guide and coordinate all post-loss efforts. The loss would be increased expenditures or decreased revenues due to the death, disability, early retirement, or resignation of a key employee. The plan should hold certain people responsible for administering programs to restore losses, which should include developing backup employees, maintaining business contacts, diversifying business activities, and being prepared to transfer control of the organization.

The most important component of the plan should be developing backup employees who are capable of replacing a key employee after a personnel loss. Backup employees can be developed by cross-training and delegating responsibility.

Cross-training enables employees to learn jobs outside of their own areas. For example, a design engineer can be trained as a manufacturing engineer. First, the design engineer learns about the manufacturing process to design products that are more easily manufactured. Second, if the training is sufficient, the design engineer could replace a manufacturing engineer if necessary.

Written standard operating procedures (SOPs) are helpful in this kind of training. Although the jobs of key people are probably too diverse and nonrepetitive for SOPs, others who report to the key person might have jobs that lend themselves to SOPs. Cross-trainees can use SOPs to learn jobs quickly. Of course, watching people at work and talking to them about their jobs are also important, but written material can provide a fast orientation.

Employees can be developed within their own departments by delegation. Delegation promotes job development *within* an employee's area. Managers with a goal of developing employees capable of assuming greater responsibilities can expose employees to diversified, higher level work. Delegation is not natural and easy for some managers who feel that they have to do everything themselves and who have trouble trusting others to do a good job. Some managers feel that they can get a job done more quickly themselves, and so they resist training others. For systems of internal development to be effective, senior management must insist that those systems be practiced throughout the organization.

Senior managers should also develop and maintain business contacts who can identify people outside the organization to key people. Maintaining those contacts is called networking. Since the replacement candidates have the support and recommendation of somebody in the network, the organization can feel comfortable hiring them.

Transferring Control of Business

When a sole proprietor, partner, or a major shareholder in a closely held corporation dies or is disabled, a personnel-related net income loss can occur.

That death might cause uncertainty or confusion about who, if anybody, will assume the key person's duties. A lengthy probate process could also tie up assets and cause short-term financial problems.

Under the laws of many states, the death of a partner automatically causes dissolution of the partnership. Any one of the partners has the power to legally obligate the others, so dissolving the partnership gives the remaining partners the chance to reevaluate their commitment to each other. If one of the partners becomes disabled, the partnership has probably lost a key executive, at least temporarily. Like any organization, the partnership must be prepared to replace this management talent and return as soon as possible to normal operations.

For a closely held corporation, a major percentage of stock could end up being owned by parties that management and the other owners disapprove of. Suppose the surviving spouse of a major shareholder inherited one-third of the stock of a corporation owned equally by three people. If that surviving spouse sells the stock to an outside party, the two remaining owners could wind up working closely with someone with whom they do not wish to do business.

Such problems can seriously affect the continued operation and profitability of a business and create a net income loss that could threaten the survival of a firm. Pre-loss legal planning can prevent many of those problems by making arrangements to transfer the business smoothly. For example, in a closely held corporation, the owners can agree in advance to purchase the shares at a specified price from the estate of any shareholder who dies. That arrangement is called a business interest purchase agreement and provides an orderly transition and peace of mind for all parties. Similar agreements can be written for proprietorships and partnerships. The details of those agreements should be worked out with the aid of appropriate legal counsel.

Summary

An organization can suffer a net income loss (a reduction in revenues or increase in expenses) through accidental events. Most of those accidents, however, will also involve a property loss, a liability loss, or a personnel loss. The extent, or severity, of the net income loss will vary with the following:

- Length of time the accident impairs the organization's normal operations
- Activity level at the time the impairment occurs
- Degree of impairment

- Amount of extra, expediting, or continuing expenses required by the impairment
- Time necessary to resume normal revenues after the organization resumes normal operations

Regardless of whether a net income loss is related to a property, liability, or personnel loss, the appropriate risk control measures to prevent or reduce net income losses fall into several categories. The first category, loss prevention, typically stresses avoiding the accident that causes the net income loss. The second category, loss reduction, stresses using contingency plans to shorten disruption time and to reduce the degree of disruption. Reducing the degree of disruption is often achieved by providing standby facilities or replacement personnel, that is, segregating exposure units to maintain the organization's operations. Both categories of loss control measures help reduce the loss of market share that can result from an event that causes a net income loss.

Chapter Note

1. Mark R. Greene, *Risk and Insurance,* 2d ed. (Cincinnati, OH: South-Western Publishing Company, 1968), p. 89.

Chapter 11

Controlling Crime Losses

Educational Objectives

1. Illustrate risk control measures that prevent or reduce an organization's crime losses in given situations.

   In support of the above objective, you should be able to do the following:

   a. Describe the distinctive features of the crime peril that create special risk management challenges.

   b. Describe the characteristics of specific crimes against property, persons, and organizational activities.

   c. Describe the general crime control strategies and apply them to specific crimes.

2. Define or describe each of the Key Words and Phrases shown in the course guide for this assignment.

Outline

Outline, continued

Appendix D—Representative Controls Against Fraud

Appendix E—Representative Controls Against Embezzlement

Appendix F—Representative Controls Against Counterfeiting/ Forgery

Appendix G—Representative Controls Against Vandalism

Appendix H—Representative Controls Against Arson (By Persons Other Than Owner or Manager)

Appendix I—Representative Controls Against Violent Attack and Homicide

Appendix J—Representative Controls Against Kidnapping

Appendix K—Representative Controls Against Terrorism

Appendix L—Representative Controls Against Espionage

Appendix M—Representative Controls Against Computer Crime

Controlling Crime Losses

Crimes, whether committed against or by an organization, can result in property, liability, personnel, or net income losses. People, business firms, and other entities all face those loss exposures from crime. To illustrate, consider the crime of burglary. Under common law and the criminal codes in most states, burglary is the act of forcefully breaking into or out of a locked building or portion of a building to commit a felony. Most burglaries involve breaking into a business when it is closed to steal money or other property. An organization that is burglarized usually suffers a loss of the property the burglars took and often damage to doors, locks, windows, or walls through which the burglars forced their entry or exit. The burglars might also take property belonging to customers, or they might injure customers or employees. The organization faces potential liability for the customers' stolen property and their injuries and for workers compensation benefits for employees.

Continuing the same example, suppose the burglars injure or kidnap a key employee to prevent detection and capture. (Intentionally injuring or kidnapping a person during a burglary is another crime.) Losing the valuable services of the key employee until the employee recovers from injuries or is freed by the kidnappers and returns to work would be a key person loss for the organization. Any extra expenses the organization incurs as a result of this burglary (such as costs of cooperating with the police or filing insurance claims) are net income losses. Additional net income losses that reduce revenues might occur if news of the burglary frightens away some customers.

Many other crimes that could strike an organization impose comparable property, liability, personnel, or net income losses. Those crimes and resulting losses might stem from robbery, embezzlement, arson, check fraud, vandalism, homicide, confidence schemes, or other crimes. The types of crimes that can victimize an organization and the ways of committing those crimes are limited only by the imagination of criminals. Staying ahead of criminals is the major risk management challenge of controlling crime losses.

An organization could also suffer loss because of legal liability for the criminal acts of its employees or others the organization directed or allowed to commit crimes on its behalf. To continue the burglary example, the president of the organization that is eager to learn a competitor's trade secrets could suggest to a few highly trusted employees that some after-hours reconnaissance of the competitor's home office could generate valuable information. Without directly participating in any break-in, that president and the organization itself could incur criminal liability as accessories to the burglary the employees were encouraged to commit.

In another illustration, if the manager of a retail store encourages sales clerks to be very aggressive in confronting suspected shoplifters, the manager (as well as the clerks) could be guilty of criminal assault if a clerk strikes or forcibly restrains a customer who has not shoplifted. The owners of the store might also share in that criminal liability if a court finds they encouraged or consciously chose to ignore company policies that abused customers' rights.

Another illustration of conduct that could impose criminal fault on an organization is improperly disposing of wastes, which can violate federal, state, or local environmental protection statutes. If those violations are willful, the organization as an entity, as well as its senior management as individuals, are likely to face criminal penalties regardless of actual intent.

An organization's losses due to crimes committed by or attributed to the organization are initially liability losses, not crime losses, in the context of this chapter. Criminal liability is likely to cause additional losses to an organization:

- Loss of property seized by law enforcement officials
- Further civil liability in tort for negligent or intentional harm to others as a byproduct of the criminal activity
- Personnel losses because key company executives must stand trial and might be incarcerated
- Net income losses because the company might need to pay criminal fines or divert some executive time and other resources to defending itself and its executives against criminal charges

For criminal charges, neither fines nor defense costs are insurable. Proper risk management strives to protect an organization, its employees, and its customers and other constituencies against the criminal intent or conduct of others, both outside and within the organization. The major sections of this chapter discuss the distinctive features of the crime peril, the characteristics of the crimes to which most organizations are susceptible, some general strategies for applying risk management techniques to controlling crime losses, and how to apply those strategies to specific crimes, particularly computer-based crimes.

Distinctive Features of the Crime Peril

How does the crime peril differ from other perils?

How do the distinctive features of the crime peril influence crime loss controls?

What are the most significant crimes against property, persons, and activities?

Crime causes many of the same types of property, liability, personnel, and net income losses discussed in other chapters of this text. Nevertheless, several distinctive features of the crime peril create hazards that require special risk control measures. Those distinctive features stem from the fact that the diverse crimes that can strike an organization (1) are directed by hostile intelligence; (2) require constant, universal loss control efforts; and (3) arise from only one hazard—hostile humans who believe they can act with impunity.

Directed by Hostile Intelligence

As a peril, crime against an organization differs fundamentally from other perils dealt with in this text. Other perils strike by chance, by accident, or as natural events. They are acts of God, not acts of humans. In contrast, crime strikes an organization because criminals intend to commit crimes. Crime is the only peril that is directed by human intelligence and is intentional. A criminal might intend to acquire property or information illegally or to injure or kill a person associated with the organization. Human actions or faults contribute significantly to other types of losses: ignorance or carelessness allows many property damage or injury hazards to go uncorrected, and a lack of reasonable care for others' safety causes many negligence liability losses. Only for crime losses, however, are hostile acts and intent to harm the essential elements of the peril.

To reduce the frequency and severity or to improve the predictability of crime losses, risk control measures must focus on hostile human conduct. For example, both accidental fires and fires set by arsonists can seriously damage a building. However, the ordinary precautions against accidental fire damage, such as controls on ignition sources and on excessive accumulations of combustibles, are not effective against fires set by arsonists. Arsonists supply their own rapidly burning fuels, fire accelerants, and ignition sources. As another example, the boards and tape that an organization stores for use in protecting exterior windows against high winds will not provide much protection against the stones and bricks that vandals or rioters hurl against those windows. To illustrate further, a computerized quality control monitoring system, designed to ensure the uniformity of products from an automated assembly line, will not be effective if the employees operating the system intentionally sabotage the company's products. To ward off arsonists, vandals, rioters, or saboteurs, effective crime loss control measures must recognize that criminals are driven by intelligent hostile intent.

Because most persons with criminal intentions are intelligent, they look constantly for new opportunities for crime. They search for high-value, easily transported items; unguarded property; vulnerable people; or unprotected key operations. To counter criminals, crime loss control programs must stay ahead of the criminals. An organization's risk management professional must anticipate new opportunities for criminals to attack the organization and must devise countermeasures before criminals strike. New opportunities for crime, and hence special needs for increased vigilance, are especially likely when an organization undergoes change (for example, acquires new facilities, develops new operating procedures, or hires new employees). Each of those changes probably creates gaps in the organization's security program that watchful criminals are waiting to exploit.

Need for Constant, Universal Control Measures

One feature of the crime peril is that criminals rapidly discover weaknesses in an organization's efforts to combat crime losses. As mentioned, that characteristic is not shared by perils that strike accidentally. To illustrate, if the automatic fire detection/suppression system in a restaurant's kitchen is defective, several months or even years could pass before a fire accidentally starts in the kitchen and causes severe damage. However, if a disgruntled kitchen employee decides to intentionally set fire to the restaurant under circumstances that appear accidental, the employee could use the defect in the sprinkler system to facilitate or conceal the arson. As another illustration, an organization's security procedures for depositing its daily cash receipts might require the organization's messenger to randomly change the routes traveled to and from the bank. If the messenger deviates from that procedure and follows more predictable routes, potential robbers might waylay and rob the messenger. The messenger or the messenger's supervisor might even conspire with the robbers. Such conspiracy demonstrates that detailed knowledge of an organization's operations can reveal many potential opportunities for criminal acts. Therefore, an organization's employees possess, and might be tempted to use, information that allows persons hostile to the organization to circumvent the organization's crime loss control measures.

Constant vigilance is crucial in preventing any breakdowns or gaps in an organization's crime loss control measures. Honest employees will report such breakdowns or gaps to management so that those problems can be corrected. Less scrupulous employees might be tempted to take advantage of those security weaknesses. Thus, no organization can tolerate dishonest or disloyal employees or other agents. Moreover, employees responsible for the daily functioning of an organization's crime loss control measures must be among its most trustworthy.

Hostile Humans as the Fundamental Crime Hazard

One significant hazard increases the likelihood and severity of all crime losses. That hazard is the hostility of persons who intend, or might be tempted, to commit crimes if they believe they can do so with relative impunity. Other hazards include the failure to physically secure valuable property, the failure to take precautions against violent attacks on employees or customers, or the failure to audit sales and other accounting records. Those hazards, however, do not increase crime losses without the criminal intent of hostile persons. Controlling that hostility tends to neutralize the other crime hazards an organization might face. Controlling other hazards that lead to crime is important, but it is not as crucial as reducing or countering the hostility of potential criminals.

Focusing on the hostility hazard provides a logical framework for categorizing possible crime loss control measures. Generally, crime loss control measures strive to manage the hostility hazard by doing the following:

- Reducing the hostility of persons who may commit crimes against the organization or others associated with it

- Shielding the organization's assets and activities against hostile persons by maintaining physical, procedural, and managerial barriers that reduce criminals' opportunities

- Reducing potential criminals' perception that they can commit crimes against the organization with legal impunity

The two remaining major sections of this chapter describe crime control measures and explain how to apply those measures to widespread types of crimes. To facilitate the description of the crime loss control measures, the crimes that serve as examples in the rest of this chapter are defined.

Characteristics of Some Common Crimes

All crimes are acts (or sometimes failures to act) that violate the peace and order of the general population. Persons or organizations *accused* of criminal acts are prosecuted in criminal courts by local, state, or federal governments on behalf of all the people. Persons or organizations *found guilty* of crimes are punished by the government on behalf of all the people. The punishments could be fines, imprisonment, loss of some civil rights (such as to serve in public office or to vote), or other penalties.

Most crimes are also torts against the victims of the crimes. The victims can sue wrongdoers in civil courts to collect monetary damages or to enforce other legal remedies. Thus, anyone committing a crime would probably be found liable in both a criminal and a civil court.

Crimes are defined either by common law precedents that are based on court decisions and recognized in most jurisdictions or by statutes that apply only in the jurisdictions whose legislative bodies enact those laws. Criminal law traditionally distinguishes between crimes against property (such as burglary and arson) and crimes against persons (such as violent attack, kidnapping, and homocide). Adding a third crime category is useful for risk management purposes. That category includes crimes against an entire activity or enterprise, such as terrorism and espionage, which strike both the persons and the property of an organization. Exhibit 11-1 summarizes, and the following subsections describe, several of the most widespread crimes against organizations and their employees.

Exhibit 11-1
Characteristics of Common Crimes

CRIME	CHARACTERISTICS
Crimes Against Property	
Burglary	Breaking into any closed building or space not open for business to commit another felony
Robbery	Taking personal property from another person by force or by threat of force against that person or against another
Shoplifting	Removing merchandise from a store by stealth without purchasing it
Fraud	Using trickery, falsehoods, or other deception to induce another person to voluntarily surrender money, other property, or rights for another's benefit and without proper compensation
Embezzlement	An employee's or other agent's fraudulent taking of money or other property for personal use when that money or property was entrusted to the employee or agent by another

Counterfeiting/Forgery	Creating or using an unauthorized copy of currency, documents, or artwork to commit fraud
Vandalism	Maliciously damaging or destroying another's property without just cause or compensation
Arson	Burning others' or one's own property for personal gain without legal purpose
Crimes Against Persons	
Violent attack	Forcefully, and physically harming or threatening to harm another person, such as by striking, wounding, or placing that person in grave danger (including sexual assault)
Kidnapping	Limiting the freedom of physical movement of a person by force or threat of force to collect ransom or to achieve some other illegal purpose
Murder (homicide)	Killing a human being through an intentional action without just cause
Crimes Against Activities	
Terrorism	Using violence, intimidation, or threats to influence others' behavior, often for a political purpose
Espionage	Using spies or mechanical or electronic techniques to obtain confidential information
Computer crime	Using or damaging computer hardware or software for an illegal purpose, such as embezzlement, espionage, fraud, or vandalism

Crimes Against Property

Crimes against property usually involve theft of or damage to tangible property. Some of the most common crimes against tangible property include burglary, robbery, shoplifting, fraud, embezzlement, forgery, vandalism, and arson. Intangible properties, such as trade secrets, copyrights, and licenses, are also subject to loss by crimes such as espionage and computer-based intrusions. Crime exposures to intangible property are treated later in this section.

Burglary

Burglary is breaking into a locked building (or a secured area within that building) when the building is not open for business with the intent to commit a felony. The intended felony is usually theft of personal property, but the intent to commit another felony, such as homicide, counterfeiting, or computer fraud, makes the forced entry a burglary. (Breaking into a house or other residence at any time is burglary because a residence is never open for business.) Burglary also includes breaking out of a locked building or area when the building is closed for business if the burglar enters during business hours to commit a felony and hides until after the building or area is closed.

The forced breaking into or out of a building or an area for a felonious purpose, and not the act of committing the intended felony, constitutes burglary. For example, if criminals break through the wall of a bank to take money from the vault but flee the bank before reaching the vault because they are frightened by alarms, they have still burglarized the bank. Even if the criminals penetrate both the bank wall and the vault, only to find that the vault is empty, they have burglarized both the bank and the vault.

Because the essence of burglary is the breaking into or out of a building or an area, many of the measures for controlling burglary losses focus on protecting the boundaries or perimeter of a building or an area. If the perimeter of a facility is not breached, no burglary has occurred, even if theft or some other crime not involving burglary occurs. As explained later in this chapter, protective measures can be physical (such as fences or locks), procedural (such as requiring everyone who enters a building to show identification), or managerial (such as educating employees about situations that might invite burglaries).

Robbery

Robbery is taking personal property (tangible property other than real estate) from persons through violence or the threat of violence. In contrast to burglars, who normally steal property from buildings or unoccupied areas, robbers harm or threaten people to steal from them. An organization's employees are usually present during a robbery but not during a burglary. Consequently, the safety of personnel and customers is usually a major concern during a robbery. In addition, the employees involved in a robbery can sometimes help to identify and prosecute the criminals. Burglaries are usually committed without witnesses.

Shoplifting

Shoplifting is the theft of merchandise by sneaking the merchandise out of a store. Shoplifters typically conceal the stolen items on their person or in some container they are carrying. Shoplifters can work alone, in teams, or in collusion with the store's employees or others. They usually pose as customers or others who have an apparent right to be in the store, such as maintenance personnel or law enforcement officers. Shoplifters typically avoid confrontation and violence, relying on stealth to achieve their thefts and remain undetected. Merchants' annual losses from shoplifting are several times their losses from robbery or burglary.

Shoplifters want their thefts to pass unnoticed, so security procedures or surveillance systems aimed at detecting the theft are strong deterrents. Such control measures are effective in catching and discouraging shoplifters. (To stay ahead of experienced shoplifters, however, a store might also use hidden safeguards. Some of these safeguards are described later in this chapter.)

Efforts to thwart shoplifters, as well as other thieves, can create other loss exposures. In striving to stop crime, risk management professionals should also control those additional exposures. For example, if a store employee challenges a shoplifter, the thief will probably leave the store and might even discard any stolen merchandise before leaving. However, a shoplifter confronted too aggressively may become violent, possibly injuring employees or customers or even creating a hostage situation. If someone is wrongfully accused of shoplifting or committing another theft, that person can have a valid tort liability claim against the store for defamation, assault, wrongful imprisonment, or malicious prosecution. Therefore, as explained later in this chapter, an organization's on-site procedures for handling suspected thieves must guard against both theft and other possible types of losses.

Fraud

Fraud is any theft by trickery, falsehood, or deception that requires another person or entity to relinquish money, property, or legal rights for another's benefit without fair compensation. *Confidence artists* can perpetrate fraud through *confidence games*. Victims are often persuaded to pay in advance for goods, services, rights such as property ownership, or other benefits that they never receive or that are worth far less than they paid. Fraud may be committed against an organization in many ways; the following are some examples:

- The organization pays a dishonest merchant in advance for goods the merchant knows will not be delivered or will be greatly inferior to what the organization is entitled.

- The organization sells and delivers goods or services to a customer who has no intent to pay for them.

- An inventor persuades the organization to purchase all rights to an invention that the inventor knows has been developed and patented by another person.

- An unauthorized person acquires and uses the account number and personal identification number for one of the organization's telephone credit cards and charges many personal long-distance calls to the organization's account (in effect, impersonating an authorized user of that card).

- A person falsely claims to have been injured by one of the organization's products and brings a large negligence suit against the organization.

As detailed later in this chapter, ways to controll fraud losses include trying to avoid dealing with dishonest persons, attempting to detect fraud promptly, and pressing vigorously for civil and criminal legal sanctions against confidence artists.

Embezzlement

Embezzlement is fraud by an employee or other agent against an employer or other principal. An embezzler usually steals by manipulating some of the employer's or principal's operating procedures or violates the trust that the employer or principal has placed in the embezzler. For example, it is embezzlement for a messenger to take for personal use the money or property entrusted to the embezzler by the employer or other principal. Embezzlement could also involve an employee or a group of employees, perhaps in collusion with others, who interfere with the organization's selling or purchasing procedures to divert cash and merchandise for the embezzlers' own use. Embezzlement is not a violent or forceful crime, like robbery or burglary, but rather a crime of stealth or deception.

Embezzlement occurs because dishonest employees find and seize opportunities to secretly compromise the organization's procedures for their or others' benefit. Therefore, controlling embezzlement involves employing honest workers, strictly enforcing the organization's procedures, and promptly discovering any violated procedures (and, ideally, the violator's identity).

Counterfeiting/Forgery

Counterfeiting and forgery are synonymous. Both involve fraudulently creating or using false or unauthorized versions of currency, documents, artwork, or other property that only specified entities or persons have the right to make or use. Thus, privately duplicating a country's currency or presenting it as genuine with knowledge that it is not is **counterfeiting**. The same is true of the unauthorized creation or use of false versions of documents such as stock certificates, birth records, lottery tickets, drivers' or other licenses, passports, or other papers that only government agencies or other entities (such as corporations or banks) have the right to issue. **Forgery** involves creating or presenting false documents, such as checks, letters, or paintings, as genuine.

Counterfeiters and forgers can cause two broad types of crime losses. First, those criminals can induce an organization to accept falsified currency, checks or other negotiable instruments, documents, or artwork. When the organization exchanges something of value for the valueless items, the organization's immediate loss is the value of whatever it relinquished in the exchange. (The further costs of trying to correct its original mistake of accepting the counterfeit or forged items are likely to increase the organization's ultimate loss.) To control losses stemming from counterfeiting and forgery, an organization must be able to verify the authenticity of the currency, documents, or other items it accepts in exchange for the values it provides.

Second, counterfeiters and forgers can create or use unauthorized or stolen copies of the organization's own documents (for example, checks, identification cards, invoices, purchase orders, or even business cards, letterhead, and envelopes). Those documents could enable the counterfeiter or forger to impersonate the organization through the mail. Criminals can use falsified documents to manipulate funds, make seemingly valid promises, and issue "official" statements that harm the organization financially or damage its reputation. To reduce this second type of counterfeiting or forgery loss, an organization must control access to and use of all its documents.

Vandalism

Vandalism involves maliciously defacing, damaging, or destroying others' property, usually out of anger or revenge or as a way of making a political statement. Vandals usually attack property to attack those who own or use the property; they do not want the property itself. Although some vandals act alone and in secret, most vandals are part of a group. Two of the most effective strategies for controlling vandalism are to avoid arousing the anger of potential vandals and to establish physical barriers to shield vulnerable property from attack and from sight.

Arson

Arson, a form of vandalism, involves intentionally damaging or destroying others' property by fire. It also includes purposely burning one's own property for some fraudulent purpose, which is fraud by arson. The latter type of arson could be committed to collect insurance on the property or to avoid having to perform some obligation, for example, an obligation to finish construction or to pay off a mortgage. Such arson is a crime against the person who is defrauded, not the owner or user of the property. If a person who owns property conspires with others to burn it, the owner commits fraud by arson and, in some jurisdictions, arson as well. When discussing arson control measures (which are similar to vandalism controls), this chapter focuses on arson, not fraud by arson.

Crimes Against Persons

The purpose of crimes against persons is to injure, kill, frighten, or restrict the physical freedom of someone else. Some crimes against persons are committed to achieve some desired result, such as learning secret information or obtaining a ransom. However, the majority of crimes against persons are committed to harm or threaten another person's physical well-being. (Robbery is not typically considered a crime against persons, even though it involves taking personal property by force or threats. A robber's goal is to acquire the stolen property, not to harm the victim.) Some common crimes against persons that often create risk management concerns are violent attack, kidnapping, and murder.

Violent Attack

In this chapter, **violent attack** is a generic term for any overt action that inflicts serious physical or psychological harm on someone. Sexual assault, running someone down with a vehicle, crimes that involve bludgeoning, shooting, or knifing, or attempts at any of these are examples of violent attacks. Robbers and burglars might also violently attack anyone who tries to thwart their crimes. Such attacks can cause losses of key personnel, workers compensation claims, property damage, loss of patronage, and general liability losses. Many courts hold that such violence, especially when committed by the organization's employees or their relatives, is becoming more foreseeable, creating a clearer duty for organizations to establish more effective safeguards to prevent or reduce that violence. That duty is also being applied by some courts even if violence is committed by someone who is not connected with the organization.

Protecting against violent attack is very difficult. Potential attackers have advantages over potential victims: they can select whom, when, and where to attack; they can surprise their victims; and they can wait until a lapse in security precautions gives them an opportunity to attack and to leave the attack scene without being captured or recognized. Moreover, attackers who are employees of the organization or who are relatives or friends of employees typically have little difficulty gaining access to the property or persons they wish to attack. To neutralize those advantages and to prevent violent attacks, organizations can implement a variety of physical, procedural, and managerial controls, such as those detailed later in this chapter.

Kidnapping

Kidnapping commonly involves seizing and detaining a person against that person's will. It is usually committed to collect a ransom or influence the behavior of a third party. For example, a kidnapper might demand the release of a political prisoner. The executives of organizations that are involved in controversial or politically sensitive activities are subject to kidnapping, especially when traveling abroad. Bank robbers and burglars might kidnap employees or the relatives of employees of the organizations they want to rob or burglarize and hold those persons hostage while they commit their thefts.

As explained later in this chapter, the best strategies for combating kidnappers are to alert potential kidnap victims to this threat, to train potential victims in how to deal with kidnappers, and to develop an emergency response plan for negotiating or achieving the victim's safe release. Vigorously prosecuting suspected kidnappers and imposing heavy criminal penalties on convicted kidnappers can deter future kidnappings.

Murder (Homicide)

Homicide involves killing someone accidentally, negligently, or intentionally. Homicide, especially if accidental, is not necessarily a crime. Intentional homicide without legal justification (such as self-defense or a legal execution of a person who has committed a capital offense) constitutes murder, which is always a crime. Negligent homicide could be a crime. Federal and state statutes define various classes of murder and negligent homicide and establish penalties for those found guilty of those acts.

When an employee, a relative of an employee, or a customer is a homicide victim, the organization is likely to suffer the same types of losses as when a violent attack occurs. The safeguards for reducing the frequency or severity of homicides are similar to those for combating violent attacks.

Crimes Against Activities

Some forms of criminal activity are directed at activities rather than specific persons or property. Those criminal activities can cause pervasive harm to the persons and properties involved in the activities. Some common examples of criminal acts against an organization's activities are terrorism, espionage, and computer crime.

Terrorism

Terrorism is the use of violence, intimidation, or threats to influence others' behavior, often for a political purpose. The same organizations whose politically sensitive or controversial activities increase their exposures to kidnappers are also targets for terrorists. Although kidnappers strike at particular kidnap victims, terrorists target an organization's overall operations, hoping to bring activities to a halt by disrupting one or more of the organization's key operations.

To protect itself against terrorists, an organization must safeguard its ability to continue the operations that terrorists are most likely to attack. As explained later in this chapter, those protective measures can include physical, procedural, or managerial measures to protect facilities and personnel and emergency steps to continue key operations created by a terrorist attack.

Espionage

A synonym for espionage is spying, that is, obtaining confidential information through personal observation or mechanical or electronic techniques that thwart efforts to protect the information's confidentiality. Many organizations keep much of their operating information confidential for the following reasons:

- To protect competitive advantages that are based on trade secrets
- To protect employees' rights to keep personal information from becoming public knowledge
- To maintain national defense secrets

Criminals try to obtain confidential information in numerous ways. Therefore, as described later in this chapter, the measures for protecting an organization's confidential data and operations must be comprehensive and must evolve to stay ahead of spies' ingenuity and the technology of electronic and other scientific espionage.

Computer Crime

Computer crime involves damaging or using computer hardware or software to achieve an illegal purpose, especially embezzlement, espionage, fraud, or vandalism. Protecting computer facilities from physical damage is similar to protecting any portion of an organization's premises against malicious damage. Common control measures include physical barriers, guards, limited access to computer equipment and programs, and other administrative and managerial safeguards. Criminals may even turn to perils to which computer hardware and software are particularly vulnerable—perils like magnetic disruption, interruption of electrical power, or water—to damage an organization's computer facilities and operations.

As detailed later in this chapter, criminals' use of computer equipment and programs to commit embezzlement, espionage, or fraud poses much greater dangers to organizations that rely heavily on computerized accounting or production processes. By manipulating computer programs, embezzlers can drain much of an organization's financial resources without being detected for years. Espionage agents can discover, record, and transmit much of an organization's highly confidential information. In collusion with other employees or outsiders, an employee can defraud an organization of sales revenue, inventories, and customer records, resulting in large property and net income losses. Attempts to control crime losses resulting from computer crimes require the following:

- Physical, procedural, and managerial controls on computer access
- Audits
- Aggressive investigation and prosecution of persons suspected of committing computer crimes

Ideally, efforts to control computer crime should evolve more rapidly than advances in computer technology.

General Crime Control Strategies

What three general strategies can you use to reduce crime losses?

How can you apply these strategies to reduce losses from crimes against property, persons, and activities?

In general, an organization suffers crime losses because persons hostile to the organization or to those associated with the organization find opportunities for committing crimes. Therefore, an organization's general strategies for controlling crime losses should focus on (1) reducing hostility against the organization, (2) reducing opportunities for committing crimes against the organization, and (3) reducing the belief that people can act with impunity because their crimes will either not be detected or not be prosecuted. The following paragraphs summarize those three basic crime control strategies. The closing section of this chapter illustrates how those strategies can reduce losses from specific types of crimes.

Reducing Criminal Hostility

A distinctive characteristic of the crime peril is hostile criminal intelligence, not random chance, as the basic cause of loss. Criminals act with intent, not negligence or mishap. In fact, criminal law defines hostile intent (*mens rea*, which is Latin for "a mind for the thing") as an essential element of all crimes. Therefore, one basic strategy for reducing the frequency or severity of an organization's crime losses is to reduce hostility.

Concerning employees, an organization should strive to (1) hire persons who are not accustomed or inclined to commit crimes, (2) treat all employees fairly so that they do not seek vengeance through crimes directed at the organization, (3) resolve grievances promptly and equitably, and (4) terminate or take other appropriate action against an employee who commits crimes against the organization. To implement those measures, the risk management professional must work closely with the human resources (personnel) department.

Particular employees can become targets of violent crime. Violence in the workplace leads not only to work-related injuries but also to property damage, net income, personnel, and other liability losses for the organization. To control hostility and violence against employees, an organization should encourage employees and their supervisors to report situations that could lead to criminal violence at work. Because such situations combine employees' personal and working lives, the risk management professional and others who address those situations must be attentive to employees' right to privacy. Wrongfully invading an employee's privacy or unduly interfering with an employee's personal relationships can expose an organization to tort liability.

Some employees might become hostile toward an organization because of *irresistible temptations*, or conflicts between their obligations to their employer and their obligations to others. For example, an employee facing financial problems might think that the only solution is to embezzle money or to kidnap and hold for ransom the supervisor whose "unfair" treatment keeps the employee from earning an adequate income. Good risk management, as well as sound personnel practices, should help a supervisor and other managers recognize potentially explosive situations. Supervisors and managers should also have the skills to help employees resolve dilemmas constructively and peaceably.

Customers, neighbors, or others who become hostile to the organization might also vent their hostility against it. They could vandalize property; tamper with products; or commit arson, computer-based fraud, or espionage. Hostile outsiders could also seek revenge through actions that are equally damaging to the organization but not illegal. For example, those hostile outsiders could organize boycotts or bring frivolous lawsuits against the organization. To reduce the resulting losses, an organization's risk management professional should work cooperatively with its public relations department in recognizing and defusing situations that could escalate into criminal activity. All employees, even their families, can help reduce general community hostility toward an organization by being positive spokespersons and by reporting complaints or other situations that could lead to overt criminal acts.

Reducing Criminal Opportunities

Reducing hostility against an organization will ideally eliminate all potential crimes against the organization. However, identifying and removing all sources of hostility that could lead to criminal conduct is not practical. An organization's crime loss control measures should therefore recognize that some people will always seek opportunities to commit crimes. Thus, the second strategy for controlling an organization's crime losses is to reduce opportunities for intentional harm. The methods for reducing those opportunities are categorized as physical, procedural, and managerial measures, although the measures often overlap.

General Physical Controls

Physical controls against crime losses place tangible barriers between would-be criminals and their targets. Walls, fences, locked doors, vaults and safes, guards and guard dogs, and automatic devices to detect intruders and to sound alarms are all examples of physical barriers. Some less apparent physical barriers include the following:

- Placing a particularly crucial or vulnerable facility in a remote location, perhaps surrounded by unoccupied properties
- Conducting sensitive activities, such as computer operations or chemical testing, near the center of an organization's facility (out of public view and away from the property's boundaries)
- Surrounding property that criminals might be tempted to attack by night with intense lighting (the surrounding pool of light acts as a protective moat between the thieves and their target)

Placing vaults or safes in public view so that potential robbers or burglars risk immediate detection is one way merchants commonly protect cash on their premises. Those merchants might also physically safeguard their cash by having all cash-register receipts fall automatically into a locked box or safe that even store employees cannot open. (Similarly, buses and taxi cabs are often equipped with locked boxes that their drivers cannot open.) Although such physical barriers can be very effective in protecting cash, their use might cause angry robbers or burglars to vent their frustration by violently attacking employees.

Specific Physical Controls[1]

Four specific physical controls against crime losses involving theft are alarms; security patrols; surveillance cameras; and locks, safes, and vaults.

Alarms

Unlike some physical controls, alarm systems do not prevent burglars from entering a building or property. Although alarms can serve as deterrents, their primary function is to indicate when an intruder has already entered the premises.

Some alarm systems use simple electrical circuits that sound an alarm when an electrical connection is made or broken. Other systems use more sophisticated electronic devices. Those devices might sound alarms when an intruder, such as a burglar, is on the premises. Others use invisible light rays that sound an alarm when the rays are broken. The principal varieties of alarms are described below.

A simple alarm system consists of electrical contacts or metal tapes on each door, window, or other building opening. The system is usually wired so that an electrical current passes constantly through the system. Opening a door or a window interrupts the electrical current, which activates an alarm. That system is called a *perimeter system*, and it sounds an alarm whenever the building is entered through a door, a window, or other opening protected by the system.

A perimeter system gives no protection against entry through a roof or a wall. To signal entry through a roof or a wall requires installing wires or other devices that protect the wall or roof areas accessible from neighboring buildings. Various sensing devices are illustrated in Exhibit 11-2. Sensing devices are usually connected to either local or central station alarms.

Alarms are not limited to preventing burglary. They can also reduce the robbery exposure. Buttons or foot pedals can be situated so that a bank teller or store clerk can send a silent alarm to a central station company or the police. (The silent alarm is silent at the location being robbed.) If the police respond rapidly enough, they could arrive while a robber is still on the premises.

Local Alarms   Many simple alarm systems are connected to interior and exterior gongs or alarms. An interior alarm system can be effective in a store with security personnel on duty at all times. The alarm system would alert security personnel to a burglar's entry. However, the outside alarm could be almost completely useless in an industrial or mercantile district where few people are present at night. Such local alarms often ring for hours before anyone pays attention to them. Sometimes neighbors call the police only because the noise eventually interferes with their sleep. In the meantime, the burglars have escaped with the stolen goods.

Central Station Alarms   A more effective type of alarm system is directly connected to a central station of an alarm company, which is monitored at all hours. All circuits are electrically or electronically monitored from the central station. When an alarm is received at the central station, a guard is sent to the alarm transmission site. The police are also notified that an alarm was received from the premises.

Exhibit 11-2
Burglar Alarm System Design

Door Switches (Contacts) These devices are usually magnet-operated switches. They are affixed to a door or window in such a way that opening the door or window breaks the magnetic field. That, in turn, activates the switch, causing an alarm.

These devices can be surface-mounted or recessed, exposed or concealed. A variety of switches exists for every kind of door or window and for all levels of security.

Metallic Foil (Window Tape) Metallic foil is the traditional means for detecting glass-breakage. Strips of thin foil are affixed to a glass surface. Breaking glass ruptures the foil and interrupts the detection circuit to signal an alarm.

Thin foil, however, is easily damaged by people or objects accidentally touching the glass surface. Also bonds at the corners and between multiple-foil strips deteriorate with time. Metallic foil, therefore, requires frequent maintenance, especially on glass doors.

Wooden Screens Openings such as air-duct passages and skylights can provide paths for an intruder. Those can be secured by a cage-like frame of wooden rods. An intruder breaks the wire embedded within the frame, which triggers an alarm.

Wood screens are custom-built for each application. They can be mounted permanently or removed when the alarm system is turned off. Wooden screens require little maintenance. They are suitable for protecting openings where aesthetics are not important.

Continued on next page.

Lacing (Paneling) Lacing can protect walls, doors and safes against penetration. Lacing is a closely woven pattern of metallic foil or fine brittle wire on the surface of the protected area. An intruder can enter only by breaking the foil or wire. That activates the alarm. A panel over the lacing protects it from accidental damage.

Photoelectric (Eyes, Beams) Photoelectric devices transmit a beam across a protected area. When an intruder interrupts the beam, the photoelectric circuit is disrupted. That activates the alarm.

Modern photoelectric devices are a great improvement over their predecessors. Today's photoelectric devices use diodes that emit infrared light, which is invisible to the naked eye. The beam usually pulses rapidly to prevent compromise by substitution.

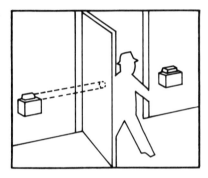

Photoelectric devices are effective and reliable. Some have ranges of more than 1,000 feet for large buildings and hallways. Those devices provide excellent protection for relatively low-risk areas.

Ultrasonic Detectors These devices also sense movement. Ultrasonic means "above the range of hearing." An intruder disrupting the ultrasonic wave pattern activates the alarm.

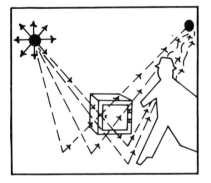

Ultrasonic devices can be mounted on the ceiling or wall. They protect three-dimensional areas with an invisible pattern. However, they are prone to false alarms, due to excessive air currents or ultrasonic noises from mechanical equipment. Again, proper application is important.

Infrared Detectors These devices are part of the motion-detection group. They sense the body heat of an intruder as the intruder passes through the protected area. A change from the area's normal heat profile triggers an alarm. Infrared detectors are relatively free of false alarms. They provide relatively inexpensive protection for confined areas.

Microwave Detectors This kind of motion detector uses high-frequency radio waves, or microwaves, to detect movement. Microwave devices have greater range than ultrasonic devices. Since microwave devices do not use sound, or air, they are not prone to false alarms from air currents. However, they can cause false alarms, because they penetrate materials such as glass, and metal objects reflect them. This means microwaves can detect motion outside the protected area if the detectors are not properly installed.

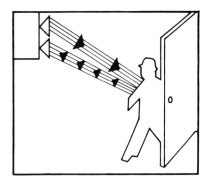

Object Protection Object protection provides direct security for individual items. It is often the final stage of an in-depth protection system with perimeter and area-protection devices. The objects most frequently protected are safes, filing cabinets, display cabinets, models, and expensive equipment.

Proximity (Capacitance or Electrostatic) With this system, the object itself becomes an antenna, electronically linked to the alarm control. When a person approaches or touches the object, its electrostatic field becomes unbalanced. That activates the alarm. Only metal objects isolated from the ground can be protected this way.

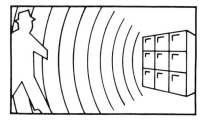

Continued on next page.

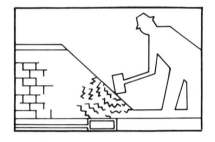

Vibration Detectors (Seismic) These sensing devices use a highly sensitive piezoelectric crystal or microphone to detect the sound pattern that a hammer-like impact on a rigid surface would generate. Those devices are attached directly to safes and filing cabinets or walls and floors.

The devices instantly detect a vibration an intruder makes. Some vibration detectors are adjustable. They can be adjusted to detect a sledgehammer attack on concrete or the delicate penetration of a glass surface.

This kind of protection is generally used for securing the perimeter surfaces of a vault. The correct number, spacing, and location of these sensors are important for suitable detection.

Adapted with permission from *Alarm Handbook for the Security Manager*, Honeywell, Inc., 1984, pp. 8-11. (Adapted from James S. Trieschmann et al., *Commercial Property Insurance and Risk Management*, 4th ed., vol. 1 [Malvern, PA: American Institute for CPCU, 1994], pp. 87-90.)

Selection of Alarm Systems   The quality and extent of protection by alarm systems vary. Insurance rate manuals generally give credits only for **approved alarm systems.** An approved system is installed by an approved burglar alarm company named in the rating manual. Underwriters Laboratories, Inc., issues alarm certificates that indicate the grade, type, and protection extent of the alarm system. Those certificates are considered when granting insurance rate credits. Regardless of its cost, an alarm system without an Underwriters Laboratories (U. L.) certificate might not receive a premium reduction, a fact too often discovered only after the alarm has been purchased.

Deficiencies of Alarm Systems   Burglar alarm systems have many problems. One of the most difficult problems is false alarms caused by accidental triggering. One survey indicated that more than half of the major police emergency calls in a large city were false alarms. As a result, police in some cities assign a low priority to calls that come in from burglar alarm systems.

Another deficiency is that an alarm system does not stop burglaries from occurring. The system merely shortens the burglar's operating time. A delay of five to fifteen minutes or more from the time an alarm sounds until a guard or police officer arrives at the premises may give a burglar ample time to complete the theft and escape. Response time is a vital consideration in determining whether the expense of a sophisticated burglary or robbery alarm system is worthwhile.

Central station contracts with merchants ordinarily require that the central station guard remain on the premises for up to two hours after the alarm has been received so that the proprietor has time to arrive and secure the premises. Sometimes the proprietor fails to arrive within the specified two hours, the alarm-company guard leaves the premises, and the burglars reenter and complete their work.

One alarm that can be used when a central station service is not available is an automatic system that dials the police telephone number and transmits a recorded message to the police department when the alarm is activated. That system can send a robbery alarm when a button is pushed or can indicate a burglary when the premises are entered. Unfortunately, the system can be deactivated by placing other telephone calls from nearby phones or by disconnecting the telephone lines. A sophisticated burglar can breach security if the telephone lines are accessible. Telephone lines in the basement of a multiple-occupancy building, overhead , or on a pole or box outside a building are easy targets for experienced burglars.

An alarm system could have a *shunt switch,* which gives the store operator a few seconds to exit the store upon closing or to enter upon opening without sounding an alarm. However, a sophisticated burglar can easily determine in advance exactly what the proprietor does in using the shunt switch. The burglar can then breach the system.

Watchman or Security Patrols

Many organizations find it worthwhile to maintain watchmen on the premises. A watchman patrols the building at periodic intervals (typically hourly) to see that the structure and its contents are secure. The watchman protects against fire and, to a degree, against other perils such as burglary. Certain devices ensure that the watchman patrols at the required intervals. In one system, the watchman carries a special clock that records his or her visits to stations throughout the building. A key is fastened to each location, and inserting the key into the special clock records the time when the watchman visited the station. By checking the records, the employer can be sure the watchman completed all rounds. The weakness of this system is that if a watchman is attacked by thieves during the night, no one knows about it until the premises are reopened the next morning. A watchman deters burglars, but does not eliminate all loss possibilities.

Central station alarm companies also maintain a **supervised system** under which a watchman signals the central station upon visiting each station throughout the premises. In that system, the central station alarm company sends a guard to the premises if the watchman at the premises fails to signal as required. Sometimes burglars or robbers will force a watchman to continue making rounds while a theft is being carried out. Most signaling systems allow the watchman to secretly signal for help even while making rounds under the burglar's scrutiny.

Large organizations might have a complete security system with a central station on the premises that supervises the watchmen. The expense of such a system would be justified only if large values were involved or if watchmen needed to be supervised for other reasons.

Surveillance Cameras

Banks and other organizations with high robbery exposure frequently install automatic cameras to photograph criminals in the process of committing a crime. Such installations are effective in two ways:

1. They facilitate the identification, conviction, and incarceration of criminals.
2. They discourage robbery by increasing the probability of identification and conviction.

Locks, Safes, and Vaults

An organization can install passive restraints, such as locks, safes, and vaults, to restrict entry. The type of lock used on doorways can make a difference of several minutes in the entry time needed by a thief. The ordinary snap lock can be manipulated in seconds. A deadbolt lock cannot be manipulated in the same way as a snap lock but usually requires picking the tumblers or using force. Lock picking requires tools and skills that many ordinary burglars do not possess.

The rear doors in a building can be barred from the inside so that access is difficult. Bars, grates, or other coverings can be put across windows or doorways. An "unbreakable" glazing material can be used for doors or windows where the proprietor wishes to maintain a clearly visible window display. (It is worth noting that any measure that impedes the burglar's entry or exit also impedes entry by firefighters or exit by members of the public during an emergency.)

Many burglaries are committed by breaking a show window and grabbing valuable items. Ordinary plate glass is easily broken. Varieties of breakage-resistant glass and plastic materials often improve protection, particularly for smaller windows. A sheet of breakage-resistant glass suspended behind the glass of a show window can impede a burglar's access to jewelry or other valuable items in display windows. The second sheet of glass is hung on chains from the top of the show window so that it swings backward when struck. The show window can be broken, but the second sheet of glass is difficult to break because of its composition and, particularly, because it swings. It is difficult for a thief to reach around such a glass when it is properly installed.

Installing good locks, grates, bars, breakage-resistant glass, and similar devices provides satisfactory protection for mercantile stocks of low value, particularly if the premises are under frequent surveillance by police and in a low crime area. However, passive restraints merely delay the burglar's entrance and do not guarantee that a burglary will not occur. The adequacy of such measures must also be considered in light of the loss exposures involved. The organization must decide whether the small volume, light weight, and high value of the merchandise make it attractive to burglars.

Safes are another type of physical protective device. Safes vary in their vulnerability to burglary. Many safes are basically fire protection devices, referred to as **record safes**, and offer little resistance to the burglar. Designed to protect money and valuable records from fire damage, **fire-resistive safes** generally have square doors and are mounted on wheels.

Money safes are designed to be burglar resistive. They generally have round doors and are not mounted on wheels. (However, some modern money safes have been designed with square doors to facilitate their use with cash register trays.) Safes come in many models with different degrees of resistance to fire and/or burglary. Exhibit 11-3 gives the classifications for safes and vaults. Like other physical protection devices, safes do not eliminate the possibility of a loss. However, they do reduce the likelihood of loss relative to the quality of the safe and the skill of the thief.

Procedural Controls

Procedural controls define how to perform particular tasks in secure ways that make it difficult for persons to commit crimes or make crime detection more prompt or certain.

Procedural controls to combat crimes involving property (robbery, burglary, shoplifting, vandalism, computer crime, or violent attack) must make it difficult for potential criminals to gain access to the property. Procedures that require everyone entering an area to identify themselves, sign in, or give passwords are access controls. Declaring particular areas, facilities, or activities *off limits* to everyone except designated persons or groups also effectively limits access, as does limiting the hours that a facility is open for business.

Exhibit 11-3
Safe and Vault Classifications

Safe, Chest or Cabinet or Vault Classification	Construction		
		Walls	
	Doors	Safe, Chest or Cabinet	Vault
B (Fire-Resistive)	Steel less than 1" thick, or iron	Body of steel is less than 1/2" thick, or iron	Brick, concrete, stone, tile, iron or steel
	Any iron or steel safe or chest having a slot through which money can be deposited		Not Applicable
C (Burglar-Resistive)	Steel at least 1" thick	Body of steel at least 1/2" thick	Steel at least 1/2" thick; or reinforced concrete or stone at least 9" thick; or non-reinforced concrete or stone at least 12" thick
	Safe or chest bearing following label: "Underwriters Laboratories, Inc. Inspected Keylocked Safe KL Burglary"		Not Applicable
E (Burglar-Resistive)	Steel at least 1 1/2" thick	Body of steel at least 1" thick	Same as for C
ER (Burglar-Resistive)	Safe or chest bearing the following label: "Underwriters Laboratories, Inc. Inspected Tool Resisting Safe TL–15 Burglary"		Not Applicable
F (Burglar-Resistive)	Safe or chest bearing one of the following labels: 1. "Underwriters Laboratories, Inc. Inspected Tool Resisting Safe TL-30 Burglary" 2. "Underwriters Laboratories, Inc. Inspected Torch Resisting Safe TR–30 Burglary" 3. "Underwriters Laboratories, Inc. Inspected Explosive Resisting Safe with Relocking Device X–60 Burglary"		Not Applicable

G (Burglar-Resistive)	One or more steel doors (one in front of the other) each at least 1 1/2" thick and aggregating at least 3" thickness	Steel at least 1/2" thick; or reinforced concrete or stone at least 12" thick; or non-reinforced concrete or stone at least 18" thick
	Not Applicable	
H (Burglar-Resistive)	Safe or chest bearing one of the following labels: 1. "Underwriters Laboratories, Inc. Inspected Torch and Explosive Resisting Safe TX–60 Burglary" 2. "Underwriters Laboratories, Inc. Inspected Torch Resisting Safe TR–60 Burglary" 3. "Underwriters Laboratories, Inc. Inspected Torch and Tool Resisting Safe TRTL–30 Burglary"	Not Applicable
I (Burglar-Resistive)	Safe or chest bearing the following label: "Underwriters Laboratories, Inc. Inspected Torch and Tool Resisting Safe TRTL–15x6 Burglary"	Not Applicable
J (Burglar-Resistive)	Safe or chest bearing the follow label: "Underwriters Laboratories, Inc. Inspected Torch and Tool Resisting Safe TRTL–60 Burglary"	Not Applicable
K (Burglar-Resistive)	Safe or chest bearing one of the following labels: 1. "Underwriters Laboratories, Inc. Inspected Torch and Tool Resisting Safe TRTL–60 Burglary" 2. "Underwriters Laboratories, Inc. Inspected Torch Explosive and Tool Resisting Safe TXTL–60 Burglary"	Not Applicable

For some crimes such as shoplifting, embezzlement, or violent attack, criminals prefer to act alone or be unobserved. Therefore, procedural controls must make it difficult for potential criminals to act alone or be unobserved. For example, guidelines for handling cash, for maintaining inventory or sales records, or for conducting audits often divide activities among two or more people to defeat a solitary embezzler. Auditing techniques themselves act as a procedural safeguard against embezzlement and fraud losses. Auditors are likely to detect crimes promptly, and criminals who know that an organization has strong audit procedures will probably target other, more vulnerable organizations. Operating rules that require at least two employees to be present when a store is open, or to work together when interviewing clients or providing medical care, provide some assurance that no single employee can attempt to defraud or to violently attack other persons. Procedures for opening and closing a building only at designated hours and only after clearance with an off-site security service help ensure the integrity of an organization's nighttime and holiday security measures.

Another group of procedural controls helps detect crimes that have already been committed and identify the criminal(s). Among those controls are cameras attached to off-site videotape recorders to film shoplifters and robbers, magnetic tags that must be removed only by authorized personnel before merchandise can be taken from a store, and specially marked packets for cash that can later be used to trace bank robbers and their accomplices. Auditing techniques can also promptly detect and facilitate the prosecution of embezzlers. Like other procedural controls, those detection methods might also deter criminals and lead them to seek other targets.

Managerial Controls

Without establishing the step-by-step operating methods that characterize procedural controls, managerial controls against crime losses establish a climate or atmosphere within an organization that deters crime or assists in its detection. Such managerial controls frequently include hiring and initial training practices emphasizing that dishonesty will not be tolerated and that all criminals, both employees and nonemployees, will be vigorously prosecuted. Making that policy clear should encourage job applicants with criminal tendencies or records to seek employment elsewhere. Requiring some or all present employees and job applicants to apply for fidelity bonds (a type of employee dishonesty insurance for employers) can also raise the general level of integrity among employees.

Other managerial controls can combat crime after an employee has been hired. For example, educating employees about the organization's exposures to

crime losses, the crime loss control measures the organization has implemented, and how employees can help reduce crime losses without endangering
themselves can raise employees' awareness of crime without providing incentives or information to commit crimes. Recognizing or rewarding employees
who report criminal activities or who make specific suggestions for deterring or
detecting crimes can also demonstrate management's commitment to crime
control. The same commitment can be shown more forcefully by keeping
employees informed of the organization's work with law enforcement officials
in prosecuting persons suspected of perpetrating crimes against the organization. Projecting a tough attitude toward crime to employees (and through
them to the public) can help an organization avoid becoming a target for
criminals.

Education

An employee education program should include three groups within the organization: senior officers, supervisors at all levels, and other employees.

Any effective crime control program must be completely supported by senior
officers. They should also understand the broad outline (not necessarily the
technical details) of the crime control measures and should appreciate the loss
exposures the organization would face if it had no crime control program.
Moreover, senior officers should convey their full support of the program to all
personnel.

Supervisory personnel should also be part of the crime control effort if it is to
succeed. Supervisors should understand and respect the crime control
program's purpose and importance. Experience shows that people who understand the reasons for a crime control program are more likely to accept it. If,
however, supervisors do not believe in the program or do not want it to be
effective, the program cannot be enforced. Risk management personnel
alone cannot enforce the program. To rely merely on an organization's risk
management personnel, without the active participation of supervisors and
managers, is much like depending only on the police of a city, and not on its
citizens, to uphold the law.

All other employees must also be motivated to support a crime control
program. Therefore, education is the cornerstone of an effective security
program. All employees should be part of the program and participate in its
enforcement.

The crime control education of employees can be formal or informal, depending on the size of the organization and the nature of its crime exposures.
Regardless of how it is conducted, education should give each employee a
full explanation of the purposes and extent of the program. However, much

of the data on the technical aspects of the crime control program should not be included in the education because it could allow an employee to subvert any crime control measure.

Educational efforts must not be limited to a lecture on crime control. An effective program should also use employee newsletters, bulletin boards, and participatory meetings. All policies and procedures should be defined in writing. For example, if the organization has a policy that prohibits employees from accepting bribes, that policy should be published and distributed throughout the organization. Employees should also be informed in writing that theft, regardless of the amount, will not be condoned. They should also know the corrective or disciplinary actions that will be taken if they violate any crime control procedures.

An organization's crime control personnel should be responsible only for *assisting* management in corrective or disciplinary actions. The primary responsibility for those actions lies with line management. Crime control procedures should include a plan for supervisors who are reluctant to act when a problem is referred to them. Such a plan often recommends that the problem be referred to higher management.

The importance of employee education in crime control cannot be overstated. The employer or supervisors must properly explain how a crime control system works and why it is needed. The explanation must emphasize that the system is designed to protect the physical safety and reputations of honest employees from violent crime and dishonest employees. After such an explanation, most employees will accept the crime control system as a normal and necessary control.

Applicant Screening

Applicant screening is one preventive measure that should precede the processes of hiring and training employees. If a mistake occurs in selecting some employees, even the best educational and supervisory programs will not prevent those employees from committing serious crime losses.

The primary objective of a screening program is to hire and retain a reasonably suitable, trustworthy, and competent work force. That objective can be met by checking personal and professional references given by prospective employees on their job applications. The organization can also verify previous places of employment, education, and other personal data given by the applicant. Because various state and federal laws that recognize employees' rights to continued employment can complicate efforts to discipline or dismiss an employee, applicant screening often provides the best opportunity to eliminate the crime threats posed by employees.

Transfer of Personnel

Transferring employees within an organization or periodically rotating them is an effective device for preventing crime losses. If employees are aware that their job assignments can be changed, they are less likely to commit crimes that might be discovered after they are transferred. A transfer is not always possible, but rotating employees who hold job positions that involve substantial opportunities for employee theft should be considered. For example, branch managers can occasionally be moved to different offices, and truck drivers can be given different routes. Factory foremen and supervisors can be rotated, and clerks and supervisors who handle the organization's financial affairs can be periodically shifted. A programmer who was responsible for a sensitive activity should be shifted from that program to another.

Some managers might object to rotations, stating that their transfer or their employees' transfers disrupt effective working relationships within departments, create unnecessary staffing and training needs, and complicate career planning. To reduce the number of those objections, rotations should be included in the job descriptions, the transfers should occur in a reasonably predictable fashion, and rotations should be made only as frequently and for as long as necessary. Employees should expect that they will be transferred so that they recognize such shifts as a routine and necessary part of the crime control system that protects them as well as the organization. Above all, it should be clear to all managers and employees that transfers do not imply any discipline problems, suspicion, or criticism of the personnel being transferred.

Reducing Criminals' Perception of Impunity

Persons planning to commit crimes generally anticipate that they will not be caught. Criminals believe they have an easy target, they can act with impunity because their crimes will not be detected, or they will not be identified or not be prosecuted. Therefore, a third fundamental strategy for controlling an organization's crime losses is to change criminals' perception of the organization as a ready target. Two ways of changing that perception are (1) to strengthen the organization's abilities to detect crimes and to identify the criminals and (2) to cooperate fully in prosecuting suspected criminals.

Improving Detection and Identification

Most crimes are easy to detect. Many of the physical and procedural barriers discussed earlier increase the likelihood that crimes will be discovered. Thieves' and violent attackers' attempts to circumvent walls, guards, alarms, dogs, bright lights, and surveillance cameras will probably be discovered. Arsonous fires are naturally spectacular and, after competent investigations, can usually be distinguished from accidental blazes. To coerce or influence others' actions, kidnappers and terrorists must make their crimes known. To succeed, these criminals must be recognized—even feared—by their victims.

Other, more stealthful crimes can easily go unnoticed, and their perpetrators welcome secrecy. Confidence schemes and other forms of fraud as well as embezzlement, forgery, and counterfeiting succeed only if the victims do not recognize that a crime has occurred. For these more devious crimes, the criminals wish to remain undetected or at least unrecognized.

Besides detecting a crime, an organization should take steps to identify the criminal(s). For crimes that occur on an organization's premises (particularly various kinds of theft and acts of violence), surveillance cameras attached to secured videotape recorders can help identify perpetrators. Employees should also be trained to remember as many details as possible (such as height, weight, eye and hair color, distinctive facial features, speech characteristics, or any references by the criminal(s) to names and places) that would help identify suspects. Because it is very difficult to remain alert to such details while a crime is in progress, providing employees with training and role-playing situations is usually helpful. That training also helps employees to maintain composure and to behave appropriately for their own protection.

For crimes of stealth such as embezzlement, confidence schemes, and computer crimes, an organization's normal operating procedures should establish an audit trail of receipts, computer logs, and other documents to trace suspected criminals. Training all employees to be alert to unusual events can also generate information that could be helpful in apprehending and convicting criminals.

Enhancing Prosecution

Organizations that actively work with law enforcement officials to convict suspected criminals reduce their crime losses in two ways. First, helping prosecute suspects can increase an organization's opportunities to recover stolen property or to receive restitution (repayment or compensation) from the criminals. Second, vigorously prosecuting criminals gives an organization a reputation for being tough on crime. Rather than risk the wrath of such a target, criminals will strike a more vulnerable organization.

There are many ways an organization can help prosecute criminals. Even though all crimes are offenses against society and are prosecuted on society's behalf by district attorneys, law enforcement officers depend on the victims. Many people, including the senior managers of many organizations, are reluctant to report crimes and to press charges against suspects. It is often easier to let the crime pass unreported, especially if lodging a criminal complaint would be embarrassing, time-consuming, lead to adverse publicity, or harm employee morale. However, the disadvantages of not prosecuting suspects are greater. Not only will the perpetrators be free to continue victimizing the organization, but other criminals and the organization's employees will also view the organization as being vulnerable to crime.

Being ready to assist in prosecuting suspected criminals requires the proper management attitude and specific procedures. Therefore, reporting suspected crimes and cooperating with law enforcement officials should be duties included in the organization's risk management and crime control policy statements. Moreover, notifying police, interviewing witnesses, and writing detailed incident reports should be part of the procedures required after a suspected criminal incident occurs.

Applications of Control Strategies

What are some of the physical, procedural, and managerial controls you should apply in controlling specific crimes?

How can those controls help reduce computer-based crimes?

Each of the physical, procedural, and managerial controls just discussed can help control many crime losses. This three-part classification of control strategies can suggest many specific measures for controlling virtually any type of crime loss. Without being exhaustive, the rest of this chapter shows some of the ways these strategies can reduce the frequency and severity of each of an organization's potential losses from each of the crimes listed in Exhibit 11-1. Among these, computer-based crimes are especially important because computers provide many opportunities for innovative criminals to perpetrate extremely large thefts. Computer-based crime therefore deserves from risk management professionals the detailed attention it receives in the concluding major section of this chapter.

Applications to Particular Crimes

Appendixes A through M (at the end of this chapter) identify specific physical, procedural, and managerial controls for the crimes to property, persons, and organizations first shown in Exhibit 11-1. These controls do not represent exhaustive lists. Making the lists complete would also make them highly repetitious, since many control measures (especially managerial controls) can be equally effective against many crimes. New ways of committing particular crimes and new ways of trying to prevent or reduce crimes are also constantly emerging. Therefore, for any one of the crimes discussed in those Appendixes, control measures from other crimes could be adopted. Moreover, additional control measures now being developed will belong under the physical, procedural, or managerial headings for several of these crimes.

Applications to Computer Crimes

Organizations of all kinds depend heavily on computers. However, in many organizations, little thought has been given to protecting computers and the information they process. Despite its great advantages, a computer can actually cause serious losses if proper crime control is not in place. This section discusses typical computer-related exposures and describes the controls that can be implemented to ensure adequate, cost-effective crime control.

The first step in designing any computer crime control program is to analyze computer-related exposures. The principal exposures that affect computers can be divided into two classes: (1) those that threaten data and (2) those that threaten the physical integrity of the computer facilities and equipment.

Data-Related Exposures

In addition to the perils that threaten the actual physical computer and its facilities, computer operations are exposed to loss through perils associated with data. Those perils include the following:

- Sabotage, fraud, and embezzlement, which occur as a result of surreptitiously manipulating data
- Time-sharing arrangements that result in unauthorized but overt access to information
- Theft of data through surreptitious listening gear or the covert removal of tapes
- Theft of computer time
- Espionage

Sabotage

Sabotage is the deliberate destruction of property or disruption of productive processes by hostile persons. Sabotage can be as obvious as a bomb or as surreptitious as the application of a large magnet to a computer's magnetic storage media. Striking computer components with heavy objects, spilling caustic solutions on circuit boards and wires, or introducing foreign matter into a computer's or printer's moving parts are acts of sabotage.

The basic hazard underlying sabotage is unauthorized access to the computer installation. Effective access control, including using positive personnel identification procedures, granting access to information on a "need to know" basis, and tightly supervising computer operations and equipment, reduces the probability of loss through sabotage. Another important risk control measure is adequately screening and selecting personnel to ensure a high level of trustworthiness in those who have regular access to the computer.

Any deliberate manipulation of data can render an entire computer program unreliable because manipulation introduces random errors. The results are dangerous and long-lasting for two reasons: (1) the crime is extremely difficult to detect, and (2) the information generated by a computer is used to make decisions and as a basis for ongoing activities in the organization. Because those activities and decisions could be based on erroneous information, sabotage is extremely detrimental to the organization.

Fraud and Embezzlement

An employee can fraudulently manipulate data in many ways. For instance, a single change in a computer program can report abnormally high inventory shortages as breakage losses. Material reported as broken can then be removed without the theft being noted. The evidence can be destroyed by reversing the computerized accounting entry. Alternatively, data processing employees in a financial institution might enrich themselves by rounding off fractions of cents in interest calculations and transferring the accumulated resulting amounts to a personal account. A computer payroll system is also a vehicle for fraud. For example, fictitious paychecks can be printed, or extra wages and overtime can be programmed to be paid to designated persons.

Examples of embezzlement include a computer manager for a pharmaceutical manufacturer who concealed a $1 million inventory shortage at a manufacturing plant, and a back-office investment house employee who embezzled more than $250,000 over seven years, becoming a vice president before his actions were discovered.

Time-Sharing Arrangements That Result in Unauthorized but Overt Access to Data

Time-sharing systems can present some of the greatest dangers to computer operations. Time sharing allows several users access to a single computer in which one or more programs are processed. Access can be through a local area network (LAN) within a single organization (for example, when various departments use the same central computer). Access can also be through a service bureau or central facility that employs a large computer to process several programs for different, unrelated customers. The ultimate time-sharing arrangement is the multiprogram, multiprocess operation in which many users have access to a single mainframe for simultaneously processing many unrelated programs.

The three basic crime control objectives associated with time sharing are (1) ensuring that only authorized persons have access to a program, (2) preventing a system malfunction from accidentally disclosing data, and (3) preventing unauthorized access that would result from the unauthorized change or manipulation of data.

The most common way to limit computer access to authorized persons only is to use a code or password. To gain access, each person using the computer must first give a personal code or password, which can be as elaborate as required and should be known only to the person who will use it. Furthermore, the code or password could be valid only if given together with some other item of personal identification, such as name or payroll number. The computer will check those two items against a stored memory table to confirm that they are the two required matching items. Making the code or password truly random, not related in any way to personal identification data, achieves a high level of access control.

Crime controls can be defeated, however, if the authorized person deliberately or negligently discloses the password or if some other person who knows the password further discloses it. Another breach of security could occur if the computer is not programmed to suppress passwords and not to repeat or print them out elsewhere in the network.

A more elaborate check on unauthorized access requires both a physical identifier and a password. For example, a card can be coded with personalized information in a magnetic format. The authorized person would insert the card into a card reader that controls the computer's electrical supply or activates an intrusion alarm. That person's card must be used along with a password to activate the terminal and/or to prevent an alarm from sounding if the terminal is used. The authorized person's fingerprints, voiceprint, or retina scan can also be used as a physical identifier.

Finally, access from remote terminals can be made more secure by restricting each person to preassigned terminals or programs. Each personal password authorizes access only to certain terminals or programs. A supervisory program within the central mainframe should signal any attempt to gain access to a program not authorized for that user, stop all data output to that terminal, and print a description of the attempted unauthorized transaction.

Each additional measure in the chain of security adds to the overall crime control cost, mostly as software costs because of the additional programming required. The extent to which crime control measures are implemented should be determined by the criticality/cost trade-offs and the availability of alternative countermeasures.

Theft of Data Through Surreptitious Listening Devices or Covert Removal of Tapes

Thieves typically steal data to learn trade secrets or to determine a competitor's marketing or financial strategy. Stealing data by computer can be devastating because most organizations with computerized operations have *all* their business data on a computer. Given access to that data, the thief is ensured of success. If a thief does not have the advantage of being part of a time-sharing arrangement, the thief could steal data by using surreptitious listening gear or by covertly removing hard copy or tapes from the computer facility.

Surreptitious Listening Devices   Vast amounts of data are in transit among computers within a facility or among computers in different facilities. Therefore, one way to steal electromagnetic data is to intercept ongoing communications by tapping into a line or an electronic signal that moves data either from unit to unit within a computer center or to other locations. To accomplish the theft, the thief must get close to the computer center or to the communications link, have suitable equipment to monitor the electronic signals and to identify the frequency used to transmit the data, and convert the electronic signal into readable messages. The thief need not do everything from the original access point. It is enough to record the transmission, carry the recording away, and, when convenient, reduce the recorded data to readable messages.

Three crime control measures to reduce or prevent theft of data are (1) to physically encase the computer facility in protective electronic shielding to suppress the transmission of signals, (2) to "harden" the communication link through which information is sent to or from the computer, which involves using shielded cables for hard-wire connections and randomly changing microwave and radio signal frequencies, and (3) to process the data to make it difficult to capture and/or read. The third option involves two techniques, simultaneous transmissions and encoding.

Simultaneous transmission is the simpler and less expensive alternative. That alternative simultaneously transmits multiple communications over the same link. The communications can be nonsense signals or legitimate mixed messages. To recover any specific communication, the receiver or interceptor must recognize and filter out all the other signals to isolate the targeted one. For anyone except the intended receiver, that process can be so difficult or expensive that it precludes any serious effort at theft by anyone outside the computer center.

Encoding is the more complex and expensive crime control option. It involves encrypting and decrypting data, which increase the chance of mistakes because of frequent changes in codes or because of human error.

Because encasing and encoding are expensive, they are usually reserved for computers running highly sensitive information. However, when proprietary information is of great value, those options should be considered, particularly as part of plans for new computer centers.

Another consideration in developing crime control measures for the theft of data is the location of the interceptor. The closer the interceptor is to the initiating or receiving terminal, the easier is the interceptor's task. Sound risk control should provide more protection at the points of origin and receipt of computer data than at other locations. If the data are transmitted by telephone line, the simultaneous transmission technique just described automatically becomes a crime control feature when the computer signal is transmitted with other signals on common carrier telephone lines. Also, the telephone company essentially provides automatic protection. Based on the signal load, the automatic telephone company switchgear selects the optimum transmission path at the moment the message is sent. Consequently, the thief has no way of knowing in advance what path the signal will take. The thief is thus faced with the dual problem of multiple signals and an unknown signal path.

A final consideration in developing crime control measures for this type of theft is the attacker who can gain access to the wires *inside* the transmitting or the receiving terminal. Accessing and retrieving data in this way is like any other telephone tap. It involves either physical or inductive electronic connections between the targeted terminal and the surreptitious listening device. That connection is possible from any point at which the target computer is accessible. The leads from the computer center to the various telephone terminal boards and from the terminal boards into cables leaving the facility are all vulnerable. Adequate physical crime control measures must also be maintained over the link from the junction points outside the facility back to the computer on one end and to the input/output terminal on the other. Achieving crime control means locking terminal and mainframe rooms, enforcing strict controls on people who have access to areas that contain communications equipment, and maintaining cooperative arrangements with the telephone company in providing acceptable protection for junction points on the perimeter of the premises. That protection will probably be some combination of lock controls, live surveillance, and intrusion alarms.

Covert Removal of Computerized Records   When there are no effective security controls, a thief with access to the computer center can quickly and easily remove or copy records or tapes. Those materials can be used by the thief or sold. The materials often include secret customer lists, invaluable product information, or crucial operating procedures.

Theft of Computer Time

The unauthorized use by employees of computer time for personal purposes is a significant kind of theft. That theft can occur when computer use is not supervised or audited. Risk control efforts to reduce the possibility of loss from this peril include keeping a continuous record of each person who has had access to computer hardware or software, along with the dates and times of their use. An **exceptions logbook** should maintain a record of program running times. Anyone can examine the log to ensure that the necessary programs were run and that unscheduled programs were not run. Sometimes computer personnel maintain records for an outside business run by themselves or others. (The unauthorized use of computer time for personal reasons also increases the probability of loss from the surreptitious manipulation of data.)

Espionage

Because computer systems now store most of the information essential to an organization's operation, espionage is a primary peril. That crime can be committed most easily from within the facility housing the computer. Copies of disks, tapes, or computer-generated reports could contain concentrations of data that would otherwise take a thief months or years to accumulate. In organizations centered around proprietary processes, data could be available from process control programs or from computer-generated management reports.

A spy can acquire information either as hard copy or in a computer-readable format, as on a magnetic tape or disk. Unsupervised access to information is usually enough for a skilled thief with a good memory. When information has been stolen but no evidence of its theft exists, the loss is doubly expensive because the victimized organization continues to operate on the assumption that the data are safe. If the breach in security had been known, additional losses and related expenses might have been avoided even if the data could not have been retrieved.

Access Controls for Computer Facilities

Most of the perils, other than natural perils, that threaten a computer facility occur because access to the building and/or to the computer is weakly controlled or not controlled at all. Risk control efforts to maintain computer security include controlling access to the following:

- The entire computer facility
- Designated portions of the facility that house especially sensitive activities
- Particular computer programs

Building/Facility Access

A physical control system should prohibit unauthorized personnel and visitors from entering any part of the computer facility. Some organizations, however, view their computer installations as showplaces. Those organizations encourage visitors and often fail to take minimum security precautions because they have not adequately considered the potentially serious losses that might result from open access.

Access controls for the computer center should deal separately with two time periods: (1) when the center is not in use and (2) when it is in use. When the center is not in use, the entrance and all other openings should be securely locked. The walls, ceilings, doors, and floors should also be constructed so that surreptitious entry is difficult and any break-in is obvious enough to signal a security center. A proper security system should also be installed, including alarms that signal surreptitious and forced entry as well as periodic, but randomly timed, inspections by human or canine guards.

When the computer center is being used, entry can be controlled in several ways. It is good practice to secure the entrance with a lock and to designate someone to monitor and keep a log of who enters and leaves the premises. If the center is occupied by only a few employees, an on-site supervisor can be given responsibility for access control. A telephone, doorbell, or other audio connection could be installed outside the center for those seeking admittance. More elaborate security controls could include closed-circuit television with a camera outside and a monitor inside the center or at a central security station. If the computer area is too large or the traffic through the entrance too heavy to be controlled from inside the center, someone at a desk outside the entrance could control entry.

Regardless of overall control, an accurate, current list of those authorized to enter is essential. That list should either be held by the employee controlling access or should be incorporated into automated access controls.

Area Access Within Buildings

Not all people working in a computer facility need free access to all its areas. Programmers, for example, will usually not require access to the main computer controls. Similarly, most operators do not need access to areas where files are maintained. Access to areas within the center should be properly controlled. Access to the entire facility should be given only to those persons whose responsibilities require it.

Because software and data files are essential to computer systems, a storage library should be established, and access controls should be implemented to protect that library. Authorized personnel should have access only to specified parts of the library, and files should be removed from the library only when needed for specific tasks. Records of file use should be kept, and a file should be checked in and out of the library in the name of the person actually taking the file.

Only one person or operating group should be responsible for any operation at any one time. Sharp distinctions of authority and responsibility are necessary among employees who authorize a computer transaction, those who produce the input, those who process the data, and those who use the output. Distinctions of authority and responsibility should also govern scheduling, manual and machine operations, maintenance of programs, and related functions. Programmers should not have access to the entire library of programs, nor should they operate the hardware without permission. If those programming and project duties are properly separated, the probability of loss to hardware or software is reduced. The technique of separating duties is discussed again at the end of the chapter as part of the section on developing an integrated crime control program.

Access to Computer Software and Output

Despite efforts to physically protect the computer center and areas within the buildings, data can still be innocently or intentionally damaged. The potential harm can be sharply reduced by controls built directly into software programs. The controls signal most types of errors or unauthorized procedures. Developing those controls is a programming task, but ensuring that the controls are used is a management responsibility with the following requirements:

- *Restrict the ability to change master files* to personnel other than those who handle day-to-day operations. That restriction reduces opportunities for fraud. If the person who handles the daily operations cannot change the master file and the person who changes the file does not have regular access to the operating programs, the chance that either person alone can make an improper change to the data is reduced. If the programs themselves automatically update master files, then copies of such files (made before updating) should be retained long enough to confirm that the updates are correct.

- *Document master data changes* by requiring authorized signatures, limiting access to serially numbered forms, and retaining the authorization document until the updating is verified.

- *Require limits to be stated on the face of checks* issued by the organization to ensure that a large disbursement cannot be made without executive approval. For example, a check might carry the message "Not Valid For More Than $100" or "No Paycheck Exceeds $2,500."

- *Establish individual users' territories* within the computer memory so that only authorized personnel have access to sensitive information and programs.

- *Test new programs* before allowing them to process actual data. Tests should not be run on line or on production files to guard against the possibility that testing a faulty program will disrupt operations or destroy important data.

- *Use batch and hash (cross-check) totals* to ensure that all required transactions have been performed but unauthorized transactions have not. Those totals use input data to verify operating processes. For example, if a given number of consecutively numbered sales orders have to be processed, the serial numbers of the individual orders can be totaled. Comparing the serial number total with a predetermined reference total would indicate any omitted or inserted order(s).

- *Maintain time and error logs* to record the time it takes to perform computer activities. Program standards, mentioned earlier, should indicate how much time is required for various normal computer runs. The time logs will then indicate how much time was actually used for various operations. If the actual time exceeds the "normal" time by a significant margin, then the accompanying error log should contain an explanation of the additional time used to correct an error. If no error is indicated, there should be some other explanation for the extra computer running time. If no explanation is found, supervisors and management should investigate the possibility of unauthorized computer use.

Summary

This chapter explains the distinctive features of crime as a peril, describes the characteristic of crimes that most often cause losses to organizations, explains general strategies for controlling crime losses, and details how to apply those strategies to control losses from specific crimes, especially computer-based crimes.

Like perils, criminal activity against an organization can cause it to incur property, liability, personnel, and net income losses. Unlike other perils that strike by chance or out of human carelessness, crime is guided by the hostile intelligence of criminals, whose constant search for opportunities to commit crime forces those who control crime losses to be continuously vigilant.

To reduce their losses from crimes, organizations and risk management professionals should (1) reduce the hostility that employees and others feel toward the organization, (2) adopt physical, procedural, and managerial controls to reduce criminals' opportunities to commit crimes, and (3) act vigorously to detect and prosecute persons suspected of crimes against the organization.

Those strategies are applicable to all crimes, but especially to computer-based criminal activity. Protecting a computer center and the equipment and information it contains requires coordinating most of the crime control measures described throughout this chapter. Thus, safeguarding a computer facility entails protecting the computer building and equipment against fire, sabotage, industrial accidents, natural disasters, and mechanical/electrical malfunctions in the equipment serving the building and in the computer hardware itself. Protecting the data processed within a computer center requires special attention to threats of embezzlement, espionage, and other forms of surreptitious theft. Controlling access to a computer center as a whole, to specific areas in a computer facility, and to particular programs or data is essential to safeguarding the facility and its operations.

Chapter Note

1. The material under this heading is drawn from James S. Trieschmann et al., *Commercial Property Insurance and Risk Management*, 4th ed., vol. 1 (Malvern, PA: American Institute for CPCU, 1994), pp. 83, 86-92.

Appendix A

Representative Controls Against Burglary

Physical Controls

- Install and maintain perimeter protection of premises (fences, lighting, alarms, guards, cleared space around premises).
- Use appropriate locks, vaults/safes, and exterior doors.
- Install surveillance cameras attached to off-site videotape recorders.
- Place "marked" cash and other property in vaults/safes to help trace and identify burglars.
- Eliminate places of possible concealment for burglars.

Procedural Controls

- Train personnel to watch for potential burglars reconnoitering premises.
- Adopt premises and safe/vault opening and closing procedures that should frustrate and trap burglars.
- Develop and practice procedures for notifying and cooperating with police.
- Caution employees against sharing information about premises with others.
- Check premises for unauthorized persons just before closing and just before opening.
- Control access to combinations to vaults/safes and change combinations frequently (especially when a senior employee leaves the organization).

Special Managerial Controls

- Inform employees about burglary peril and hazards.
- Keep records of burglary losses.
- Include burglary loss control in managerial performance standards.

Appendix B

Representative Controls Against Robbery

Physical Controls

- Install physical barriers inside premises to shield personnel from potential robbers.
- Install safes and vaults with time locks that only a few employees know how to open.
- Place surveillance cameras in vulnerable locations.
- Employ guards and/or plainclothes security personnel.
- Place "marked" cash or other valuables in registers or other locations to help trace and identify robbers.
- Install silent alarms that signal police or a private security service.

Procedural Controls

- Decrease the amount of cash and other valuables at any one vulnerable location.
- Make effective use of any vaults or safes (do not leave them unlocked and do not leave valuable property in the open).
- Run bank errands involving cash deposits or withdrawals at random times, and travel by varying routes to and from bank so that robbers cannot predict bank visits and wait in ambush.
- Train personnel in surreptitiously sounding silent alarms.
- Train personnel in dealing with robbers for their and others' safety (remember features, speech, names, and other details that can help track robbers and delay their departure until police arrive, provided delay does not endanger others).
- Post in public areas prominent signs indicating that employees cannot open safes/vaults.

Special Managerial Controls

- Screen present employees and job applicants for records of past crimes.
- Educate employees about general precautions the organization has taken against robbery.
- Assist law enforcement personnel in apprehending and prosecuting burglary suspects.

Appendix C

Representative Controls Against Shoplifting

Physical Controls

- Install surveillance cameras (some obvious to discourage potential shoplifters and others hidden to record actions of actual shoplifters).
- Employ plainclothes security personnel to watch for shoplifters.
- Attach magnetic tags or other markers to vulnerable items of merchandise to signal alarms if merchandise is removed from premises without payment or other authorization.
- Arrange store, installing mirrors as needed, so that all areas are directly visible from at least one cash register station.
- Post prominent public signs indicating that shoplifters will be prosecuted.

Procedural Controls

- Train employees in how to spot and discourage potential shoplifters and in how to deal effectively with actual shoplifters without exposing themselves or the store to tort liability.
- Screen present employees and job applicants for records of past shoplifting.
- Establish procedures to prevent employees from sneaking merchandise out of the store at the end of their shifts.
- Staff each cash register with at least two employees, with rotating assignments, to discourage employees from colluding among themselves or with others in committing, encouraging, or allowing shoplifting.

Special Managerial Controls

- Make all employees part of an organization-wide "team" to combat shoplifting because it directly or indirectly lowers all employees' take-home pay.

- Educate customers about how shoplifting raises costs and prices.
- Encourage regular customers to alert store employees to possible shoplifters, but not to take "vigilante" action themselves.
- Prosecute suspected shoplifters vigorously but carefully to avoid tort claims for assault, battery, false arrest, or wrongful arrest and prosecution.

Appendix D

Representative Controls Against Fraud

Physical Controls

- Control access to premises to be sure only legitimate persons enter.
- Use videotape cameras to record retail sales and members of public entering premises.

Procedural Controls

- Apply the procedural controls for embezzlement (shown in Appendix E) and computer crime (shown in Appendix M).
- Confirm identity of persons entering premises and their reasons for entering.
- Conduct frequent, unannounced audits to detect any unusual transaction.
- Verify good business reputation of persons and firms with which organization deals either as a buyer or a seller of goods and services.
- Keep complete, accurate, detailed business records to discourage fraud, detect fraud when it occurs, and identify and trace perpetrators.
- Transfer or rotate employees among positions to safeguard against collusion among them or with outsiders.

Special Managerial Controls

- Apply the managerial controls for embezzlement (shown in Appendix E) and computer crime (shown in Appendix M).
- Keep managers and employees who deal with the public alert to the many possibilities for fraud.
- Stay informed of new varieties of fraud, especially those new to the organization's industry or activities.
- Bring criminal and civil charges against persons suspected of fraud.

Appendix E

Representative Controls Against Embezzlement

Physical Controls

- Keep under lock and key all documents used in making or recording all the organization's incoming or outgoing cash or credit transactions (checks, receipts, purchase orders, bills of lading, vouchers, and customers' records) so that embezzlers cannot use them to drain funds from the organization.

- Use locked doors, guards, cameras, or other barriers to control physical access to areas or operations where vulnerable property and records are kept or processed, especially computer operations.

- Install and use vaults and safes, keeping valuable property under lock and key except when it is being used or processed.

- Monitor employees who are handling cash, jewelry, or highly vulnerable property or performing other sensitive tasks with video cameras on a continuous or random basis.

- Implement physical controls for computer crimes, since much embezzlement is done through computers.

Procedural Controls

- Number consecutively all documents related to incoming or outgoing cash or credit transactions so that any misuse of these documents to embezzle funds can be readily recognized and traced.

- Divide among several employees responsibility for performing and documenting all tasks related to incoming or outgoing cash and credit transactions so that no employee has complete control over both doing and recording any activity related to cash.

- Require all employees to take vacations so that one employee's control over any task is not continuous for long periods.

- Rotate employees among tasks for this same purpose.
- Conduct regular, unannounced audits by both internal and external auditors.
- Conduct independent checks of payroll and other payment records to ensure that those records accurately reflect payments to actual persons or organizations that have provided the organization with the goods or services for which the payments have been made.
- Verify records of sales, deliveries, and purchases of goods and services to confirm that these records reflect real transactions and do not mask embezzlements.
- Maintain strict controls of inventories of goods in process, merchandise, and supplies to counter embezzlement of property other than cash.
- Inspect incoming and outgoing shipments of goods, supplies, and raw materials to detect shortages or defects through which employees, alone or through collusion with outsiders, may embezzle.
- Implement procedural controls for computer crime losses, since much embezzlement is perpetrated through computers.
- Screen job applicants or present employees seeking job transfers for records of past embezzlement convictions or attempts.

Special Managerial Controls

- Educate employees about the threat of embezzlement, its effects on the organization's profits (and therefore employees' compensation), and the organization's efforts to prevent it.
- Encourage supervisors and other managers to counsel with, or call to management's attention, any employee who is under such financial or other personal pressure that he or she may be tempted to embezzle.
- Prosecute or dismiss suspected embezzlers or, if this is impractical, transfer them to positions that offer less opportunity for embezzlement.
- Remain alert to changes in operating procedures or technology that might offer new opportunities for embezzlers.

Appendix F

Representative Controls Against Counterfeiting/ Forgery

Physical Controls

- Maintain very strict security over organization's documents (checks, vouchers, bills of lading, purchase orders, and receipts), which, if stolen, would facilitate counterfeiting or forgery against the organization.
- Use a clearly visible camera to make a videotape recording of all customers at cash registers or other points of payment to help identify persons suspected of forgery or counterfeiting.
- Photograph all checks, money orders, and other noncash forms of payment to aid in identifying and tracing forged or counterfeit documents.
- Post prominent public notices that forgers and counterfeiters will be vigorously prosecuted.

Procedural Controls

- Accept payment in the form of only certified or cashiers' checks, if possible and without losing customers.
- Train employees in (1) recognizing counterfeit currency or checks with irregularities that indicate they may have been forged and (2) delaying, questioning, or otherwise dealing with suspected forgers in ways that discourage them from completing their transactions or trace them after their transactions have been completed.
- Train employees in recognizing altered or expired credit cards.
- Instruct employees never to depart from standard procedures in making credit card transactions.

- Require valid forms of identification from all persons not paying in cash.
- Alert employees to distracting or disconcerting tactics through which counterfeiters and forgers can lead employees to depart from standard precautions when accepting and obtaining authorization for check or credit card payments.

Special Managerial Controls

- Educate personnel in general methods and importance of controlling forgery and counterfeiting losses.
- Give special recognition or other appropriate rewards to employees who make special efforts to control these losses.
- Assist authorities in prosecuting forgers and counterfeiters and also initiate private tort suits for such wrongs as fraud and conversion (tortious theft of personal property) where appropriate.
- Remain alert to new methods of making payments or other technological changes that may open new opportunities for forgery and counterfeiting.

Appendix G

Representative Controls Against Vandalism

Physical Controls

- Establish perimeter safeguards for premises like those established to protect against burglary.
- Minimize amount or value of property that invites vandals (large windows, signs, or items of great value that are visible from streets or sidewalks).
- Keep videotape records and maintain logs of all visitors entering the property.
- Garage vehicles and movable equipment in secure locations that vandals cannot enter.

Procedural Controls

- Search persons entering premises for weapons or other means of causing damage (such as strong magnets in computer facilities).
- Escort visitors at all times while on premises.
- Remove keys, passes, passwords, identification cards, and other forms of authorization from any employee who retires, becomes disabled for an extended period, is discharged, or is given disciplinary leave.

Special Managerial Controls

- Remain alert to, and try to defuse, signs of hostility from the community or political activists.
- Maintain friendly (or at least not overtly hostile) relationships with all employees, their families, suppliers, customers, and others who may seek vengeance against the organization.
- Communicate any specific concerns about possible vandalism to police and public fire officials.

Appendix H

Representative Controls Against Arson (By Persons Other Than Owner or Manager)

Physical Controls

- Adopt measures for preventing or reducing accidental fires (presented in Chapter 3) so that property will not burn readily and any fires can be quickly extinguished.
- Install locks for vulnerable areas, especially storage areas where arsonists might find flammable liquids and combustibles with which to set fire.
- Apply physical controls for combating vandalism (arson being an extreme form of vandalism).

Procedural Controls

- Frequently inspect premises, especially storage areas.
- Screen present employees and job applicants for past arson activities or tendencies toward pyromania.
- Post guards, especially when the organization is closed for several days (as during holidays or labor union disputes).
- Work with police and fire departments on arson control procedures, particularly with respect to persons considered hostile to the organization.
- Implement fire emergency response plans to reduce damage and the time operations are interrupted after any fire (including arson).

Special Managerial Controls

- Seek to identify and counsel or terminate relationships with any employees, customers, suppliers, or other persons who may be so hostile to the organization that they may be tempted to commit arson against it.

- Avoid, or be very careful in undertaking, activities so controversial that they may trigger political activists to commit arson against the organization.

- Alert employees to arson threat and to the measures the organization is taking to counter that threat.

Representative Controls Against Violent Attack and Homicide

Physical Controls

- Provide doors, walls, locks, fences, guards, guard dogs, and lighting, as appropriate, to keep attackers out of areas occupied or traveled by people.
- Install alarms, intercom systems, or telephones in these areas so that victims or threatened persons may summon help.
- Use videotape cameras linked to monitors in guard stations to record activities in vulnerable areas, and keep a visual record of events that occurred in the past twenty-four hours.
- Equip vulnerable personnel (especially executives when traveling) with appropriate personal protective devices (such as bulletproof automobiles and vests).

Procedural Controls

- Limit access to protected areas (use keys, passwords, badges, guards, or similar measures) so that only authorized persons can enter.
- Search all persons entering premises for weapons.
- Train personnel in how to avoid or how to escape areas or situations where they are particularly vulnerable to attack.
- Train personnel in self-defense measures that do not endanger them.
- Provide escorts to visitors or employees occupying or traversing hazardous areas.
- Encourage personnel to avoid statements or conduct that may invite attack.

- Encourage personnel to inform their supervisors or other appropriate personnel of family situations or other circumstances that might make them targets for attacks.

- Discourage personnel from working or walking alone in areas of the organization's premises that might attract attackers.

- Train executives and other vulnerable personnel in techniques for evading attackers.

Special Managerial Controls

- Keep informed of workplace and other community violence and appropriate countermeasures.

- Support community efforts to control violent public attacks.

- Cooperate in prosecuting violent attackers and, when appropriate, assist in pursuing tort claims against them.

Appendix J

Representative Controls Against Kidnapping

Physical Controls

- Implement the same perimeter and access controls as those implemented to prevent burglary and vandalism.
- Provide bodyguards for vulnerable personnel when traveling.
- Install silent alarms, concealed video cameras, and other devices that enable executives and vulnerable personnel to signal the organization's security personnel or public law enforcement officials if they feel threatened by potential kidnappers.

Procedural Controls

- Educate executives and other vulnerable personnel in recognizing and avoiding situations where they may be kidnapped.
- Train executives and other vulnerable personnel in techniques for evading kidnappers.
- Have vulnerable personnel travel at random times by varying routes (both to and from work and on business trips) so that kidnappers cannot easily plan where to wait in ambush.
- Train executives and other vulnerable personnel (together with their families) in appropriate ways of dealing with kidnappers when in their custody and, if safely practical, escaping from them.
- Develop and practice techniques for coded communication between kidnap victims and their employers and families (secret words or gestures that may be communicated by telephone or television).
- Work with local, national, and international law enforcement officials on procedures for avoiding kidnapping, appropriate conduct while in kidnappers' custody, determining optimum strategies for negotiating with kidnappers, and paying ransoms when appropriate.

- Arrange with the organization's bankers and other sources of funds procedures for obtaining funds needed to pay ransoms, for delivering the ransom money, and for marking it so that the funds and kidnappers can be traced and identified.

Special Managerial Controls

- Ask senior management to decide on the extent of kidnapping hazard the organization should tolerate as a risk when doing business.
- Evaluate the ability and willingness of present executives, vulnerable persons, and their families (as well as new applicants for those positions) to deal with being kidnapped.
- Remain alert to changes in the political and economic environment that might change the level of kidnapping hazard to which the organization's personnel are exposed.

Representative Controls Against Terrorism

Physical Controls

- Disguise premises or operations in order to operate in secrecy or anonymity.
- Establish extremely strong perimeter protection to control entry, comparable to that of a military facility.
- Implement the same physical controls that combat robbery, kidnapping, and vandalism.
- Establish alternative emergency facilities for continuing crucial activities and protecting vital executives and other personnel.

Procedural Controls

- Communicate with law enforcement and other government officials about the potential for terrorist actions and the range of appropriate responses to various situations.
- Inform employees of the potential for terrorism, and train them and their families in proper conduct (on and off the job) for reducing the threat of terrorism and for dealing with actual terrorists.
- Implement the same procedural controls that combat robbery, kidnapping, and vandalism.

Special Managerial Controls

- Formulate organizational policies and crisis response plan for dealing with terrorism.
- Develop, or secure from an outside source, expertise in negotiating with terrorists.
- Inform employees of the potential for terrorism, and train them and their families in proper conduct (on and off the job) for reducing the threat of terrorism and for dealing with actual terrorists.

Appendix L

Representative Controls Against Espionage

Physical Controls

- Implement the same physical controls that combat embezzlement and vandalism.

- Erect physical barriers to hide sensitive activities and information.

- Keep sensitive information in vaults or other locked areas.

Procedural Controls

- Convert most sensitive records and communications to codes (encryption) and create false substitute records if appropriate.

- Implement the same procedural controls that combat embezzlement and vandalism.

- Involve as few people as possible in sensitive activities.

- Ask law enforcement officials to perform security checks on persons who have, or apply to have, access to sensitive activities and information.

- Limit access to sensitive activities and information so that only authorized persons see or work with it.

- Spread portions of sensitive information and of each sensitive activity among several persons so that no one person has access to all aspects of a sensitive project.

- Educate employees about the espionage threat, how the organization is combating that threat, and what employees should do, on and off the job, to reduce that threat.

Special Managerial Controls

- Implement the same managerial controls that combat embezzlement and vandalism.

- Decide whether sensitive activities that attract espionage generate sufficient revenue or other benefits to outweigh the loss exposures those activities create.

Appendix M

Representative Controls Against Computer Crime

Physical Controls

- Limit access to computer facilities using locked doors, badges, and guards so that only authorized persons have access.

- Screen all new hardware and software for computer viruses before allowing their use in the organization's computer system.

- Employ computer passwords, and restrict physical access to software so that each user is able to use only the software he or she needs to carry out that user's responsibilities.

- Locate computer facilities in a structure that is relatively safe from vandals or other attack and that blocks external electronic or radio signals.

- Install devices to electronically shield computer operations from external interference or eavesdropping.

- Monitor and record users, each user's time, and software programs used.

- Implement the same physical controls that combat embezzlement, espionage, and vandalism.

Procedural Controls

- Screen present personnel and new job applicants for records of any past computer-related crime.

- Implement the same procedural controls that combat embezzlement, espionage, and vandalism.

Special Managerial Controls

- Educate personnel about the general features of computer-related crime, how the organization is combating it, and how employees' conduct (on and off the job) can reduce exposures to computer-related crime.

- Implement the same managerial controls that combat embezzlement, espionage, and vandalism.

- Remain alert to innovations in computers and other technology, as well as changes in the organization's operations, that may create new opportunities for computer-related crime and therefore call for innovative crime loss controls.

Chapter 12

System Safety

System Safety

Almost everything in the universe, from the largest galaxy to the smallest subatomic particle, can be considered a **system**, that is, a set of interacting elements that perform some function. One authority has related the system concept to general management (and, by extension, to risk management) by noting the following:

> Almost anything can be viewed as a system. Recently, a new cigarette was prominently advertised as a "Total System" in which tobacco, filter, and paper are arranged in perfect balance with each other. An automobile is a mechanical system of hundreds of parts. A flower is a botanical system. A horse is a zoological system. A human being is a physiological and psychological system consisting of cells, a heart, lungs, attitudes, expectations, and many other elements. A business firm is a sociotechnical system because it combines human organization and a technology of machines, materials, production, marketing processes, and so forth.[1]

The organizations that risk management professionals strive to protect from loss are systems. Their machines, organizational structures, transportation networks, production processes, inflows of raw materials, outflows of finished products, and services are also systems. A core duty of all risk management professionals is to keep these systems operating, thereby preventing system failure and maintaining system efficiency.

Viewing an organization as a set of systems (from an organization's steam boiler thermostat to its global marketing network) enables risk management professionals to apply many system-related concepts to reduce the frequency or severity of accidents. In a system context, these accidents are viewed as disruptions, that is, full or partial system failures. The system-related concepts are grouped under the term "system safety."

System safety includes various techniques for analyzing potential accidents and reducing the frequency or severity of those accidents. The term is a misnomer because it focuses on the failures and not the successes of a system.

Adding to its seeming complexity, the term is also used to refer to many different techniques. For example, the Systems Safety Society recognizes at least thirty techniques of system safety analysis, each having its own name and many being restricted to particular applications.[2] Rather than emphasizing the specific techniques, this chapter describes the fundamental purpose and logic of all system safety techniques.

To illustrate how the concept of system safety can help to prevent system failures, consider an accident that a computer manufacturer might experience: the brakes on one of the manufacturer's trucks fail while the truck is transporting a computer mainframe to a customer, thus preventing delivery by a specified contract date. This accident can be viewed within several systems, including the following:

- The brake mechanism itself, consisting only of its mechanical parts

- The brake system for the truck, including the brake mechanism, the driver's foot on the brake pedal, and the truck tires on the highway

- The driver/vehicle/highway system that transports the computer mainframe

- The transportation system (truck, rail, ship, or air) through which the computer manufacturer delivers its products to customers

- The overall management system of the computer manufacturer

- The overall economic/legal system of the United States

A system-oriented analysis of this accident allows a risk management professional to view the accident from many perspectives. Each system suggests different ways in which this accident might occur and how the frequency or severity of such accidents could be reduced. The following are the systems that can be analyzed and examples of control measures related to each system:

System	*Control Measure*
The mechanical system of the brake mechanism itself	Purchase better mechanisms or replace them more often
The truck's brake system	Purchase trucks that use a better kind of brake
The driver/vehicle/highway system	Select routes that require less braking
The manufacturer's transportation system	Find a more cost-effective way to transport goods to customers
The manufacturer's overall management system	Focus senior management's attention on transportation safety
The United States' economic/legal system	Revise the manufacturer's contracts of sale to excuse delays in delivery caused by specified types of accidents

This example illustrates at least three advantages of system safety to risk management programs:

1. By considering how an accident impairs various systems, risk management professionals can follow an orderly process for developing a range of risk control measures that improve the reliability of interrelated systems.

2. Since systems differ in scope, risk management professionals can use the system safety approach to enlist the cooperation of many people within and beyond the organization. In this case, those asked would include (1) the computer manufacturer's purchasing and mainframe personnel (responsible for buying and maintaining trucks with adequate braking systems), (2) the manufacturer's senior management (responsible for coordinating the work of all departments), (3) legal experts (responsible for reviewing contracts with the customers), and (4) legislative and possibly judicial officials (responsible for interpreting contracts).

3. By using safety analysis, risk management professionals can reduce accident frequency and severity rates by defining and preventing events that lead to particular accidents.

Given these advantages of system safety, this chapter first describes the characteristics common to all systems and explains how system safety can protect the integrity and reliability of any system whose failure can bring losses to the organization. The chapter then reviews popular techniques of system safety analysis.

Characteristics of a System

What are the components of a system?

What is the purpose of a system?

How do changes in an organization's environment affect safety efforts?

What is the life cycle of a system?

All systems are characterized by their components, purpose, environment, and life cycle. By understanding the characteristics of systems, risk management professionals can protect the integrity and reliability of any system.

Components

Since systems vary, care must be taken to describe the components of systems in ways that are broad enough to include all the activities of the system yet sufficiently specific to be meaningful. All systems have three **components:**

1. The physical elements of the system
2. The subsystems that compose major systems
3. The forces that energize movement within the system

Physical Elements

All systems that concern risk management professionals have physical components, such as machine parts, sections of highway, or bones and sinews. Some systems might also contain nonphysical elements, such as the system of traffic laws, which are often considered part of the environment of a system, its purpose(s), or the energy powering the system.

The system's physical elements deserve special risk management attention because any impairment of a physical element of a system can jeopardize the system's ability to perform. Accidental impairments have traditionally been a risk management or safety responsibility. Other forms of impairment (deterioration or technological obsolescence, for example) have been the responsibility of other managers. The system approach eliminates this distinction.

Subsystems

Virtually all systems consist of **subsystems**. The skeletal, muscular, circulatory, nervous, and respiratory systems are subsystems of the larger system known as the human body. The accounting, data processing, production, maintenance, and utility supply systems are among the subsystems of a business. Any organization is also a subsystem within its industry.

Subsystems can be nested at several levels within one another. Within the organization's accounting subsystem, "payroll records" is a sub-subsystem. Regardless of how deeply nested, all systems are typically also subsystems. For example, a single pressure relief valve on one tank is a subsystem within the larger system of a petrochemical complex.

The subsystem concept is essential to effective risk control. Operating even the largest system reliably can be jeopardized when a single, deeply nested subsystem fails. For example, an entire petrochemical complex can explode because of a faulty pressure relief valve. Therefore, an organization's risk management professional must understand all the organization's systems. The risk management professional must also understand how these systems interact and how the failure of any subsystem can endanger other, larger systems, including the entire organization.

Energy and Movement

Systems are powered by energy. For example, a pressure relief valve must release when pressure becomes excessive, and a transportation system must move persons or cargo. Risk management professionals must protect the integrity of organizations' systems by ensuring the reliability of energy and movement. To do this, risk management professionals (1) protect the ability of a system's parts to move as planned, (2) ensure a supply of energy to power a system when needed, and (3) guard against this energy escaping and causing harm.

Purpose

Every system has one or more purposes. For example, a food product container must protect the food from temperature extremes and allow the consumer to see the product before purchasing it. As another example, a fire detection/suppression system must be designed for the type of fire it will combat, the interior design of the structure in which it is installed, and the building contents being safeguarded.

To assess the adequacy of physical components or energy sources of a system, risk management professionals must know the purpose of that component or energy source. Each physical element must be sufficiently strong and properly adapted to its purpose, including unintended but foreseeable purposes. The energy sources must be sufficient but not excessive for powering the system.

Environment

Every system has an **environment** in which the system fulfills its purpose(s). For example, when the volume of current flowing through the circuit (the fuse environment) becomes dangerous or excessive, the fuse interrupts the circuit to change its environment and fulfill its purpose.

Similarly, a thermostat keeps the temperature of the environment it monitors within a predetermined range, activating heating or cooling equipment as needed. An organization's industrial accident prevention program responds to changes in its environment (increases in the frequency or severity of accidents) by increasing attention to safety or by giving rewards to employees who compile outstanding safety records. The accident prevention program is itself a system, affecting the level of safety within the industrial environment it protects.

Life Cycle

Just as systems exist in a spatial environment, systems also exist in time. System safety recognizes four phases in the life of any system:

1. The **conceptual phase** (when the basic purpose, mission, and preliminary design of the system are formulated)

2. The **engineering phase** (when the design of the system is constructed and tested)

3. The **operational phase** (when the system is implemented)

4. The **disposal phase** (when the system's use elapses and the system is disposed of)[3]

The system approach to safety applies differently to each of these life cycle phases. The conceptual phase provides the greatest number of cost-effective opportunities for designing a relatively hazard-free system. In the engineering phase, the system progresses into the prototype stage. Its precise dimensions, specifications, and procedures are tested for full-scale use. The particular safety design features, such as machine guards or a fire detection/suppression system, also become integral parts of the system during this phase.

In the operational phase, when the system is fully functional, safety features built into the system during the earlier phases must be maintained in operational condition. For example, fire detection/suppression systems must be supervised, fire doors must remain closed, and periodic fire drills must be conducted to keep personnel trained in emergency procedures. Many of the traditional hygiene controls, such as personal protective equipment and good housekeeping, can also help to ensure safe and reliable system operation. However, the opportunities for adding safety options in the operational phase are not as numerous as in the earlier phases. These opportunities are more limited because the system's features have already been implemented and are therefore harder to change.

The importance of disposal as the fourth phase of a system's life cycle has been highlighted by its growing popularity. A system-oriented approach designs each product and process so that their disposal or obsolescence creates little hazardous waste or environmental harm, their raw materials can be recycled efficiently, and their newer replacement system is readily implemented.

Techniques of System Safety Analysis

What techniques are commonly used in system safety analysis?

How can you apply those techniques in different situations?

As mentioned, system safety includes a large and growing number of specific techniques.[4] Some techniques apply to virtually all systems, while others are limited to particular ones. This chapter focuses only on the more broadly applicable techniques. Some of the basic techniques of system safety closely parallel common sense, and many people are surprised to find that they have been practicing system safety for years without realizing it. The following sections describe and explain how to apply the eleven techniques of system safety analysis found in Exhibit 12-1.

Exhibit 12-1
Summary of Some Techniques of System Safety Analysis

Technique	Applied by
Change analysis	Projecting the effects that specified proposed changes in an existing system—each considered separately and then in all feasible combinations—can be expected to have on the system's level of safety and reliability
Energy/Flow analysis	Analyzing the flows or transfers of energy within an existing or proposed system—or between a system and its environment—checking for hazardous accumulations or escapes of energy
Prototype analysis	Constructing a partial- or full-scale model of a system and testing it under a wide range of conditions to find limits of safe operation and forms of likely failure
Job safety analysis (JSA)	Dissecting a repetitive task (usually in a person/machine industrial context) to determine potential hazards if each action is not performed
Scenario analysis	"Brainstorming" conceivable severe accidents, tracing their possible causes and consequences, and identifying feasible preventive measures
Cost/benefit analysis	Assigning dollar (or other measurable) values to the costs and benefits expected from proposed changes in a system and selecting the change(s) promising the greatest excess of benefits over cost
Criticality analysis	Categorizing conceivable system failures in a particular system into predetermined classes and assigning probabilities to these failures so that the "expected criticality" of each projected system failure can be determined and alternative systems ranked by their "expected criticality" of failure
Program Evaluation and Review Technique (PERT)	Developing a network of sequenced, time-critical events essential to the success of a project so that these events can be scheduled to ensure timely project completion
Fault tree analysis (FTA)	Identifying some negative result of system performance and tracing back through a logic tree every failure of a system component that can produce this negative result
Failure mode and effect analysis (FMEA)	Identifying conceivable failures of each system component and, through a logic tree, projecting the effects of these failures on system performance
Technique of Human Error Rate Prediction (THERP)	Dissecting human activity into specific tasks, determining the probabilities of specific errors while performing that task, and computing the overall probability of some error during that activity

Adapted with permission from P. L. Clemens, "A Compendium of Hazard Identification and Evaluation Techniques for System Safety Applications," *Hazard Prevention*, March/April 1982, pp. 11-18.

Although this exhibit uses current, popular names for the techniques shown, the reader should recognize that (1) many other system safety techniques are not shown, (2) a technique might also be known by other names (for example, scenario analysis is also known as maximum credible accident analysis or worst-case condition analysis), and (3) new system safety techniques of analysis continue to be developed.

These techniques help risk management professionals to analyze how accidents occur and how they can be prevented. The techniques do not require calculations, although some practitioners prefer to supplement them with calculations. Because these techniques and their applications often require insight into organizations' operations, risk management professionals should include several other managers and employees in at least the initial considerations involved in these techniques.

Change Analysis[5]

Change analysis projects the effects a given change is likely to have on an existing system. Change analysis asks a series of "What if?" questions and projects the consequences for each of the changes and for all feasible combinations of change. For example, suppose an automobile manufacturer is considering using diesel engines instead of gasoline-powered engines for its automobiles. Risk management professionals can ask how the change will affect the safety of the drivers, the employees assembling the automobiles, the operators of service stations, and perhaps the general public.

As another illustration, risk management professionals might join the personnel department in asking, "If the company changes to flextime, what will happen to the frequency or severity of automobile or train accidents our employees suffer while commuting?"

The risk management professional for a manufacturer of processed foods might ask, "If we market our grape juice in glass bottles rather than metal cans, how will this affect deterioration of the product before reaching retail markets, injuries to employees in the distribution chain, injuries to consumers using the product, and product deterioration in consumers' homes?"

Change analysis can also apply to various combinations of changes in systems. To illustrate, the automobile manufacturer considering the diesel engine option might recognize that an automobile's safe performance partially depends on its weight. Change analysis can evaluate the safety implications of switching from gasoline to diesel engines, changing the weight of the vehicles, and various combinations of weight changes and diesel engine options. This analysis might reveal that a particular combination of engine options and weight changes is safer than any engine option or weight change alone.

Energy/Flow Analysis[6]

Energy/flow analysis originated in hydraulic engineering, which deals with designing and constructing tanks, pumps, pipes, valves, and other components of systems for holding and transporting liquid and gaseous fluids. Safely and reliably operating these systems requires that correct pressures exist at certain times at different points within the systems. To illustrate, assume that both a hydraulic engineer and a risk management professional are concerned about maintaining correct pressure in the organization's steam power plant. To work with the hydraulic engineer most effectively, the risk management professional needs a basic understanding of how fluids move and of the hazards of deficient or excessive hydrostatic pressures.

The usefulness of a flow-oriented safety analysis can be enhanced by combining it with energy analysis. The concept that unifies hydraulic engineering and the energy-release theory is that energy flows like a fluid. More precisely, the energy inherent in a static or moving fluid behaves much like any form of energy. To prevent accidents or reduce the harm they cause, the risk management professional can apply one or more of the ten energy-release strategies that were detailed in Chapter 1 to prevent the buildup of energy to excessive levels, to channel that energy, to protect susceptible structures (including persons) from that energy, or to counteract the damage that escaped energy can cause.

Energy/flow analysis is particularly useful to assess demands on a system or set of subsystems that is largely mechanical and whose failure is likely to result from some internal inadequacy rather than from human error.

Prototype Analysis[7]

A prototype is a physical test model. It can be a full- or partial-scale example of a product that will be produced in greater numbers if it proves successful. A prototype can also be an existing product or process tested in a new environment (for example, when a United States retailer opens one store in a European country to decide whether to open stores throughout Europe).

A **prototype analysis** provides an opportunity to discover and correct any defects in a product or process while it is still in its early stage, before committing substantial resources to it. A prototype airplane can be test flown or a new type of food processor can be test marketed in a typical community. In essence, a prototype affords real-world testing of performance with a relatively minor commitment of resources before full-scale production and marketing.

In principle, anything that can be done on a small scale can be prototyped. Prototype analysis is therefore widely applicable. However, to reveal potential hazards and defects reliably, the prototype must meet the following criteria:

- Be sufficiently realistic (that is, be enough like the final full-scale version to reveal any flaws in the final product or process)

- Be tested realistically in a representative environment, including being subjected to all the operations the final product will have to perform (perhaps even tested more rigorously than normal to provide some margin for safety)

- Be subjected to detailed analysis before, during, and after the testing so that the test procedure yields all of the reasonably available information it can

Risk management professionals or other managers often identify opportunities for prototype testing that others might have overlooked and in this way contribute significantly to organizations' risk control efforts.

Job Safety Analysis[8]

Any highly repetitive human task performed in a stable environment is amenable to **job safety analysis (JSA)**. In this type of analysis, a trained observer of industrial processes (preferably someone who is also familiar with the organization) divides the task into specific actions or steps. After this first step, the person doing the JSA identifies hazards and accident potentials associated with each step and develops a procedure for performing each step in the safest way (provided that the added benefits of the safest procedure outweigh its incremental costs). As suggested by Exhibit 12-2, which shows a JSA for operating a hand fire extinguisher, JSA helps risk management professionals determine the task to be analyzed and each possible hazard.

Although JSA applies best to repetitive human tasks performed in an environment sufficiently stable to allow most hazards to be foreseen, a JSA can also be applied to systems in which human error is not a significant factor. Repetitive tasks and person/machine systems are so common that JSA is applicable in almost every case where a person must act safely to avoid causing injury or property damage.

Scenario Analysis[9]

Scenario analysis requires the analyst to brainstorm the worst set of catastrophes that could befall a system, to project the consequences of those events, and to suggest ways in which those catastrophes could be prevented.

The primary goal of scenario analysis is to encourage participants to think creatively about what accidents might happen, what their consequences might be, and how they can be prevented or their consequences minimized.

Exhibit 12-2
Job Safety Analysis Worksheet

Job: Using a Pressurized Water Fire Extinguisher

What To Do	How To Do It	Key Points
(Steps in sequence)	(Instructions) (Reverse hands for left-handed operator)	(Items to be emphasized. Safety is always a key point)
1. Remove extinguisher from wall bracket.	1. Left hand on bottom lip, fingers curled around lip, palm up. Right hand on carrying handle palm down, fingers around carrying handle only.	1. Check air pressure to make certain extinguisher is charged. Stand close to extinguisher, pull straight out. Have firm grip, to prevent dropping on feet. Lower, and as you do, remove left hand from lip.
2. Carry to fire.	2. Carry in right hand, upright position.	2. Extinguisher should hang down alongside leg. (This makes it easy to carry and reduces possibility of strain.)
3. Remove pin.	3. Set extinguisher down in upright position. Place left hand on top of extinguisher, pull out pin with right hand.	3. Hold extinguisher steady with left hand. Do not exert pressure on discharge lever as you remove pin.
4. Squeeze discharge lever.	4. Place right hand over carrying handle with fingers curled around operating lever handle while grasping discharge hose near nozzle with left hand.	4. Have firm grip on handle to steady extinguisher.
5. Apply water stream to fire.	5. Direct water stream at base of fire.	5. Work from side to side or around fire. After extinguishing flames, spray water on smoldering or glowing surfaces.
6. Return extinguisher. Report use.		

Adapted with permission from *Accident Prevention Manual for Industrial Operations: Administration and Programs*, 9th ed. (Chicago, IL: National Safety Council, 1988), p. 190.

This analysis focuses on the chain of events leading to and from accidents. By encouraging the study of accidents as causal sequences of events, scenario analysis helps participants, especially those new to system safety, to intuitively understand the causal logic underlying most techniques of system safety analysis.

To illustrate scenario analysis, recall the computer manufacturer mentioned earlier in this chapter. The manufacturer's truck became involved in an accident that damaged a mainframe computer, preventing its timely delivery to a customer. Assume a group of managers or other employees were asked to imagine worst-case circumstances that would greatly increase the severity of the accident. Among other possibilities, this group might devise the following scenario:

- The firm that was to receive the computer was the manufacturer's principal customer. Because of the delayed delivery, it canceled its long-term contract, forcing the manufacturer to cut back its operations by 60 percent.

- The manufacturer's employee who was driving the truck was killed in the accident.

- The accident, caused by the deceased driver's negligence, also involved a loaded school bus. Fifty passengers were killed, and the manufacturer was held legally responsible for their deaths.

- The accident occurred directly outside the manufacturer's front gate, with a resulting fire and explosion that destroyed the only access road to the manufacturer's facilities and forced the manufacturer to close for three weeks during road repairs.

This scenario or any of its elements does not need to be realistic. Instead, the objective is to envision a worst case for analysis. This analysis should help risk management professionals elaborate on the circumstances that could have led to each of these worst-case conditions and then specify how each of these underlying circumstances could have been prevented. For example, one customer's cancellation of its contract for nondelivery would not have been such a serious consequence if the manufacturer had developed a more diversified market base, either by having more customers or by offering more diverse product lines. The contract might not have been canceled if the manufacturer's personnel had formed more congenial relationships with this customer so that one late delivery would not have been viewed as a major problem.

The accident with the school bus occurred because the truck and the school bus were traveling the same road. A possible corrective measure would have been for the manufacturer's trucks to avoid school bus routes or, if this were not possible, to travel those roads at times when school buses did not.

The basic causes of all these worst cases might be identified as a personal failure of the driver or a mechanical failure of the truck. This scenario analysis should specify ways such failures can be prevented.

Cost/Benefit Analysis[10]

Cost/benefit analysis (also called cost-effectiveness analysis) assesses the contributions that safety measures make to an organization by determining whether and by how much the benefits these measures generate exceed their costs. The greater the benefits for a given cost, or the lesser the cost to achieve a given benefit, the more cost-effective the safety measure.

Cost/benefit analysis can be used to evaluate any measure whose distinct costs and benefits can be determined. Cost/benefit analysis has been used throughout this text and the entire ARM program as a decision rule for selecting among risk management techniques for which the costs have been stated in cash outflows and the benefits have been stated in cash inflows.

When assessing system safety, these costs and benefits must be expressed as expected values (to account for the uncertainty of some outcomes) and discounted to present values (to account for the time value of money). The procedures for determining expected present values were discussed in the Appendix to Chapter 1.

Criticality Analysis[11]

Certain components of a system are critical to its operation, while others might be necessary but not critical. For example, any failure of the static control device on a petroleum fuel truck can cause the truck to explode, destroying it and nearby property, and perhaps causing death or serious injury. In contrast, a temporary illness of the driver is likely only to delay delivery of the petroleum products aboard the truck.

To rank failures, four categories have been developed as part of a **criticality analysis**:

- Category 1—Failure resulting in excessive unscheduled maintenance
- Category 2—Failure resulting in delay or loss of operational availability
- Category 3—Failure resulting in potential mission failure
- Category 4—Failure resulting in potential loss of life

An explosion caused by defective static controls aboard the truck may be classified as a Category 4 failure (most severe), while the driver's temporary illness may be classified as a Category 1 or 2 failure. These categories can be used either subjectively to establish priorities among hazards and their controls or objectively to measure how a given risk control technician can alter the expected criticality of a system failure.

To rank hazards, criticality analysis can be used to identify the following:

- Items that should be studied more intensively to eliminate the hazard that could cause the failure and to develop fail-safe design, failure rate reduction, or damage containment

- Items that require special attention during production, tight quality control, or protective handling at all times

- Special requirements for suppliers concerning design, performance, reliability, safety, or quality assurance of their goods

- Acceptance standards for components received from subcontractors and for product characteristics that should be intensively tested

- Cases in which special procedures, safeguards, protective equipment, monitoring devices, or warning systems should be implemented

- Cases in which accident prevention efforts and funds can be most effectively applied

To estimate how a given risk control measure affects the level of safety within a system, the hazard rankings serve as *approximate* measures of the severity of the loss a particular system failure might cause. These loss severity rankings can be substituted for dollars to compute an expected criticality of a system. This is similar to how the expected value of a risk control device can be measured by its effect on the expected dollar value of the losses to a system. An effective risk control measure reduces both a system's expected criticality and the expected dollar value of accidental losses to that system. Calculating the expected criticality of a system is illustrated in the Appendix to this chapter.

Gauging the extent to which a risk control measure reduces the expected criticality of a system failure can sharpen risk control decisions in two ways: (1) by comparing the relative effects of two or more risk control measures on a system's level of safety and (2) by comparing the cost-effectiveness of two or more safety measures. The first use of this analysis, comparing the relative effects of two or more risk control measures, can be illustrated using static guards on a petroleum truck. The guard just analyzed reduced the expected criticality of system failure by eight percentage points. If another device reduces this criticality of system failure by ten percentage points, then this second device would be better by two percentage points of expected criticality.

The second use of this analysis, comparing the cost-effectiveness of two or more safety measures, can be illustrated by comparing the effects of the safety measures with the costs of those measures. Suppose that the technologically best static control device, one that would reduce expected criticality of system failure by eight percentage points, costs $30. Another static control device that would reduce expected criticality of system failure by six percentage points costs $15. Computing a ratio of reduced expected criticality per dollar shows that the device producing the six-percentage-point improvement with a 0.06/$15 (or 0.0040) reduced expected criticality per dollar is a better buy than the device producing the eight-percentage-point improvement with a reduced 0.08/$30 (or 0.0027) expected criticality per dollar. Thus, the technologically best device is not always the most cost-effective. The priorities indicated in the organization's safety policy can provide some guidance for specific risk control decisions, like the choice of a device to control the build-up or release of static electricity.

Program Evaluation Review Technique (PERT)[12]

Process-oriented systems usually contain a number of time-sensitive events whose timing is critical, especially if the system is complex. Each of these important events must occur on schedule or within a specified time period for the system to continue operating smoothly. If this time sequence is interrupted, the entire system fails.

For example, an automobile manufacturer anticipates the necessary lead times and possible delays in obtaining all the parts to assemble an automobile. The supplier has also planned so that all the parts can be shipped to the manufacturer on time in the quantities required. Any disruption of these plans can cause the system to fail. If an accident prevents a headlamp manufacturer from securing enough of the proper bulbs on time, the headlamp assembly and ultimately the entire automobile manufacturing process could come to a halt.

To help schedule particularly complex projects, system safety specialists have developed several forms of network analysis. The most widely used is the **Program Evaluation Review Technique (PERT)**. A PERT network identifies the necessary accomplishments, called events, of a project, defines when the events must be finished for the project to be on schedule, and identifies those events that are time-sensitive and those that are not.

Time-sensitive events, particularly those whose delay will lengthen a project, are part of the critical path. These events must be done in sequence, cannot be done simultaneously, and cannot overlap. The expected total time for the events in the critical path is also the expected time for completing the entire project.

To illustrate, consider Exhibit 12-3, which estimates the time needed to rebuild a soft-drink bottler's plant if it and its machinery are heavily damaged by fire.

The first step in developing a PERT network for this project is to identify each of the events in the process. The second step is to distinguish those events that must occur in sequence from those that can be done concurrently with other events. For example, the events in the horizontal path running from left to right through the middle of Exhibit 12-3, beginning with the fire loss, must occur sequentially. No concurrency among these particular events is possible.

In contrast, developing job specifications for operating new machinery, recalling previous employees and hiring new ones, and training employees to use the new equipment (a separate sequence of events shown along the top of the exhibit) are necessary to link the development of machinery specifications with the later restoration of the production process. Similarly, obtaining bids for and constructing machinery (shown in the lower looping portion of the PERT network) is an independent sequence of events that can be done concurrently with the events of restoring the plant and acquiring and training qualified personnel. (Note that Exhibit 12-3 uses networking analysis symbols. Rectangles indicate events within the organization's control; ovals indicate events beyond the organization's control.)

The third step in developing a PERT network is to estimate the time required for each event. For example, in Exhibit 12-3, fourteen events must occur after the fire loss. The expected time requirements for these events might be as follows:

Event	Time Required
Conducting the inspection and developing insurance reports	One week
Removing debris	One week
Developing specifications for new machinery and equipment	Four weeks
Developing specifications for new building(s) to house the equipment	Five weeks
Selecting contractor(s) for machinery	Three weeks
Selecting contractor(s) for buildings(s)	Three weeks
Constructing machinery	Eighteen weeks
Constructing building(s)	Twenty-eight weeks
Installing machinery	Four weeks
Developing job specifications for new equipment operators	Four weeks
Recalling old and hiring new employees	Three weeks
Training employees on the new equipment	Three weeks

Exhibit 12-3
PERT Network

Time Expressed in Weeks

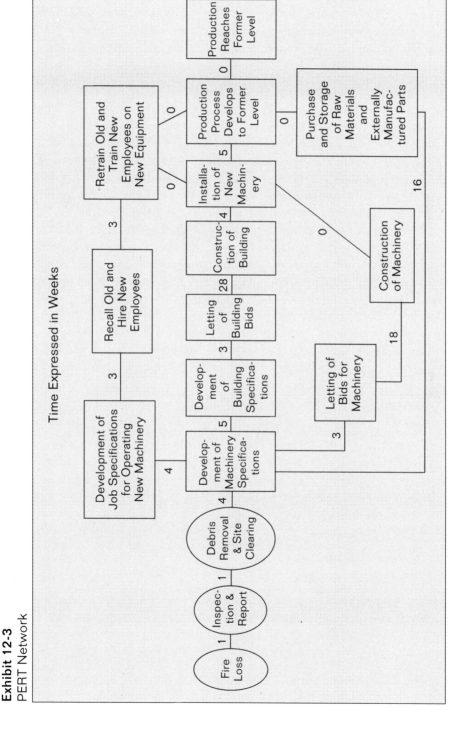

Reprinted with permission from Darwin B. Close, "PERT Networks' Use Can Help Reduce Business Interruption Down Time," *Risk Management*, March 1982, pp. 26-30.

Purchasing, delivering, and storing raw
    materials and externally manufactured parts   Sixteen weeks

Resuming production process and restoring
    production to its pre-loss level   Five weeks

The critical path is constructed by inserting these time requirements along the paths that connect the events in Exhibit 12-3. The four possible paths are the paths running horizontally along the top, the middle, and the bottom and the path looping below the central horizontal path. Each path includes the three events and times at the far left of the exhibit. The four paths consider the time required to obtain bids on and construct the machinery. The estimated time required from fire loss to restoration of pre-loss production levels is sixteen weeks for the top horizontal path, fifty-one weeks for the center horizontal path, twenty-two weeks for the bottom horizontal path, and thirty-two weeks for the looping path. The critical path, which involves the most time and events that cannot be done simultaneously, takes fifty-one weeks, leaving sufficient time for the events involved in the other paths of this network. In this example, the critical path (traced in the exhibit as a bold line) lies in the middle of the diagram; this need not be the case. The top horizontal path has thirty-five (fifty-one minus sixteen) weeks of slack time, the bottom horizontal path has twenty-nine weeks, and the looping path has nineteen weeks. Some delay in the activities along these other, noncritical paths can be tolerated without lengthening the overall time to restore pre-loss production, but any delay along the critical path will postpone the project.

Knowing what times are required and what delays are tolerable helps risk management professionals to (1) concentrate risk control measures on the events in the critical path of the PERT network (especially duplicating facilities or suppliers), (2) define the net income consequences of a delay at any point in the PERT network, and (3) estimate the time required to restore the normal operations.

Fault Tree Analysis[13]

Fault tree analysis (FTA) takes one particular system failure and traces the events leading to the system failure backwards in time. The purpose of this analysis is to identify various ways of breaking the fault tree, that is, interrupting the sequence of events leading to system failure so that the failure itself can be prevented.

Exhibit 12-4 illustrates a fault tree for a system failure in which a press operator's hand is injured. This system failure (the injury) appears at the top of the fault tree, and the events necessary to produce this failure are branched lower on the tree. The tree's branches are connected by *and* gates (shaped like beehives) and *or* gates (shaped like fishtails). These gates describe the causal relationships between the events in rectangles within the tree. For example,

Exhibit 12-4
Fault Tree for Hand Injury to Press Operator

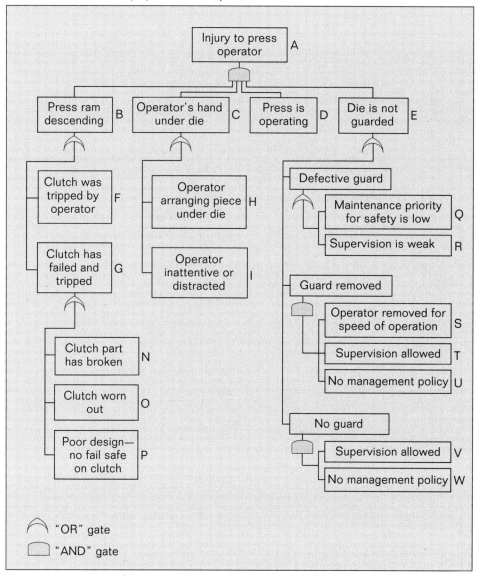

Adapted with permission from Dan Petersen, *Techniques of Safety Management,* 2d ed. (New York, NY: McGraw Hill Book Company, 1978), p. 174.

the *and* gate directly below the injury found in rectangle A indicates that event A can occur only if all four of the events in rectangles B, C, D, and E occur first. If any one of those four events does not occur, the hand injury to the press operator also cannot occur.

In contrast, an *or* gate signifies that any one of the events leading to the gate is sufficient to cause that event. For example, the operator's hand will be under the die (rectangle C) either if the operator is arranging a piece under the die (rectangle H) or if the operator is inattentive or distracted (rectangle I). To break a fault tree at an *or* gate, none of the events below this gate can be allowed to occur. To prevent the operator's hand from being under the die, the operator must remain alert and must always use some tool (other than his or her hands) to arrange pieces under the die. Breaking a fault tree at an *and* gate requires preventing any one of the events directly below that gate from occurring. For example, effective supervision (rectangle T) will prevent the press guard from being removed because all three events in rectangles S, T, and U must occur for the guard to be removed.

Because fault tree analysis depends as much on logic as on experience, it can be used to analyze exposures to accidental loss before they actually occur. (The fault tree diagrammed in Exhibit 12-4 is also known as a logic tree.) This prospective analysis requires identifying all the conditions necessary and suffi-cient for a particular accident to occur. For example, if the fault tree in the exhibit is accurate, then the four events in rectangles B through E are *suffi-cient* to cause a hand injury: every time these four events occur together, an operator's hand will be injured. These four events are also *necessary* for such an injury: if any one of the four is missing, no injury will occur.

To ensure that the fault tree is correctly constructed (all necessary and suffi-cient events are included), risk management professionals (or other profes-sionals responsible for making the analysis) should take the following steps:

1. Identify the system failure as specifically as possible so that all the events contributing to this failure can be fully described.

2. Move down the tree from the system failure, and diagram the events that are necessary and sufficient to cause the events that immediately follow them.

3. Determine whether the events leading to any other event on the tree are connected by an *and* gate or by an *or* gate. (Although logic trees using more complicated causal connectives than *and* and *or* gates can be con-structed, these two basic connectives are sufficient for most purposes.)

Because fault tree analysis identifies the events leading to a system failure, it naturally suggests loss prevention measures. The distinctions between *and* and *or* gates provide some guidance in choosing among loss prevention alternatives. For example, to prevent a clutch from failing (rectangle G), all three of the conditions in rectangles N, O, and P must be prevented because the *or* gate above these three indicates that any one of them is sufficient to cause a clutch to fail. In contrast, a press will lack a guard (the "No guard" rectangle at the bottom right of the fault tree) only if the conditions in both rectangles V and W exist. Consequently, preventing either one of these two conditions (through active supervision or through a strong management policy on such guards) will prevent the absence of a guard.

To encourage sound risk control decisions, a fault tree must be as complete and accurate as possible. An incomplete fault tree might entirely omit a chain of events that would make risk control measures applied to some other branch ineffective. For example, if a branch of events leading directly to the system failure in rectangle A of Exhibit 12-4 were unintentionally omitted from the fault tree, then risk control measures to prevent events B through E would not be sufficient to prevent the system failure represented by rectangle A.

A fault tree can also be defective if a gate is incorrectly labeled. For example, if the gate connecting rectangles V and W to the "No guard" rectangle should have been an *or* gate rather than an *and* gate, then loss prevention measures directed at either V or W would not prevent the absence of a guard.

If probabilities are attached to the lower rectangles in a fault tree, then the probabilities of events successively higher in the tree can be calculated. An *and* gate requires calculating the joint probability that all the events immediately below this gate will occur. If the probabilities of events in rectangles S, T, and U of Exhibit 12-4 are 0.15, 0.20, and 0.30, respectively, then the probability of the guard being removed is:

$$0.15 \times 0.20 \times 0.30 = 0.009$$

An *or* gate requires calculating the probability that any one or more of the events directly below the gate will occur. This probability is also the probability that the chain of events will proceed through that gate to the next higher level of the tree, bringing the system failure that much closer. The *or* gate connecting rectangles H and I to rectangle C in the exhibit indicates that if the probabilities H and I are 0.40 and 0.20, and if these two events are not mutually exclusive, then the probability of one or the other (or both) of them occurring is the sum of the probabilities of either one of them occurring alone minus the probability of their both occurring together. Thus, the following equation results:

$$p(\text{H or I or both})$$
$$= p(H) + p(I) - p(H)p(I)$$
$$= 0.40 + 0.20 - (0.40)(0.20)$$
$$= 0.60 - 0.08$$
$$= 0.52$$

An alternative, equivalent calculation of the same result rests on the fact that there are three, and only three, mutually exclusive ways in which the result "H or I or both" can occur. These are (1) H and not I, (2) I and not H, and (3) both H and I. Because these three ways of achieving this result are mutually exclusive, their probabilities can simply be added to compute the overall probability of the outcome "H or I or both." Thus,

$$p(\text{H or I or both})$$
$$= p(H)p(\text{not I}) + p(I)p(\text{not H}) + p(H)p(I)$$
$$= (0.40)(0.80) + (0.20)(0.60) + (0.40)(0.20)$$
$$= 0.32 + 0.12 + 0.08$$
$$= 0.52$$

To properly use fault tree analysis, risk management professionals must recognize its underlying assumptions and limitations. Fault tree analysis assumes that (1) all components exist in only one of two conditions, success or failure (operational or not operational); (2) any failure of a system component is independent of the failure of any other component; and (3) each failure has an unchanging probability of occurrence. Moreover, to keep FTA manageable, many logic trees limit the number of potential causes of failure they examine, perhaps overlooking other causes.

Failure Mode and Effect Analysis (FMEA)[14]

Failure mode and effect analysis (FMEA) resembles fault tree analysis with the direction of reasoning reversed. Fault tree analysis reasons from consequence to causes; failure mode and effect analysis reasons from cause to consequences. FMEA selects a failure within a system component and then, using a logic tree, projects the effects of this one failure on other system components and on the overall system. Instead of the FTA approach of tracing the events that must precede a particular system failure, FMEA projects the consequences of some failure of a system component.

Exhibit 12-4 illustrates the reasoning that underlies FMEA. Suppose, as is shown in rectangle R, supervision is weak. FMEA projects that one of the consequences of this weakness is probably a defective press guard. FMEA would then project a number of other consequences of weak supervision. Beginning at either rectangle T or V of the fault tree, weak supervision can lead either to the absence of a guard from the outset or to the guard being removed. Rectangles R, T, and V represent three different ways in which weak supervision, when combined with other circumstances, can lead to a particular kind of injury (and, by extension, to many other kinds of injuries or failures of other risk control measures).

Failure mode and effect analysis and fault tree analysis both use logic trees and are therefore subject to the assumptions and the limitations of fault tree analysis.

Technique of Human Error Rate Prediction (THERP)[15]

In any system, human error can be a significant cause of failure. Everyone makes mistakes, and some of those mistakes can cause an entire system to malfunction. The possibilities of making mistakes can be analyzed through the **Technique of Human Error Rate Prediction (THERP)**, which subdivides a particular person/machine activity into specific tasks, identifies the probability of error for each task an employee performs, and applies fault tree or failure mode and effect analysis to determine the likelihood that the error will cause a system failure.

To illustrate in the context of the logic tree in Exhibit 12-4, assume that the probability that the press operator will be attentive is 0.995. Conversely, the probability that the operator will be inattentive (the condition shown in rectangle I) and place a hand under the die (as shown in rectangle C) is 0.005 (or one in two hundred). If the operator's hand is under the die when the events in rectangles B, D, and E occur, then the operator's hand will be injured.

This example of THERP is highly simplified. In practice, the procedure for applying THERP involves the following:

1. Segmenting the standard operating procedure for a particular activity or operation into its simplest components

2. Assigning a probability of success (likelihood of human reliability) to each task based either on extended study of the particular person(s) performing the task or on some standardized average human error rate

3. Determining the probability of completing the entire operation without error by using the probabilities of success for each task

The resulting probability of human error during each repetition of an activity can be added to a logic tree for either fault tree analysis or failure mode and effect analysis. The probability would help to assess the effect of a human error during that particular activity on the overall reliability or safety of the system.

THERP has wide applications in deciding how to improve the reliability of a system. For example, THERP can help risk management professionals decide whether to concentrate on improving the reliability of human actions within the system or on redesigning the system so that human error is less of a cause of potential system failure. If human errors currently cause many system failures, and if the probability of those errors can be reduced through proper training, then training efforts can be focused cost-effectively on removing potentially serious errors. However, if the human errors that might cause system failure are difficult to correct through training, removing employees from the system by mechanizing their tasks might be more cost-effective.

Summary

Every organization is a system of human and mechanical components. Every organization also contains subsystems and is itself a subsystem within a larger system. An important responsibility of risk management professionals is to ensure the continued reliable performance of all subsystems within organizations so that the organizations can remain productive, value-producing components of national and international socioeconomic communities. Understanding basic concepts related to systems, and more specifically the particular techniques of system safety, can assist risk management professionals in performing this important responsibility.

Studying the characteristics common to all systems (components, purpose(s), environments, and life cycle stages) enables risk management professionals to see more clearly how the parts of a system must work together to be fully productive and how failure of a component in one part of a system is likely to affect the remainder of that system. Knowing of these interrelationships helps risk management professionals to discern specific measures for either preventing the failure of a particular component or reducing the adverse effects of the failure of that component.

Within this framework, causes and effects build on one another. The effects of one component failure might cause further failures. These cause-effect relationships suggest a number of specific techniques of system safety analysis, methods of determining whether and how accidents or system failures will occur, and how failures can be prevented. The distinguishing features of these techniques, some of which are highly intuitive while others use considerable quantitative analysis, were highlighted in Exhibit 12-1, which summarized major portions of this chapter.

Chapter Notes

1. Robert Albanese, *Managing: Toward Accountability for Performance*, 3d ed. (Homewood, IL: Richard D. Irwin, Inc., 1981), pp. 530-531.

2. P. L. Clemens, "A Compendium of Hazard Identification and Evaluation Techniques for System Safety Applications," *Hazard Prevention*, March/April 1982, pp. 11-18.

3. William Shakespeare, *As You Like It*, act 2, scene 7, in which the Duke speaks of the seven ages of man.

4. Rex B. Gordon, "System Safety," in Frank E. Bird, Jr., and Robert G. Loftus, *Loss Control Management* (Loganville, GA: Loss Control Institute Press, 1976), p. 466.

5. The discussion under this heading is based on Charles H. Kepner and Benjamin B. Traigo, *The Rational Manager* (New York, NY: McGraw-Hill Book Company, 1965), pp. 189-197.

6. The discussion under this heading is based on Willie Hammer, *Handbook of System and Product Safety* (Englewood Cliffs, NJ: Prentice-Hall, Inc., 1972), pp. 159-164.

7. Hammer, pp. 170-180.

8. The discussion under this heading is based on Frank E. McElory, ed., *Accident Prevention Manual for Industrial Operations—Administration and Programs*, 8th ed. (Chicago, IL: National Safety Council, 1981), pp. 144-151.

9. The discussion under this heading is based on Clemens, pp. 15-17.

10. The discussion under this heading is based on Pierre Masse, *Optimal Investment Decisions: Rules for Action and Criteria for Choice* (Englewood Cliffs, NJ: Prentice-Hall, Inc., 1962), pp. 29-41.

11. The discussion under this heading is based on Hammer, pp. 156-159. Note that here Hammer's categories of criticality have been reversed.

12. The discussion under this heading is based on Albanese, pp. 130-239 and Darwin B. Close, "PERT Networks' Use Can Help Reduce Business Interruption Down Time," *Risk Management*, March 1982, pp. 26-30.

13. The discussion under this heading is based on Hammer, pp. 238-246.

14. The discussion under this heading is based on Willie Hammer, *Occupational Safety Management and Engineering* (Englewood Cliffs, NJ: Prentice-Hall, Inc., 1976), pp. 466-468.

15. The discussion under this heading is based on Hammer, *Handbook of System and Product Safety*, p. 198.

Appendix

Calculating the Expected Criticality of a System

Assume that some deficiency in the static control device on the petroleum delivery truck creates a 0.02 probability of a Category 4 failure and a 0.04 probability of a Category 2 failure. Simplifying the analysis to consider only these two possible system failures, the expected criticality (E) of a system failure under this first set of circumstances, C1, can be computed as follows:

$$E(C1) = (0.02)(4) + (0.04)(2) = 0.08 + 0.08 = 0.16$$

Improving the static controls aboard the truck may reduce the criticality of a related system failure by either reducing the probability of some system failure of a given category or lowering the category ranking of a given type of failure (reducing the severity of the resulting losses).

To continue the example, installing a better static control device on the petroleum truck might reduce the severity of the Category 4 failure to Category 3 while simultaneously reducing the probability of the Category 2 failure from 0.04 to 0.01.

Consequently, the overall expected criticality of some system failure under this second set of conditions, C2, can be computed as follows:

$$E(C2) = (0.02)(3) + (0.01)(2) = 0.06 + 0.02 = 0.08$$

Thus, the improved static control device can be said to reduce the criticality of system failure by eight percentage points (from 0.16 to 0.08).

Chapter 13

Motivating and Monitoring Risk Control Activities

Educational Objectives

1. Illustrate effective programs to motivate an organization's personnel to implement appropriate loss control measures in given situations.

   In support of the above objective, you should be able to do the following:

   a. Distinguish between motivation as a person's psychological condition and as a managerial activity.

   b. Explain and illustrate the challenges involved in motivating others to fulfill their risk control responsibilities.

   c. Describe and illustrate how specific motivational theories motivate personnel to fulfill their respective risk control responsibilities.

2. Illustrate appropriate controls to monitor the effectiveness of an organization's risk control measures in given situations.

Outline

Motivating Risk Control

   Scope of the Challenge

   Some Theories of Motivation

   Applying the Theories of Motivation

Monitoring Risk Control

   Controlling Performance

   Adapting to Change

Overview of the Risk Control Function

   Changes in Exposures

   Changes in Risk Control Options

   Changes in the Risk Control Measures Selected

   Changes in Risk Control Implementation

   Changes in Risk Control Monitoring

Summary

In support of the above objective, you should be able to do the following:

a. Describe the importance of the two fundamental purposes of monitoring an organization's risk control program.

b. Distinguish between results standards and activity standards and illustrate risk control for each.

c. Explain the nature and risk control importance of each of the three steps in the classical managerial function of control.

d. Describe and illustrate the four major sources of standards of acceptable risk control performance for an organization.

e. Describe and give risk control examples of each of the characteristics of a good performance standard for any organizational activity.

f. Describe and explain when it is appropriate to apply effective strategies for adjusting for substandard risk control performance.

3. Illustrate the importance of adapting a risk control program for changes in loss exposures, legal requirements, organizational resources, and the relative costs and benefits of risk management techniques.

4. Define or describe each of the Key Words and Phrases shown in the course guide for this assignment.

Motivating and Monitoring Risk Control Activities

A risk control program requires personnel throughout an organization to take specific actions. For example, front-line employees must follow established work safety rules, supervisors must conduct safety training programs and encourage work safety, and senior executives must emphasize risk control as an integral part of evaluating employees' performance. Because personal responsibility for risk control is essential, motivating employees is an important element of any risk control program. Furthermore, an organization must monitor and report the effects of risk control measures. Monitoring helps an organization to determine whether decisions have achieved their desired results and to adjust past decisions to changing conditions. It also enables managers to recognize and appreciate the value of risk control.

This concluding chapter focuses on motivating and monitoring risk control measures. Regarding motivation, the basic objectives of this chapter are to enable the risk management professional to understand why people disregard worksafety or other risk control measures and to help managers improve employees' attention to these two areas. Regarding monitoring risk control measures, this chapter's objectives are to increase the risk management professional's ability to establish and strengthen procedures for monitoring a risk control program and to improve others' risk control performance.

Motivating Risk Control

How do differences among people affect your responsibility to motivate those people to practice risk control?

What theories explain how and why people are motivated?

How do those theories of motivation apply to risk control?

A **motive** is a psychological state, somewhat similar to an attitude, that compels a person to satisfy a perceived deficiency. **Motivation** may be defined as a a person's level of energy or determination in accomplishing a personal goal or as the managerial process of energizing people to accomplish an organizational goal. A highly motivated person pursues a goal with great energy while a less motivated person pursues a goal with little or no enthusiasm. Thus, with respect to worksafety, some employees may be very committed while others are apathetic or even hostile.

The motivation process, diagrammed in Exhibit 13-1, is based on the above definitions of motive and motivation. In this process, each person perceives deficiencies, or unmet needs, in his or her environment. These unmet needs activate the person's psychological energies, or motives, which compel the person to correct the deficiencies. This behavior is graphically shown in the exhibit by the arrow that runs to the left from "Actions to meet individual needs" to "Perceived deficiencies." The arrow that runs to the right indicates that an employee's actions may also serve the organization's goals, may not affect those goals, or may be contrary to those goals. When a manager effectively uses motivation, the manager increases the proportion of an employee's actions supporting the organization's goals and decreases the proportion of actions detracting from its goals. A good manager removes conflicts, or establishes congruence, between the organization's goals and the employee's perceived needs so that the employee wants to behave in ways that serve both sets of needs.

Exhibit 13-1
The Motivation Process

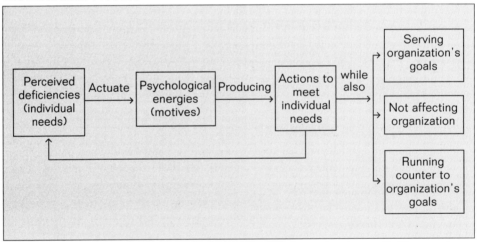

Adapted with permission from John R. Schermerhorn, Jr., James G. Hunt, and Richard N. Osborn, *Managing Organizational Behavior* (New York, NY: John Wiley & Sons, 1982), p. 107.

Motives and motivation are studied in a risk control context to explain past or present behavior and to affect future behavior. The first purpose is illustrated by a risk management professional's study of why a group of front-line employees have or have not obeyed a safety rule. To understand past behavior, a risk management professional might want to know why some supervisors regularly attend safety briefings while others do not. Once the risk management professional establishes motives for past behavior, he or she can use this information for the second purpose, to influence future behavior. Influencing behavior includes reinforcing behavior that supports risk control and attempting to change behavior that does not. Changing inappropriate behavior generally involves creating situations in which appropriate behavior is perceived to be more rewarding than inappropriate behavior.

Because individuals are so diverse, no single theory of motivation applies to everyone. Instead, many diverse theories have been proposed, each seemingly applicable to at least some people in some situations. In applying any theory, risk management professionals must realize that a theory of motivation is useful only if it explains past behavior or provides an appropriate way to influence future behavior. The more people and situations to which a theory applies, the greater its usefulness. This section discusses the challenge of motivating employees, some common theories, and how these theories may be applied.

Scope of the Challenge

Motivating others to practice risk control is a multifaceted challenge. One of the challenges, the absence of a uniform theory of human motivation, has already been mentioned. Other challenges stem from differences among individuals, differences within individuals that evolve over time, and difficulties in applying theories of motivation to employees' risk control conduct.

Differences Among Individuals

One person's ability to motivate another depends on the characteristics (unmet needs) of the person to be motivated and the characteristics of the motivator. To motivate employees, a manager must show employees how work can fulfill their personal needs in ways that also serve the organization. The following sections explain the differences among persons being motivated and the differences among managers who seek to motivate.

Differences Among Persons Being Motivated[1]

Although general theories of motivation identify certain universally applicable systems of motives, no single motive compels everyone's on-the-job behavior. The question "Why should I work safely or care about safety in my job?" has no single answer that is equally satisfying to everyone. For any two employees, that answer will vary, even if only slightly.

On the other hand, a distinctly different motivation system does not exist for each employee. Rather, several common needs motivate most employees. The challenge for risk management professionals is to identify those common needs and to create situations in which practicing risk control satisfies them.

Management scholars have suggested that the level a person occupies in an organization's structure influences the person's motives for job performance. Front-line employees tend to be most concerned about how their work will enable them to lead fuller personal lives, for example, through higher pay or more leisure time. In contrast, senior managers are motivated by the organization's profitability, fulfillment of its basic mission, or ability to serve its customers, employees, or the general public. Most employees, who are neither near the top nor near the bottom of the organization's structure, are often motivated by a mixture of personal and organizational needs. However, personal needs can conflict with equally demanding needs for promotion or other recognition within the organization.

Employees at different organizational levels will therefore have different motives for fulfilling their risk control responsibilities, including complying with recommended safe operating procedures, conducting safety training programs, or developing an organization's overall risk management policy. For example, senior management will probably support risk control efforts that increase operating efficiency, improve the quality of the organization's products or services, enhance employees' well-being, or serve the general public. In contrast, most front-line employees will probably support risk controls linked to their personal and family well-being. Examples include protection from personal injury, safety-related pay increases and bonuses, or awards and recognition from peers.

Employees in the middle of the organization's hierarchy will probably respond best to motivators that are both personal and organizational and directly linked to risk control performance. Examples include promotions or pay raises based on risk control performance, budgeting techniques that provide incentives for practicing risk control, and personal recognition by top management of those whose risk control performance is particularly outstanding.

Differences Among Managers Seeking To Motivate Others

Motivation is an interpersonal process. Therefore, successfully motivating others depends on the characteristics of the employees being motivated and the managers attempting to motivate them. In considering the characteristics of managers and their attitudes toward those they manage, one management scholar, Douglas McGregor, identified two contrasting sets of assumptions that managers could make about the characteristics of others. McGregor labeled these two sets of assumptions Theory X and Theory Y. Their differences are illustrated in Exhibit 13-2.

Exhibit 13-2
McGregor's Theory X and Theory Y

Two sets of assumptions or propositions concerning management's task of harnessing human energy to organizational requirements

Conventional view: **A new view:**
Theory X   **Theory Y**

1. *A Proposition Common to Theories X and Y.* Management is responsible for organizing the elements of productive enterprise—money, materials, equipment, people—in the interest of economic ends.

2. With respect to people, this is a process of directing their actions, modifying their behavior to fit the needs of the organization.

2. People are *not* by nature passive or resistant to organizational needs. They have become so as a result of experience in organizations.

3. Without this active intervention by management, people would be passive—even resistant—to organizational needs. They must therefore be persuaded, rewarded, punished, controlled—their activities must be directed. This is management's task. We often sum it up by saying that management consists of getting things done through people.

3. The motivation, the potential for development, the capacity for assuming responsibility, the readiness to direct behavior toward organizational goals are all present in people. Management does not put them there. It is a responsibility of management to make it possible for people to recognize and develop these human characteristics for themselves.

4. The average person is by nature indolent—working as little as possible.

4. The essential task of management is to arrange organizational conditions and methods of operation so that people can achieve their own goals *best* by directing *their own* efforts toward organizational objectives.

5. The average person lacks ambition, dislikes responsibility, prefers to be led.

6. The average person is inherently self-centered, indifferent to organizational needs.

7. The average person is by nature resistant to change.

8. The average person is gullible, not very bright, the ready dupe of the charlatan and the demagogue.

Adapted with permission from Robert Albanese, *Managing: Toward Accountability for Performance*, 3d ed. (Homewood, IL: Richard D. Irwin, Inc., 1981), p. 231, adapting material in Douglas McGregor, *The Human Side of Management* (New York, NY: McGraw-Hill Book Company, 1960).

The theory a manager believes influences how that manager's views motivate others. For example, a manager who subscribes to Theory X believes that employees are not trustworthy and are generally inferior to the manager. This manager also believes that employees will not work any harder than necessary, lack ambition and loyalty to the organization, avoid responsibility, and strongly resist change. With this outlook, the Theory X manager gives others very detailed instructions, supervises them closely, and uses fear or threats of punishment to motivate.

In contrast, a Theory Y manager has a much better opinion of his or her colleagues and considers others equal and deserving of respect. The Theory Y manager also recognizes the values of social and humanitarian goals. This manager believes that an employee receives many forms of job satisfaction, including accomplishment, growth, camaraderie, and opportunities for leadership. In motivating others, the Theory Y manager does not reward those who follow rules and threaten those who do not. Instead, this manager motivates employees to achieve their own goals and the goals of the organization by working voluntarily to fulfill responsibilities, which is rewarding in itself.

Differences Within Individuals Over Time

Motivating others to practice risk control is a challenge because of differences among individuals and inconsistencies in their motivations. The concerns (perceived unmet needs) that prompt a person to act can also change over time.

A new front-line employee whose pay is relatively low and seniority uncertain might agree to wear eye protection to earn a safety bonus. As this employee's financial security improves, however, the employee might attach less importance to the safety bonus and more to status. The employee might try to gain status by refusing to wear goggles to demonstrate superiority over less experienced employees.

Managers also change. For example, a manager might shift from believing Theory X to believing Theory Y, might become motivated by different unmet needs, or might acquire a new set of motivational skills. Perceptive managers recognize that these changes in themselves and in other employees can complicate employee-manager relationships.

Applying Theories of Motivation to Risk Control

Another challenge facing managers is that motivation of risk control activities has received relatively little attention compared with motivation of production-oriented objectives such as product quality or cost control. The few management experts who have offered guidelines for motivating safe workplace conduct, such as those shown in Exhibit 13-3, have not provided a consistent set of motivational theories or principles. Because effective managers must know how and why actions motivate others, the following section describes several alternative theories of motivation.

Exhibit 13-3
Practical Guidelines for Motivating Safe Job Performance

Guideline	Application
1. Use appropriate methods of enforcement.	1. Provide rewards, in moderation, for good safety performance.
2. Eliminate unnecessary threats and punishment.	2. Stress positive effects of work-safety, not negative effects of non-compliance with safety procedures.
3. Recognize accomplishment adequately.	3. Praise or reward progress, even if slight.
4. Provide support when needed.	4. Where feasible, allow participation in selecting and implementing safe work procedures.
5. Let employees make decisions (or participate).	5. Become personally involved in safety, encouraging others to ask for needed help.
6. Assign responsibility/account-ability.	6. Make employees responsible/accountable for enforcing their own safety procedures.
7. Encourage others to set own personal goals.	7. Use employee participation to set acceptable safety levels.
8. Link others' job performances to personal/organizational goals.	8. Give bonuses or other motivating rewards for good safety records.
9. Inform employees of what is expected of them.	9. Remind employees of importance of safety; praise safe conduct.
10. Provide appropriate mix of external/internal satisfaction.	10. Reward safety (external) and instill sense of pride for safety (internal).
11. Design tasks and environments to meet individuals' needs.	11. Provide variety of safety motivators, tailored to individuals' unmet needs.
12. Individualize supervision.	12. Provide personal safety coaching.
13. Provide immediate and relevant feedback.	13. Praise or punish good or bad safety behavior without delay.
14. Recognize and eliminate barriers to individual achievement.	14. Provide training and equipment for safe work practices as needed.

Continued on next page.

Guideline	Application
15. Exhibit confidence in employees.	15. Demonstrate that safety on the job is expected and achievable.
16. Increase likelihood that employees will experience accomplishment.	16. Set initial goals that are easily reached and praise or reward achievement.
17. Exhibit interest in and knowledge of each subordinate.	17. Comment to employees personally on good/bad safety performance.
18. Encourage employee participation in decisions affecting them.	18. Where feasible, let employees select among specific models of safety equipment.
19. Establish climate of trust and communication.	19. Be honest with employees and encourage honesty from them on safety matters.
20. Minimize emphasis on statutory regulation.	20. Find better reasons for safety than "It's the law."
21. Help employees see personal contributions to organizational achievements.	21. Recognize particular individual's contributions to department's/ organization's achievements.
22. Listen and respond to others' complaints.	22. Request feedback on work procedures and take corrective action promptly.
23. Point out improvements in performance, no matter how small.	23. Praise/reward improved safety, even if still substandard.
24. Demonstrate own motives through behavior and attitude.	24. Show enthusiasm for safety; respond to motivators provided by senior management.
25. Criticize behavior, not people.	25. Show respect for an unsafe employee as a person, but do not tolerate unsafe behavior.
26. Make sure that effort pays off in results.	26. Recognize employees' honest attempts to work safely, even if below standard.
27. Encourage employees to engage in new, challenging activities.	27. Conduct brainstorming sessions on how to improve job safety.
28. Never eliminate anxiety completely.	28. Always point to some unmet safety goal.
29. Do not equate happiness with performance.	29. Liking for job or for fellow employees has no bearing on safety effort; a happy employee may not be a safe employee.
30. Provide both short-term and long-term motivators.	30. Always have available some further reward for improved safety performance, now and in the future.

Adapted with permission from Dean R. Spitzer, "Thirty Ways to Motivate Employees to Perform Better," *Training, The Magazine of Human Resources Development* (Minneapolis, MN: Lakewood Publications), March 1980.

Some Theories of Motivation

Several motivation theories are explained here because (1) the scholars who have studied human motivation do not agree on one theory, (2) risk management professionals and others will apply one or more of these theories, and (3) risk management professionals who have not succeeded in motivating others to make safety a priority can find these theories helpful.

This section focuses on three theories of human motivation: (1) Maslow's hierarchy of needs, (2) Herzberg's two-factor theory of motivators and hygiene factors, and (3) Skinner's theory of conditioned response. These theories have been chosen because they directly apply to motivating risk control and because they are widely recognized. However, all of them indicate that people act to satisfy unmet needs, and effective motivation depends on linking the satisfaction of those needs to appropriate behavior.

These theories present different explanations about why people are motivated. Maslow describes a hierarchy of needs ranging from basic survival to more growth-oriented goals. Herzberg focuses on the satisfaction of working as an end in itself. Skinner emphasizes rewards, earned through proper job performance, that reinforce or motivate appropriate behavior. The challenge of each theory is to motivate others by convincing them to make risk control a priority.

Maslow's Hierarchy of Needs

As depicted in Exhibit 13-4, Abraham H. Maslow postulates that all persons have five major categories of needs and that these needs fall into the following hierarchy or sequence:

- Physiological (such as food, shelter, and biological necessities)
- Safety (such as protection from threats to self or property)
- Social (such as acceptance, belonging, the esteem of others, and love)
- Esteem (such as personal accomplishment, self-esteem, and privacy)
- Self-actualization (such as creativity, growth, and recreation)

Only when a lower category of needs is satisfied does a person become motivated to satisfy the next higher category. Once the needs in a category are satisfied, they are not a motivating force unless a new situation threatens the existing needs. For example, if safety needs are met, a person will not be motivated by concerns for safety but will be motivated by social, esteem, or self-actualization needs until safety is threatened again. Under Maslow's theory, an employee can be motivated only if management can either appeal to an unmet need or negate a previously met need.

Exhibit 13-4
Maslow's Hierarchy of Needs

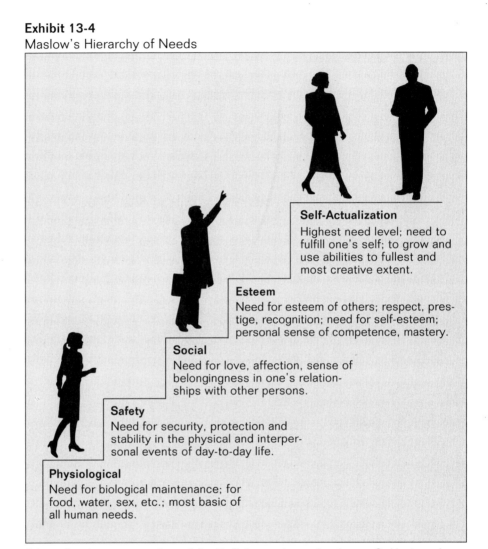

Adapted with permission from John R. Schermerhorn, Jr., James G. Hunt, and Richard N. Osborn, *Managing Organizational Behavior* (New York, NY: John Wiley & Sons, 1982), p. 108.

An employee whose safety needs have been met and who is currently striving to meet social, esteem, or self-actualization needs may act contrary to safety. For example, an employee may purposely disobey a safety rule (such as properly using a machine guard) and encourage others to do the same. The reasons for this might include gaining social status from peers, a social need; demonstrating leadership of an informal group, an esteem need; or achieving higher output to surpass a production quota (a self-actualization need). Not until the job situation changes and the safety need becomes a priority will the employee follow the safety rule. The situation can change if the employee is injured, sees a colleague injured, or is threatened by the loss of his or her job.

Herzberg's Two-Factor Theory—Motivators and Hygiene Factors

Frederick Herzberg believes that people are motivated to perform a task to achieve satisfaction for a job well done. Maslow calls this satisfying an esteem or self-fulfillment need. Herzberg says that a person is motivated by the responsibility, achievement, advancement, and personal growth that are the consequences of successfully completing a task. Good managers must therefore use those motivators if they want employees to perform well. Herzberg's model of motivation consists of two components—motivators and hygiene factors. **Motivators** relate to the satisfactions derived from the job itself (**job content**). **Hygiene factors** relate to the conditions of the job (**job context**).

Herzberg argues that although people want to perform a task well for its own sake, they will not work well if doing so produces too much discomfort. This discomfort may take forms such as inadequate pay, poor supervision, uncomfortable working conditions, hostile relationships with fellow employees, or lack of job security. These adverse conditions are hygiene factors, which dissuade a person from completing a task he or she would otherwise be willing to do for its own sake.

Herzberg contends that effective managers should create jobs that offer responsibility, achievement, and personal growth and ensure that work can be performed under positive hygienic conditions. Together, the presence of motivators and the absence of adverse hygiene factors create the greatest satisfaction and, in Herzberg's view, the best job performance (see Exhibit 13-5).

Skinner's Conditioned Response Theory

B. F. Skinner and his followers developed a theory of human behavior that was inspired by Pavlov's study of animal behavior. Pavlov noted that an animal could be made to respond in a particular way by giving it a specific stimulus. The classic example is inducing a hungry dog to salivate (a response) by exposing it to the sight or smell of meat (a stimulus). By controlling the stimuli given to an animal, a person can elicit a desired response. If a bell is rung when a hungry dog is exposed to the sight or smell of meat, for example, the dog learns to salivate at the sound of the bell, regardless of whether meat is present. Such learned behavior is known as **operant behavior**. The animal displays this behavior in response to a particular stimulus to experience a favorable consequence or to avoid an unfavorable one.

Exhibit 13-5
Herzberg's Two-Factor Motivation Theory

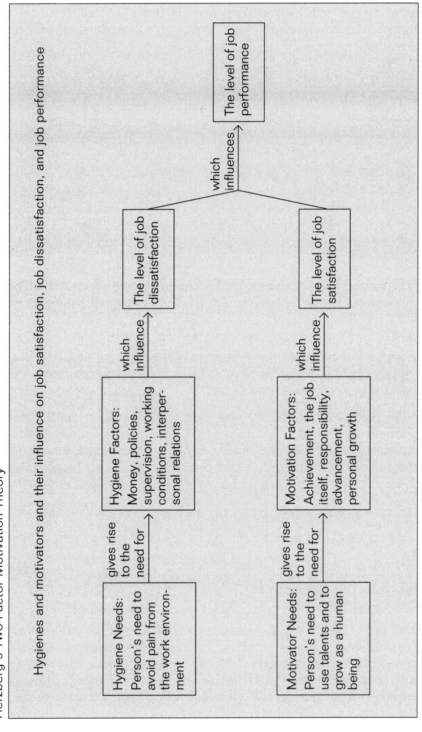

Hygienes and motivators and their influence on job satisfaction, job dissatisfaction, and job performance

Adapted with permission from Robert Albanese, *Managing: Toward Accountability for Performance*, 3d ed. (Homewood, IL: Richard D. Irwin, Inc., 1981), p. 242.

Without implying that people are on a par with animals, Skinner's theory of human motivation says that a manager can directly or indirectly influence employees to behave in certain ways. In the context of this theory, a manager can influence employees' behavior by rewarding appropriate behavior and punishing inappropriate behavior. The consequences (reward or punishment) may vary from one employee to the next. More money (a reward) or less money (a punishment) might be a meaningful consequence for some employees; for others, bestowing or withholding praise can stimulate appropriate behavior. Collectively, these rewards or punishments are known as **reinforcers**.

According to Skinner, using reinforcers to motivate employees provides the most efficient basis for causing appropriate behavior. Managers typically control many areas that influence an employee's behavior, including financial compensation, working conditions, social contacts, and job responsibilities. Managers can also relate desired or undesired behavior to positive or negative reinforcers so that employees realize the causal connection between satisfactory or unsatisfactory job performance and the resulting rewards or punishments.

Exhibit 13-6 illustrates how the timing and regularity of various reinforcement systems affect the consistency of the desired response. Varying rewards, especially those tied directly to desired performance, usually produces a higher level of motivation and more consistency in performance than does providing just one type of reward.

Applying the Theories of Motivation

The foregoing discussion implies that employees can be motivated to practice risk control. Such motivation requires controlling the consequences of employees' safe or unsafe behavior. Behavior that controls losses is rewarded; behavior that is contrary to effective risk control is punished (or not positively reinforced with rewards).

How consequences are controlled depends on the particular theory of motivation a manager uses. Each theory of motivation provides guidelines for influencing employees' safe or unsafe job behavior.

For example, a manager using Maslow's theory would motivate an employee concerned with esteem needs to focus on safety needs by showing the employee that his or her safety needs are not fulfilled. Reminding the employee of a colleague's recent injury might be effective. The manager could also appeal to the employee's esteem needs and connect those needs to safety. This might be done by informing the employee that his or her job status

Exhibit 13-6
Conditioned Responses: Effects of Different Schedules of Reinforcement

Schedule	Description	Example	Effects on Performance
Continuous	Reinforcer follows every response.	A manager watches an employee learning to use a new machine; praise is given each time the process is done perfectly.	Rapid and positive influence on behavior; behavior weakens rapidly when reinforcement is stopped.
Intermittent	Reinforcer does not follow every response.		Slow in establishing a desired behavior, but behavior is more permanent when reinforcement stops.
Fixed interval	The first response after a specific period of time has elapsed is reinforced.	A paycheck is received at the end of a week's work; a grade is received at the end of a semester.	Produces an uneven response pattern varying from a very slow, unenergetic response immediately following reinforcement to a very fast, vigorous response immediately preceding reinforcement.
Fixed ratio	A fixed number of responses must be emitted before reinforcement occurs.	A person is paid on a "piece-rate." Examples: For every 10 units produced, a certain amount of pay is received; "commission" sales.	Tends to produce a high rate of response that is vigorous and steady.
Variable interval	The first response after varying or random periods of time have elapsed is reinforced.	A manager takes periodic but unscheduled walks around the unit; compliments are given to employees displaying desirable work behaviors.	Tends to produce a high rate of response that is vigorous, steady, and durable.
Variable ratio	A varying or random number of responses must be emitted before reinforcement occurs.	A worker's output is checked at random according to the number of units produced; when quality is 100%, a small monetary bonus is paid.	Capable of producing a high rate of response that is vigorous, steady, and durable.

Adapted with permission from Fred Luthans and Robert Kreitner, *Organizational Behavior Modification and Beyond* (Glenview, IL: Scott, Foresman & Co., 1985), p. 58.

(and, by implication, fulfillment of esteem needs) depends not only on meeting the job's technical requirements but also on meeting organization-wide safety requirements.

According to Skinner's theory, motivating safe job performance requires rewarding safe behavior (the appropriate response) at least occasionally while also punishing unsafe behavior (the inappropriate response) at least occasionally. Similar action would be appropriate under Herzberg's approach to motivation. The choice of the most effective consequences should ideally be tailored to employees' unmet needs.

Monitoring Risk Control

How do you establish appropriate standards for risk control activites?

How do you adapt risk control activities to changes in loss exposures, legal requirements, organizational objectives, and costs/benefits?

The fifth and final step in the general risk management process, which is the focus of the entire ARM program, is monitoring the effectiveness of the chosen risk management techniques. Monitoring has two objectives: to control performance (confirm that the chosen risk management techniques are achieving their desired results) and to adapt the chosen techniques to change. The first objective of monitoring establishes standards, measures performance against these standards, and adjusts them for substandard performance. The second objective of monitoring analyzes the factors that influenced the chosen risk management techniques: loss exposures, legal requirements, the organization's resources, and the relative costs and benefits of alternative risk management techniques. The remainder of this chapter discusses the objectives of the final step of the risk management process—monitoring the effectiveness of the chosen risk management techniques.

Controlling Performance

The principles of management indicate that every activity within an organization should be controlled to ensure that it is being performed correctly. Controlling any activity entails (1) establishing standards of acceptable performance, (2) measuring actual performance against these standards, and (3) making adjustments either by correcting substandard performance or by modifying an inappropriate (unattainable or insufficiently challenging) performance standard.

Establishing Standards

Few risk management practitioners or scholars agree on how to determine whether an individual risk management professional did a good job in a particular year. Judging a risk management program by one year's performance leaves too much to chance. Judging a risk management professional on how he or she performs specific activities focuses too much on the business of the risk management department and not enough on effectiveness. Because that dilemma has not been resolved, using standards that focus both on results and on activities is probably best.

In establishing standards for risk control, risk management professionals must consider the types, sources, and characteristics of standards.

Types of Standards

The two basic types of standards are results standards and activity standards. A **results standard** focuses on accomplishments rather than on the means of achieving those accomplishments. An **activity standard** focuses on the activity undertaken to achieve a particular result regardless of the success of that activity. Lowering the disabling injury frequency rate in a production facility by five percentage points and reducing the concentration of carbon monoxide to a given level at a worksite are examples of results standards. Conducting five safety meetings a month and inspecting all fire extinguishers once a year are examples of activity standards.

Results standards and activity standards tend to be mutually reinforcing. Controlling concentrations of carbon monoxide in a workplace atmosphere on a regular basis reduces the frequency and the severity of work-related illnesses from this gas. The precautions taught or reinforced in safety meetings presumably reduce the disabling injury frequency rate. Maintaining fire extinguishers in good condition presumably lowers the severity of fire losses.

Because the causal connection between preventing accidents and reducing accident frequency rates is not always immediately evident (a significant element of luck is involved), many risk control programs are evaluated by both results standards and activity standards. For example, a supervisor may be responsible for conducting a specified number of safety meetings (activity standard) and may also be evaluated on reducing the disabling injury frequency rate (results standard). Rather than focusing just on the supervisor's activities or just on results, many managers believe that risk control programs should focus on both. Therefore, many risk management professionals feel uncomfortable when they are congratulated on achievements such as reducing a year's accident frequency or severity rate, producing a credit for the organization on a year's retrospectively rated liability insurance, or reducing the cost of property insurance by increasing the organization's levels of retention. Their discomfort comes from knowing that, if they are congratulated for being lucky in a good year, they may be criticized in an unlucky year, even though the *quality* of their performance is the same in both years.

Risk management professionals believe that their contributions are as significant in unlucky years as in lucky years. In fact, they believe their contributions may be even more valuable to their organizations when losses are severe. Consequently, risk management professionals tend to advocate using activity standards to evaluate their performance because such standards are independent of the organization's somewhat uncontrollable loss records. Activity standards focus mainly on the quality and quantity of the tasks of the risk management department.

However, activity standards have a major disadvantage: they do not relate directly to the standards, financial or otherwise, used to evaluate other departments. If risk management professionals ask to be judged on their own activities, rather than on their effect on the organization's bottom line, senior management might mistakenly assume that risk management activities are not making the same contributions as the activities of other departments. This perception can be detrimental to the risk management program.

Sources of Standards

Most standards for risk control, whether results standards or activity standards, originate from four sources: the law, industry practices, the organization's goals, and the attitudes of managers and employees.

Some federal and state statutes specify activity standards and actions to be taken to reduce accident frequency or severity. Many standards pertain to safe work practices, pollution controls, product safety features, transportation of hazardous materials, and life safety aspects of building construction. Other statutory and regulatory requirements specify minimum safety-oriented results, such as maximum permissible levels of airborne workplace contaminants, allowable noise levels in areas surrounding airports, and minimum nutritional requirements for prepared foods.

These legal requirements establish a uniform level of minimally acceptable safety performance (that is, a standard) for all applicable organizations. (New or small organizations might be subject to less demanding standards.) All organizations must adhere to these standards regardless of cost, secure a special exemption, or lobby to alter overly demanding standards.

To help maintain the activity standards created by state and federal laws, special groups have established detailed procedures for keeping accident records, especially for workplace injuries or illnesses. One of these groups, the federal Occupational Safety and Health Administration (OSHA), has developed procedures for keeping and reporting statistics on the frequency and severity of occupational injuries and illnesses. (The procedures for gathering these statistics and the resulting frequency and severity ratios were described in Chapter 5.) These statistics give an organization one plausible measure of how its current level of workplace safety compares to its own past level of safety and to that of other organizations. Few, if any, organizations are content with a workplace safety record that is deteriorating or that is significantly worse than that of comparable firms. Therefore, although these statistics do not establish legal requirements for actual workplace safety results, they do establish targets for improvement within an organization.

Trade, industry, and safety-oriented associations are also important sources of risk control standards. These standards are often promulgated as guidelines or codes that members can choose to adopt. This choice is often accompanied by an association's seal of approval or endorsement. Most of these codes, such as those in the construction, toy, and clothing manufacturing industries, are voluntary. Others, such as those for electrical safety or life safety, have been incorporated by reference into local, state, and federal legislation. Incorporating the latest versions of these association-generated codes into the law makes them mandatory and helps to keep legal standards for safety consistent with state-of-the-art risk control practices.

An organization's own policies and procedures are a third important source of standards for risk control. These policies and procedures should match or exceed legal standards. They might also adhere to applicable voluntary codes on safety and other risk control aspects.

Senior management's commitment to risk control is probably the most important determinant of the standards of risk control performance within an organization. This commitment influences the resources and attention given to reducing the frequency and severity of accidental losses. Therefore, to be effective, risk management professionals must motivate senior management to pay attention to risk control.

The fourth, and in some ways the most important, source of standards are the personal standards of managers and front-line employees. Their actions in implementing risk controls energize the organization's efforts to reduce losses. Ideally, managers and front-line employees should adopt the organization's policies and procedures relating to risk control. They might even strive to exceed these standards. The motivational techniques discussed earlier in this chapter can influence how employees work to surpass the organization's safety standards. However, when a person's risk control performance consistently falls below the organization's standards, the risk management professional should recommend appropriate educational, motivational, or even disciplinary actions.

In practice, the standards for acceptable risk control performance are usually a combination of minimum legal requirements, industry and association standards, senior management's expectations, and employees' commitments to risk control. In a sound risk control program, the standards from all four sources are consistent. If they are not, and particularly if the standards of senior management fall below industry or legal standards, the risk management professional(s) must help the organization to reassess its commitment to risk control.

Characteristics of Good Standards[2]

The principles of general management suggest that ten characteristics are common to well-conceived standards of performance for any activity. A results or activity standard for acceptable performance should be (1) objective, (2) quantifiable, (3) reasonably sensitive, (4) sufficiently stable, (5) reliable, (6) valid, (7) flexible, and (8) economical and should (9) highlight significant exceptions and (10) indicate appropriate corrective action.

Objective   Objective standards of performance focus on aspects of performance that can be measured. To illustrate, rather than simply stating that a driver's actions must be reasonably safe, the standard of acceptable performance for safely operating a vehicle specifies the particular kinds of driving errors that constitute poor performance. Similarly, a safety standard indicating that employees working near an assembly line should not wear dangerously loose clothing or dangling jewelry should be clarified through examples. Standards that are objective facilitate the task of measuring actual performance and reduce the likelihood of disputes over the accuracy of such measurements.

Quantifiable   An objective standard is quantifiable (for example, the number of safety training sessions conducted during a month, the parts-per-million concentration of an airborne contaminant at a workstation, or the percentage of defective products in a sample of a factory's output). Quantifiable measures of employee performance are likely to be accepted by those whose performance they measure, provided the process for measuring performance is clear and the measurements are reasonably accurate. Therefore, evaluating performance by quantitative standards, rather than qualitative ones, enhances the objectivity of the monitoring process. For example, measuring safety training efforts by the number of training sessions or by attendees' test scores is better than evaluating training on the basis of an observer's opinion of its effectiveness.

Reasonably Sensitive Any standard for safety must be based on a measure of performance that is reasonably sensitive. This means that the measure responds quickly and accurately to changes in safety performance. For example, relying on a device that continually measures the concentration of a dangerous airborne contaminant in a workplace is more sensitive than relying on quarterly physical examinations of employees for signs of adverse physiological effects. In fact, if the contaminant is immediately hazardous to life, periodic medical surveillance can be an inadequate measure of risk control performance. A minute-by-minute evaluation is essential under potentially lethal conditions.

As another example, accident frequency and severity ratios computed on a monthly basis might not be sufficiently sensitive to signal important changes in hazard levels. Therefore, many organizations establish certain danger signs that require immediate action, even though no actual loss has occurred. Two examples of danger signs are reaching a maximum tolerable level of defective output and nearly having a highway accident. Although sensitivity is desirable, a proper standard for safety performance must not give too many "false alarms." Sensitivity must be balanced with stability.

Sufficiently Stable A good standard should be based on a stable measure of performance. A measure should give different *reported* results only if *actual* results have changed significantly. Furthermore, the indicated direction of change should be the same as the actual direction of change. To ensure stability, for example, workplace disability frequency and severity rates are typically computed monthly or annually, rather than daily or weekly, so that results are based on reasonable statistical credibility. Similarly, any erratically fluctuating gauge of temperature or airborne contamination is neither a useful indicator of actual conditions nor a guide to corrective action. A standard based on a measure of performance that is not sufficiently stable will probably indicate corrective change when none is needed.

Reliable A standard should be based on a reliable measure of performance, one that reports the same results under the same conditions. For example, a reliable dosimeter reports, on two or more different occasions, the same parts-per-million of an airborne contaminant in an unchanging workplace atmosphere; an unreliable dosimeter shows varying results even though the conditions are unchanged. As another illustration, an organization's record of serious workplace injuries provides a reliable measure of safety performance only if the criteria that distinguish serious from minor injuries remain constant and if those responsible for classifying injuries apply those criteria consistently. In contrast, criteria of safety performance are unreliable if a given set of work injuries is classified differently on one occasion than on another when conditions have not changed.

Valid   A standard must be based on a valid measure of performance, one that is meaningfully related to what it is intended to measure. For example, the noise hazard to employees in a workplace increases as the loudness, pitch, and duration of the sound increase. Therefore, a record of only the loudness or only the pitch of noise is not a valid measure of the noise hazard. A record that reports both loudness and pitch is somewhat more valid. A record of all three factors (loudness, pitch, and duration) is even more valid as an indicator of noise hazards. A valid standard for noise should also specify acceptable levels of loudness, pitch, and duration of a sound.

Flexible   The standard should be sufficiently flexible to adjust to unanticipated changes in the environment. Keeping an injury frequency rate below a specified level might be reasonable under normal levels of factory output, but if unanticipated product demand requires that output increase by 50 percent, keeping the injury rate below the specified level might not be possible. The standard does not fit the new environment.

Occasionally, line managers might claim that the pressure for added production or other demands on their departments does not allow enough time for safety. The concept of a flexible standard does not mean abandoning the standard in favor of production demands. Indeed, pressures to increase output tend to intensify hazards to persons and property, requiring greater efforts to counter these hazards. Business pressures might therefore indicate that *results* standards need to be relaxed while *activity* standards for risk control are maintained or increased.

Greater flexibility might be appropriate when the existing level of safety performance is substantially below or above acceptable standards for some time. For example, sustained substandard performance could indicate that the performance standard is too high. Similarly, sustained excellent performance (especially if accompanied by complaints from outside the department or organization) could indicate that the standard is too low. Both conditions can work against the goal of achieving the best possible level of performance. The former discourages employees because the standard precludes any recognition for their work. The latter accepts and thus encourages mediocre performance. In both situations, flexibility means redefining acceptable performance based on *change* from past performance. When past performance has been substantially below standard, perhaps a specified amount of improvement (or even any improvement) would be acceptable and worthy of praise. Conversely, when excellence has prevailed in the past, continuing the standard of acceptable performance or even raising it might be appropriate.

Economical   Establishing and applying standards of performance for any activity costs money and is justified only if the benefits from those efforts exceed their costs. Therefore, activities that monitor risk controls should generate benefits greater than their costs. Moreover, the greater the excess of benefits over costs that the activity generates (proportionately or in absolute dollars), the greater the attention that should be paid to the activity.

An organization should consider the costs and benefits of monitoring its risk control program and should favor standards of performance that allow data to be easily obtained, minimally disrupt productive activities, identify substandard performance quickly (so that it can be corrected promptly), and are easily interpreted and applied by management. Economical performance standards are also those that conform to the other nine characteristics of a good standard. On the other hand, performance standards that are difficult to apply or that focus on relatively insignificant features of an organization's risk control program do not typically represent the best use of the resources devoted to monitoring risk control.

Highlight Significant Exceptions   Most standards of performance for risk control or any other activity specify a range of acceptable performance. Corrective action is required when actual results fall outside this range. For example, the quality control program for a rivet assembly line might specify a target of no more than ten defective units per hour. However, management wishes to take no action unless defective output rises above fifteen units per hour or falls below three units per hour. These upper and lower control limits are shown in Exhibit 13-7.

Exhibit 13-7
Asymmetrical Upper and Lower Control Limits for Manufacturing Process

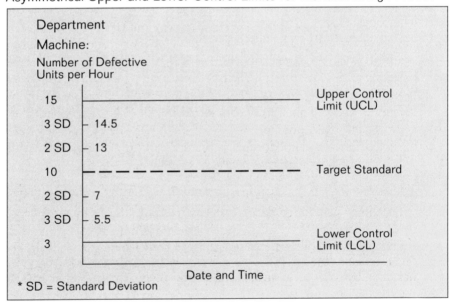

In this exhibit, output that falls anywhere between the upper and lower control limits is defined as acceptable performance. This range of performance is important because it requires no action until performance goes beyond random, uncontrollable variations and permits ranges of fluctuation above and below the target standard. The degree and direction of fluctuation will typically require different management actions, depending on whether the deviation represents particularly bad or particularly good performance. For example, in Exhibit 13-7, the upper control limit is only five units per hour above the standard of ten, but the lower control limit is seven units per hour below that target standard.

Management will not respond to insignificant, random events if the upper and lower control limits are set at least two or three standard deviations from (above or below) the target standard. The random fluctuations in mechanical processes like assembly lines fall within the normal, bell-shaped curve (probability distribution). As a result, and as detailed in the Appendix to Chapter 1 of this text, only an approximate 2.8 percent probability exists that purely random fluctuations will exceed two standard deviations from the mean (expected value) of a normal probability distribution (here, ten defective units per hour) and a less than 0.2 percent probability that random events will exceed three standard deviations from the mean. Therefore, if an upper or lower control limit is set more than two or three standard deviations above the target standard, management can be virtually assured that any performance that exceeds these limits is not a random event.

For example, if the standard deviation of the number of defective units per hour on the assembly line is 1.5 units, then one standard deviation above the target standard is 11.5 defective units per hour, two standard deviations is 13 units per hour, and three standard deviations is 14.5. Conversely, below the target standard, the corresponding values are 8.5, 7, and 5.5 defective units per hour. These random, managerially insignificant fluctuations in the number of defective units per hour are shown in Exhibit 13-7. Note that both the upper control limit of 15 units per hour and the lower one of 3 per hour are both beyond three standard deviations from the mean, or expected number of defective units per hour that is the target standard.

The upper and lower control limits are not equidistant from the target standard because management is much more concerned about increases in the number of defective units than about decreases. A statistically significant increase in the number of defective units could signal a flaw in the production process. This flaw, if not immediately corrected, could generate products liability claims or at least dissatisfied customers. On the other hand, if the number of defective units falls to the lower control limit of only three per hour, the assembly line is performing unexpectedly well. No urgent problem needs to be solved. Nonetheless, such a consistently low rate of defects could indicate a favorable change in the production process that management might want to identify and incorporate into its future production. Further, the employees responsible for such excellent output probably deserve special recognition to reward them and to motivate others.

Pointing to Corrective Action   Monitoring risk control or any other activity is not an end in itself. Instead, it is a means to maintain and, if possible, to improve performance. Therefore, effective standards go beyond indicating a problem. They pinpoint as precisely as possible the time, location, and nature of substandard performance. For example, for the product quality limits charted in Exhibit 13-7, the data on performance show the location of the assembly line and the date and time for each measurement of quality control. Therefore, when actual performance goes beyond an upper or lower control limit, knowing the time and location of each significant deviation from the standard helps management to determine the causes of those deviations and correct them.

Other standards for risk control performance should also be specific to help identify the problem. For example, inspection reports on the fire detection/suppression system in a building should not merely indicate that the inspector considers the system deficient or inadequate. Instead, the report should detail why the system is inadequate, including the information that sprinkler heads at location A-12, B-17, and E-64 are blocked by stacked supplies or that extinguishers 104, 719, and 812 have not been inspected for twelve months. Similarly, evaluating a truck driver's performance should specify the occasions when the driver exceeded the speed limit, failed to signal, improperly negotiated a turn, and made other specific driving errors.

Specifying the nature of any faulty risk control performance also helps to objectify the evaluation, thus strengthening the basis for discussing the situation unemotionally with those who may be responsible. In general, standards of performance that are specific and objective tend to be those that also clearly indicate the correctiive action needed. Imprecise standards cannot suggest what corrections should be made.

Measuring Performance Against Standards

Establishing standards of acceptable performance is the first, and arguably most important, of the three steps in controlling performance. Without appropriate standards, the other two steps, measuring actual performance and correcting substandard performance, become very difficult. However, despite the importance of the standards themselves, the remaining two steps are not automatic and also require special attention.

Four conditions must be met to measure performance and compare it with standards:

1. Performance must be objectively measurable.
2. Performance must be measured in ways and at times that are understood and accepted by those whose performance is being measured.
3. The measurements taken must represent actual performance over the period to which the measurements apply.
4. Only significant deviations from performance should trigger managerial action.

These four conditions imply that measuring performance should be a cooperative activity.

Adjusting Standards for Substandard Performance

If performance is measured against a standard and is shown to be below that standard, adjustments must be made. Any risk control performance that is consistently below standards should be improved and/or a more realistic standard should be set. Conversely, any risk control performance that consistently exceeds standards should be explored to find the causes of this excellence and to modify standard operating procedures so that this excellence can become the basis for a higher attainable standard.

When actual risk control performance is deficient, the following are appropriate steps to improve performance:

1. *Confirm the accuracy of the data* documenting the substandard performance.
2. *Identify the probable cause(s)* of this performance.
3. *Discuss these causes* with the manager and/or employee who is responsible to identify or explain
   a. the extent to which this performance is within each person's control.
   b. the change in operating procedures that could improve performance if the situation is within either person's control.
   c. the other causes of this substandard performance if the situation is not within either person's control.
4. *Implement corrective actions* with the cooperation of those responsible for the substandard performance.
5. *Continue monitoring* to verify that the corrective actions have restored acceptable risk control performance.

Line supervisors, usually with the advice and often with the assistance of risk management professionals, should take these five steps to correct substandard performance. This will help risk management to become an integral part of every employee's and every individual's job responsibilities.

In correcting substandard performance, managers should emphasize that the deficiency being corrected is in a procedure or way of doing a particular job, not in the employee. As indicated in guideline 25 in Exhibit 13-3, any criticisms should be aimed at the performance, not at the employee.

If substandard performance still occurs despite good operating procedures and efforts to improve performance, the standard itself could be unreasonable. Establishing proper standards at the start should decrease substandard performance. However, problems can occur when the initial standards are too high or if some change in operating conditions makes a previously proper standard unattainable. These cases are probably characterized by performance that is consistently below acceptable levels despite the genuinely best efforts of the supervisor and the employee. Good management in those cases requires revising standards.

The process for revising an unreasonably high standard is the same as that for initially establishing a standard:

1. Select one or more variables for which results or performance standards will be developed.
2. Establish target values that constitute acceptable performance for those variables and establish control points above or below those values that require managerial action when exceeded.
3. Confirm that standards meet the ten criteria discussed in the previous section.

Similar to establishing an initial standard, revising an existing standard should be a participative activity, designed to develop consensus that the new standard is reasonable.

Adapting to Change

Beyond controlling and improving actual performance, the second purpose of monitoring an organization's risk control program is to help the organization adapt to changes. Although a correct choice in the past, a particular risk control might stop being cost-effective because of some change in (1) loss exposures, (2) legal requirements, (3) the organization's objectives or resources, or (4) the relative costs and benefits of alternative risk management techniques. Changes in these areas are discussed below.

Changes in Loss Exposures

Identifying and analyzing loss exposures is the first step in the risk management decision process; consequently, these exposures are the primary determinants of an organization's risk control needs. Changed exposures will probably alter the optimum combination of risk control measures. For example, starting a new activity probably requires new risk controls appropriate for that activity, just as discontinuing some activity means that its risk control measures might no longer be necessary.

Changes in risk control measures are probably appropriate when the following other changes occur:

- An organization moves to a new area, which brings changes in the quality of public fire protection, natural hazards to which the area is susceptible, or the characteristics of the indigenous work force.

- The number of shifts or hours of work during which the organization operates is modified, which changes the levels of employee fatigue, exposures to nighttime crime, or availability of outside police, fire, medical, or pollution control assistance.

- The means or routes of transportation change, which might require different kinds of packaging, altered production schedules, or increased values exposed to loss during transport.

Virtually any modifications in an organization's operations will probably change its loss exposures, increasing some and reducing others, thereby shifting the mix of risk control measures appropriate for that organization.

Changes in Legal Requirements

Because the law is an important source of standards for risk control performance, changes in the law are likely to mandate changes in an organization's risk control practices. When an organization's compliance management program (discussed in Chapter 8) identifies a new statute, regulation, or court decision demanding a higher level of safety performance, the organization should promptly move to comply. Compliance not only raises the level of safety within an organization's operations, but it also reduces potential civil or criminal fixed liability for noncompliance.

When a new law imposes a new standard of activity or results, an organization's management does not usually need to decide whether to comply with the new requirements. Instead, the organization must decide only on the most cost-effective way of complying.

Changes in the Organization's Objectives or Resources

An organization's resources available for risk control could increase or decrease over time. Moreover, the annual budget for overall risk management and risk control might fluctuate with business cycles or budget considerations. Despite these changes, risk management professionals are responsible for designing and maintaining cost-effective risk control programs. Risk management professionals should therefore develop a list of priorities for existing and proposed risk control measures and be prepared to drop or add measures depending on either decreases or increases in risk control resources.

Risk management professionals should categorize priorities to distinguish between risk control measures that are legally required and those that are not. The risk control measures required by law and already in place presumably meet all legal requirements and will presumably stay in place regardless of any decrease in resources available for risk control. However, the other existing risk control measures are subject to being discontinued if resources are cut back severely. When retrenchments are necessary, the risk control measures with the lowest cost-effectiveness should be the first to be discontinued so that the remaining measures continue to give the organization the greatest protection for the resources available.

To be prepared for increases in risk control budgets, risk management professionals should have ready some proposals for additional risk control measures. (These proposals should be ranked in decreasing order of cost-effectiveness.) Being prepared to demonstrate the cost-effectiveness of additional expenditures for risk control can demonstrate to senior management the value of risk control and make the risk management department able to compete with other departments' demands for funds.

Changes in Relative Costs and Benefits of Risk Management Techniques

To choose specific risk management techniques, an organization weighs the costs and benefits of each feasible option in terms of its expected present values of cash inflows and outflows. In selecting a technique, the organization should choose measures that promise the highest internal rate of return or net present value of cash flows from the asset or activity to which each risk management technique is applied. This decision rule typically leads the organization to choose some combination of risk control and risk financing measures.

The same decision rules and procedures apply when monitoring the continuing appropriateness of past decisions. When the costs or benefits of risk control measures change, their continuing effectiveness needs to be reevaluated. These changes might occur for reasons such as cyclical changes in the costs of insurance, the new availability of risk control technology, or new safety regulations. Any or all of these or other changes affect the projected present value of cash inflows and outflows (and, hence, the costs and benefits) attributable to a risk control measure. Determining whether some new risk control measure would be more cost-effective than an existing measure requires applying the decision rule to a new set of cost and benefit conditions.

Overview of the Risk Control Function

What role does a review of the entire risk management process have in monitoring risk control activites?

Properly monitoring the risk control aspects of a risk management program requires confirming that effective, cost-efficient measures are in effect. Therefore, monitoring, although the final step, requires reviewing the entire risk management process to ensure that (1) loss exposures have been thoroughly identified and analyzed, (2) risk control alternatives for managing those exposures have been fully examined, (3) risk control measures have been chosen, (4) the chosen risk control measures have been implemented, and (5) the proper use and continuing effectiveness of the risk controls are being carefully evaluated.

To illustrate, consider the case of Valence Chemical Company, a medium-sized manufacturer of specialized chemicals. In the past, Valence's operations have occasionally been halted for many weeks by the labor union strikes of the truck drivers. These truck drivers were employed by the common carrier with which Valence customarily contracted to transport its raw materials and finished goods. To avoid these work stoppages, Valence's senior management has decided to change its operations significantly. Instead of relying on outside transporters, Valence will purchase its own trucks and hire its own drivers.

One of the fundamental purposes of monitoring risk controls is to adapt these controls to changes in an organization's operations. Therefore, when Valence's risk management professional first hears about the transportation changes, he or she should explore how these changes can be expected to affect the following:

- The company's transportation loss exposures
- The risk control options for handling these exposures
- The company's choices of risk control measures for transportation hazards
- The implementation of new risk control measures
- The monitoring of these new measures

(Valence's change in transportation methods would raise similar concerns about the risk financing aspects of the company's risk management program, but the following discussion focuses only on the risk control aspects of that program.)

Changes in Exposures

Two of the most significant loss exposures that will change for Valence when it undertakes its own transportation will be the property values of the trucks the company will purchase and the work injury hazards faced by its own drivers. The vehicles and drivers will be exposed to transportation perils.

Putting aside new or altered exposures, assume that the new conditions require the risk management professional to consider risk control measures to counter the following:

- Highway accidents
- Theft of trucks and their cargoes
- Fire damage to the trucks and their cargoes
- Natural perils that might strike the company's trucks while in transit or while garaged
- Improperly designed workstations (cabs) for truck drivers
- Uncontrolled releases of toxic substances
- Net income losses from the unavailability of Valence trucks to meet transportation needs
- Increased liability to owners/operators of vehicles and to owners of real property adjoining highways who may suffer bodily injury or property damage from highway accidents involving Valence vehicles

Specific actions for controlling the frequency and/or severity of such losses have been discussed throughout this text.

Changes in Risk Control Options

The next step in monitoring how Valence's risk control program responds to its decision to handle its own transportation would be to list the specific risk control measures for each major exposure related to transportation. The risk control measures directly applicable or adaptable to transportation settings should be highlighted for analysis. Analyzing existing risk control measures can also suggest alternatives for exposure avoidance, loss prevention, loss reduction, segregation of exposure units, or contractual transfers for risk control. The purpose at this stage is to develop as extensive a list of specific risk controls as possible so that no option is overlooked.

Changes in the Risk Control Measures Selected

The next step in adapting Valence's risk control program is to evaluate the feasibility of all options for controlling losses from each of these transportation exposures. Some options will clearly not be feasible for various reasons. The projected costs and benefits (usually expressed as differential cash inflows and outflows) of the feasible options that remain should be examined. Valence should select the risk control measures that promise the greatest excess of benefits over costs (usually the greatest present value of expected future net cash flows) if it has the financial resources to implement them. To simplify the remaining discussion, assume that Valence selects the following options:

- A thorough training program (complete with regular refresher courses) for all drivers of its new trucks that focuses on avoiding highway accidents and on appropriate procedures when accidents occur

- Automatic fire suppression systems for all trucks

- Antitheft alarm devices for all trucks

- Routing and scheduling all trucks to avoid particularly dangerous or congested sections of highway

- New, ergonomically designed instrumentation, controls, and seating for the cabs of all trucks

Changes in Risk Control Implementation

As Valence undertakes its own transportation operations, it must also modify the responsibilities of many company employees. An appropriate share of risk control responsibility should be included among the new duties of those affected by the change. For example, the purchasing department must obtain vehicles having suitable safety equipment. The traffic department will need to schedule deliveries at convenient times over the safest reasonable routes when roads are the least congested. Maintenance will have to ensure that the trucks are in safe operating condition and that their fire suppression and theft alarm devices are operational. The drivers and their supervisors will need to stress highway safety throughout their activities, and senior management will need to review and approve policies and procedures for safe, efficient transportation operations.

Valence's risk management professional will have additional staff responsibilities for advising line managers in the risk control aspects of their daily work, thereby acting as a coordinator for the transportation safety program. He or she will likely decide many technical matters independently, including the type of training drivers should receive, the appropriate locations and types of fire and theft control devices, and the ergonomic specifications for truck cabs. On administrative matters, Valence's risk management professional will probably be a staff advisor to line managers outside the risk management department who are directly responsible for safety-related activities involving fleet operations.

Changes in Risk Control Monitoring

To monitor the effectiveness of risk control measures, these measures should be evaluated by activity and results standards. As illustrations, consider two of the risk control measures Valence will implement: installing antitheft alarm devices for all trucks and routing and scheduling deliveries to reduce accidents and delays. For the alarms, appropriate activity standards would include installing and regularly testing these devices. Results standards would indicate whether the alarms rang during an attempted theft (and did not give false alarms) and whether the timely sounding of the alarms assisted Valence's drivers or the police in identifying or apprehending thieves. For the routing and scheduling of trucks, appropriate activity standards would verify whether detailed routes and schedules were developed in the traffic department and would indicate whether drivers actually adhered to these schedules. A results standard would indicate how often and for how long trucks were delayed by accidents or by traffic congestion. These records, compared with past performance, would reveal whether the routing and scheduling activities were helping Valence maintain smooth transportation operations. (Similar activity and result standards could be developed for the other risk control measures listed previously or for other feasible risk control measures.)

Summary

Two essential aspects of administering a risk control program are motivating personnel to give high priority to their risk control responsibilities and monitoring risk controls to ensure that they are achieving their desired results (and, if necessary, to adapt to changes that might require new risk control measures).

The concepts of motive and motivation apply both to employee management and to the overall management of an organization. Within any person, a motive is an energized psychological state that leads to actions aimed at satisfying perceived unmet needs. Organizational management, including sound management of a risk control program, involves creating situations in which employees' efforts to meet their own needs also serve the organization's objectives.

No single theory or technique of motivation is universally applicable. Motivating others within an organization is particularly challenging because of differences among individuals (managers and employees alike), differences

that occur within individuals over time, and disagreement among management scholars about the kinds of unmet needs that motivate employees.

Among widely held theories of motivation, Maslow's hierarchy of needs postulates that people do not respond to their higher social, esteem, and
self-actualization needs until they have satisfied their lower physiological and
safety needs. In contrast, Herzberg's two-factor theory says that employees
need to find satisfaction in doing a job for its own sake. Employees are therefore motivated by a sense of accomplishment, pride, and recognition at work
and continue to perform well as long as any discomforts (or hygiene factors
such as pay, working conditions, and relations with fellow employees) are
within tolerable limits. The stimulus/response/consequence theory of Skinner
holds that employees learn certain patterns of appropriate behavior (including
safe work habits and attention to other risk controls) in response to rewards for
appropriate behavior or punishments for inappropriate behavior.

Monitoring an organization's risk control efforts consists of the classical management function of control and the modern management responsibility of
adapting to change. The control function involves setting standards, measuring performance against those standards, and adjusting standards for substandard performance. To set standards for a risk control program, risk
management professionals must work with others to (1) decide on appropriate
types of standards (results standards or activity standards), (2) locate appropriate
sources for these standards (such as the law, association and industry codes, the
organization's own policies and procedures, and each person's commitment to
risk control), and (3) design standards that are objective, quantifiable, reasonably sensitive, sufficiently stable, reliable, valid, flexible, and economical and
that highlight significant exceptions from acceptable performance and identify
appropriate corrective action. Once these standards have been set, they can be
compared against actual performance. Based on this comparison, adjustments
for substandard performance can be made either by raising levels of actual
performance or by easing unattainable standards.

Modern management scholars and practitioners also emphasize the responsibility of executives to help the organization adapt to changes. For a risk control
program, the most significant changes are in the loss exposures stemming from
modifications to the following: the organization's operations, legal requirements for specific risk control measures or levels of safety, the resources available for risk control, and the relative costs and benefits of risk control
techniques. Changes in these variables require re-examining the
organization's original decisions, that is, reviewing and repeating the entire
risk management decision process—including both risk control and risk financing choices—and possibly renewing the risk control program.

Chapter Notes

1. The discussion under this section draws on Frank E. Bird, Jr., and Robert G. Loftus, *Loss Control Management* (Loganville, GA: International Loss Control Institute, 1976), pp. 139-165 and Dan Petersen, *Techniques of Safety Management*, 2d ed. (New York, NY: McGraw-Hill Book Company, 1978), pp. 141-161.

2. The discussion under this section draws on two sources. The first is Harold Koontz, Cyril O'Donnell, and Heinz Weihrich, *Management*, 7th ed. (New York, NY: McGraw-Hill Book Company, 1980), pp. 734-739. The second is William E. Tarrants, *The Measurement of Safety Performance* (New York, NY: Garland Publishing, Inc., 1980), pp. 16-18.

Bibliography

Albanese, Robert. *Managing: Toward Accountability for Performance.* 3d ed. Homewood, IL: Richard D. Irwin, Inc., 1981.

Bird, Frank E., Jr., and George L. Germain. *Practical Loss Control Leadership: The Conservation of People, Property, Process, and Profits.* Loganville, GA: International Loss Control Institute, 1985.

Bird, Frank E., Jr., and Robert G. Loftus. *Loss Control Management.* Loganville, GA: International Loss Control Institute, 1976.

Clemens, P.L. "A Compendium of Hazard Identification and Evaluation Techniques for System Safety Applications." *Hazard Prevention.* March/April 1982, pp. 11-18.

Close, Darwin B. "PERT Networks' Use Can Help Reduce Business Interruption Down Time." *Risk Management.* March 1982, pp. 26-30.

Cote, Arthur E., ed. *Fire Protection Handbook.* 16th ed. Boston, MA: National Fire Protection Association, 1986.

Dul, Jan, and Bernard Weerdmeester. *Ergonomics For Beginners.* London: Taylor & Francis, 1993.

Ergonomics: A Practical Guide. Chicago, IL: National Safety Council, 1988.

Garb, Solomon, and Evelyn Eng. *Disaster Handbook.* 2d ed. New York, NY: Springer Publishing Company, 1969.

Gordon, Rex B. "System Safety." In Frank E. Bird, Jr., and Robert G. Loftus, *Loss Control Management.* Loganville, GA: Loss Control Institute Press, 1976.

Grandjean, Etienne P. "Fatigue." *American Industrial Hygiene Association Journal,* vol. 31, no. 4. July-August 1970, pp. 401-411.

Greene, Mark R. *Risk and Insurance.* 2d ed. Cincinnati, OH: South-Western Publishing Company, 1968.

Haddon, William, Jr., M.D. "On the Escape of Tigers." *American Journal of Public Health and the Nation's Health.* December 1970, pp. 2229-2234.

Hammer, Willie. *Handbook of System and Product Safety.* Englewood Cliffs, NJ: Prentice-Hall, Inc., 1972.

———. *Occupational Safety Management Engineering.* Englewood Cliffs, NJ: Prentice-Hall, Inc., 1976.

Heinrich, H.W., Dan Petersen, and Nestor Roos. *Industrial Accident Prevention—Safety Management Approach.* 5th ed. New York, NY: McGraw-Hill Book Company, 1980.

Hollingsworth, E. P., and J. J. Launie. *Commercial Property and Multiple-Lines Underwriting.* Malvern, PA: Insurance Institute of America, 1984.

Kepner, Charles H., and Benjamin B. Traigo. *The Rational Manager.* New York, NY: McGraw-Hill Book Company, 1965.

Koontz, Cyril O'Donnell, and Heinz Weihrich. *Management.* 7th ed. New York, NY: McGraw-Hill Book Company, 1980.

Lathrop, James K., ed. *Life Safety Code Handbook.* 5th ed. Quincy, MA: National Fire Protection Association, 1991.

Masse, Pierre. *Optimal Investment Decisions: Rules for Action and Criteria for Choice.* Englewood Cliffs, NJ: Prentice-Hall, Inc., 1962.

McElroy, Frank E., ed. *Accident Prevention Manual for Industrial Operations: Administration and Programs.* 8th ed. Chicago, IL: National Safety Council, 1981.

Mehr, Robert I., and Bob A. Hedges. *Risk Management in the Business Enterprise.* Homewood, IL: Richard D. Irwin, Inc., 1963.

———. *Risk Management: Concepts and Applications.* Homewood, IL: Richard D. Irwin, Inc., 1974.

Petersen, Dan. *Techniques of Safety Management.* 2d ed. New York, NY: McGraw-Hill Book Company, 1978.

———. *Techniques of Safety Management.* 3d ed. Goshen, NY: Aloray, Inc., 1989.

Plog, Barbara A., ed. *Fundamentals of Industrial Hygiene.* 3d ed. Chicago, IL: National Safety Council, 1988.

PREPARE: Pre-Emergency Plan and Recovery. Hartford, CT: Hartford Steam Boiler Inspection and Insurance Company, 1977.

Shakespeare, William. *As You Like It.* Act 2, scene 7.

Snook, Stover H. "Approaches to the Control of Back Pain in Industry: Job Design, Job Placement and Education/Training." *SPINE,* vol. 2, no. 1. September 1987, pp. 45-59.

Tarrants, William E. *The Measurement of Safety Performance.* New York, NY: Garland Publishing, Inc., 1980.

Trieschmann, James S., et al. *Commercial Property Insurance and Risk Management.* 4th ed. Vol. 1. Malvern, PA: American Institute for CPCU, 1994.

Walker, Jasen M. "Injured Worker Helplessness: Critical Relationships and Systems Level Approach for Intervention." *Journal of Occupational Rehabilitation,* vol. 2, no. 4, 1992, pp. 203-206.

Index

S